GRAND NATIONAL

GRAND NATIONAL

THE OFFICIAL CELEBRATION OF 150 YEARS

ANNE HOLLAND

Macdonald Queen Anne Press

A Queen Anne Press BOOK

© Anne Holland 1988

First published in Great Britain in 1988 by
Queen Anne Press, a division of
Macdonald & Co (Publishers) Ltd
3rd Floor
Greater London House
Hampstead Road
London NW1 7QX

A Pergamon Press plc Company

Jacket photographs – Front: All-Sport
                      Back: Rex Coleman

British Library Cataloguing in Publication Data

Holland, Anne
    Grand National: the official celebration of 150 years.
    1. Grand National
    I. Title
    798.4'5   SF359.7.G7

    ISBN 0–356–15571–4

Typeset by MS Filmsetting Limited, Frome, Somerset
Printed and bound in Great Britain by
Purnell Book Production Ltd
Member of BPCC plc

CONTENTS

ACKNOWLEDGEMENTS

FIRST AND FOREMOST go grateful thanks to ALL the subjects of this book and those connected with them who gave willingly and enthusiastically of their time during the research. Without their unfailing help and co-operation, the end result could not have been achieved.

Thanks also go to Aintree Racecourse, Derek Ancil, Ascot Bloodstock Sales, Rosemary Berry, Jim Bidwell-Topham, Aubrey Brabazon, Dorothy Castro (USA), Cheltenham Racecourse, Mrs A. N. G. Clarke (NZ) Doncaster Bloodstock Sales, Peter Doyle, Merrick Francis, Sir Martin Gilliat, Reg Green, *Guinness Book of Records*, the late John Huston, Irish Turf Club, Mrs Jane Liddell, National Steeplechase and Hunt Association (USA), New Zealand Racing Conference, Nick and Sharon Saville, Patsy and Peter Smiles, Messrs Weatherbys (G. Bivens), Mark and Sandy Wilkinson.

AUTHOR'S NOTE: Although most of the chapters concern undisputed record-makers, some accolades are the author's own choice and therefore can be contended. For instance, I make no apologies for finding an excuse to include Crisp, whereas Golden Miller's feats, I feel, belong more to the Cheltenham Gold Cup. But for all those worthy of inclusion and not here this time, I can only hope their turn will come in due course.

While every attempt has been made to trace holders of copyright material reproduced in this book, this has not always been possible. Macdonald and Co. Publishers therefore offers its apologies to any person or organisation to whom it has failed to give the appropriate acknowledgement.

H.M. Queen Elizabeth the Queen Mother: 7; Arthur Ackermann & Son Ltd: 10–11; Allsport: 193 (Peter Greenland), 148B, 192T (both Trevor Jones; The Associated Press Ltd: 72, 78–9, 82, 86, 133, 137, 139; BBC Hulton Picture Library: 12–13, 14, 55, 68–9, 80, 85, 87; Courtesy Mrs P. Biegel/Claude Berry: 75; Charlotte Brew: 150, 151; Bridgeman Art Library: 34B, 38T (Oscar & Peter Johnson Ltd, London) 36–7; Rex Coleman: 79, 146B, 186, 188B, 191B; The Courtauld Art Institute: 22; Gerry Cranham: 40, 73, 76B, 78T, 80B, 115, 143, 145, 151T, 152, 158–9, 160, 164–5, 203, 208, 210, 212, 215, 186B, 188T, 189, 192B; Mary Evans Picture Library: 27, 38B; Messrs Fores, London: 20, 39T; Richard Shaw/*Financial Times*: 190T; taken from *The Grand National* by Clive Graham and Bill Curling, published by Barrie and Jenkins, London 1972: 7, 8, 11, 17T, 21, 25, 26, 38, 58; *The Illustrated London News*: 8, 16, 23, 24, 39B, 40, 49, 52–3, 54, 57, 62–3, 64, 66, 67, 102, 103, 185, 216; Mrs W.G. Jameson: 25; Mr John Longe: 58; The Mansell Collection Ltd: 28–29; Paul Mellon Collection, Upperville, Virginia: 33T; Bernard Parkin: 17B, 19B, 107; Photosource: 92, 120–1; Popperfoto: title page, 34, 35, 83, 132, 135, 148, 177; Press Association: 33, 36, 97, 108, 109, 123, 127, 130, 141, 155, 156, 161, 178, 179, 180, 184, 187, 198, 204, 207, 209, 212–213B; Regional Magazines Ltd: 15, 19T; E.B. Richardson: 21, 26; W.W. Rouch & Co Ltd: 18, 51, 56, 60, 71, 90, 124; D. Saunders: 150T; George Selwyn: 146T, 148T, 150B, 187; Sport and General Press Agency: 31, 37, 86T, 75, 77, 78B, 101–1, 104, 110, 111, 112–13, 116, 117, 119, 122, 125, 128–9, 130, 134, 145, 146, 157, 168, 183, 195, 196, 199, 200; Sporting Pictures (UK) Ltd: 80T; Sunday Express, Manchester: 142; Bob Thomas: 76T, 147, 149, 151B, 185, 186T, 190B; Captain Robin Thompson: 59; Triple Crown Agency, Oxford: 191T; Major F. Tyrwhitt-Drake: 38; National Museums and Galleries on Merseyside, the Walker Art Gallery: 33B; Gordon Whiting: 140L; United Press International: 140R.

LOTTERY

1839: First winner

'Dandy' Jem Mason, first winning rider of the Grand National.

IF ONE QUALITY is needed above all others to win the world's greatest steeplechase, the Grand National, it is 'heart', that intangible will to win; only then come luck and ability...

So it was with the very first winner, Lottery, and Jem Mason, a highly spirited pair with as much will as talent. There was nothing foppish about 'Dandy' Jem, as he became known, when, at the age of fourteen, he set off with his cob to travel the 80 miles from Stilton, Leicestershire, to his parents' new home near Harrow. Having scorned a lift in the carriage, the lad completed the journey on horseback in one day.

His father was a horse jobber and so it was natural that Jem and his brother, Newcombe, should grow up nagging and making horses, schooling them and showing them off in the hunting field. Horses were in Jem's blood, and so when he discovered that a dealer called Mr Tilbury had about 200 horses near their new home, and that Mr John Elmore, a great steeplechasing figure of the time, had horses only 4 miles away, he was soon to be found 'rough-riding' for them – if it happened that Jem found his way more frequently to Elmore's, it might just have been that the owner's pretty daughter had something to do with it.

Soon Jem had but two ambitions: to be a famous jockey and to win the hand of the fair Miss Elmore. Being a determined sort of chap, with that inherent will to win, he succeeded in both.

'The 'orse can jump from 'ell to 'ackney.'

Jem learned much about horse coping from Mr Elmore, who had an old-fashioned manner but knew how to win races, often working his horses in hand. When Mr Elmore acquired Lottery, Jem set about training him in a fashion that would be considered cruel today but raised few eyebrows at the time. Not that then, before the birth of the Grand National, he was considered a likely top horse. None could have foreseen that he would still rank among the immortals 150 years later.

Bred in Yorkshire on the Jackson farm near Thirsk, the mealy-brown colt, who was originally called Chance, was by another horse called Lottery out of an unregistered mare, Parthenia. He was unfurnished, narrow and rather long-backed but showed modest promise by winning a flat race at the Holderness Hunt meeting of 1834 as a five-year-old. He was then sent to Horncastle Fair and offered for sale as a hunter.

John Elmore was the only dealer to take much interest in the leggy horse; he had him trotted up, then got Newcombe Mason to jump him over some rails. He was a bit green, but Newcombe reported, 'The 'orse can jump from 'ell to 'ackney,' and a deal was done for £120.

Not that Lottery's jumping lived up to much when he arrived back at the Harrow stables: in his first schooling session he fell over a gate and was out of action for some months.

It was at about this time that Jem Mason set out on the path towards his first ambition: to be a famous jockey. At the St Albans meeting of 1834, he was offered the ride on a rogue reject from the flat, a hard puller called The Poet, owned by Lord Frederick Beauclerk, the hunting vicar of St Albans. The ground was a quagmire, and it was all Jem could do to carry his saddle and the 4 stone of lead needed to build his weight up to the required 12

Lottery makes light of the massive wall in front of the stands.

stone. Things went badly for him at the start, for the horse was slowly away and refused the first fence. Lord Beauclerk, wanting to do well on his local track, wrung his hands in despair, probably wondering why he had put up such an inexperienced young jockey, when suddenly everything changed, for, as Ivor Herbert and Patricia Smyly said in *Winter Kings*, 'Mason had magic in his hands and quicksilver in his heels and few horses would not run sweetly for him.' He won by 20 lengths.

No wonder, after such a debut, everyone in racing was talking about Jem Mason. His name was made. There was not a big race he did not go on to win in his career, and he even went to France, where he won the big steeplechase in Paris on St Leger.

With fame came Jem's love of clothes and of a gentlemanly image. He found tailors in Savile Row who were only too happy to cut him fine suits for nothing, knowing he would be a walking advertisement for them. As for his boots (free, of course), he had the feet made by Messrs Wren in Knightsbridge and the legs by Messrs Bartley in Oxford Street; history does not record which maker stitched the two together. On his hands, he wore white kid gloves.

None of this finery prevented Jem from getting on with his job of schooling young horses, and with Lottery he had plenty of wrangles. The jockey always made sure he won the battles, but he took many falls in the process. The first thing he did when the horse arrived was dispense with the severe curb bit, using instead a double-reined snaffle, and set about converting the 'uncouth brute' into a 'balanced, cracking hunter', regularly following Mr Anderson's fast-running staghounds. If Lottery fell at a fence, Jem would give him such a hard knock that the horse made sure he jumped it clean

'Mason had magic in his hands and quicksilver in his heels and few horses would not run sweetly for him.'

next time. Should he refuse, Jem kept at him until he jumped, even if it ended in a fall. He even made him jump the garden table, set for a meal, and chairs – which became quite a party piece – and anything else he could find to school over.

Soon Lottery detested the sight of Jem so much that, when they went racing, Jem had to hide his racing silks under his jacket until the last minute before mounting, lest he should be savaged. But then the horseman kidded him into tractability, Lottery responding to what were described in *Winter Kings* as Jem's 'magic hands and the hypnotic power in the soul of all great jockeys'.

Lottery's early racing career was inauspicious: he raced round little local tracks, today mostly covered by London suburbs, even indoors at the Bayswater Hippodrome; he dead-heated in a steeplechase at Kensal New Town, but it was when he bolted off the course at Finchley and leaped right across a lane that Jem told John Elmore that this was no ordinary hunter.

In 1837 he ran in the St Albans Steeplechase, the precursor of the Grand National, but his saddle slipped. Before the 1838 race he was 'amiss' and, as was the custom of the day (for both humans and equines), he was 'bled'. Even with this drastic treatment he finished third (and was placed second after an objection). When fully recovered, he won a big steeplechase at Barnet in 'a common canter', and then caused a minor sensation by beating Captain Becher on his great Vivian at Daventry, more famous today for its radio mast than any trace of a racecourse.

So John Elmore's sights were firmly set on the big new steeplechase that was to be run at Aintree the following year, a similar race having taken place at nearby Maghull for the past three years. He sent Lottery to the Epsom yard of George Dockeray, who had won the Derby with Lapdog. There, none of the speedy flat-racers could get away from the raw-boned half-bred chaser called Lottery.

The new race was all the rage and over fifty of the best steeplechasers in the land were entered, including some from Ireland. Called the Grand Liverpool Steeplechase (in 1843, the Liverpool and National Steeplechase), it was a sweepstake of 20 sovereigns, forfeit 5 sovereigns, with 100 sovereigns added; weights 12 stone each for gentlemen riders; 4 miles across country; the second to save his stake, the winner to pay 10 sovereigns towards expenses; no rider to open a gate or ride through a gateway or more than 100 yards along any road, footpath or driftway.

Aintree was a veritable Mecca.

Long before the time of radio and television, cars or planes, sponsorship or mass media, the whole racing fraternity was talking about the race and, on the day, Aintree was a veritable Mecca. From north, south, east and west, Scotland, Ireland and Wales they came, by railway, steamer, coach, gig, wagon; the gentry arrived in 'swell turn-outs' and stayed in fine mansions. The Liverpool hotels and boarding houses were overbooked to the extent that some slept four to a bed; the Waterloo and Adelphi Hotels each let 100 beds. Omnibuses and horse-drawn

cabs were so full that even offers of half a guinea for a 2/6d seat failed – with the result that, on Tuesday 26 February 1839, droves of people walked the 3 miles from Liverpool to Aintree in the bright early morning sunshine, ready for a scheduled 1.00 p.m. start. Piemen mixed wich chimney sweeps, cigar sellers with thimble riggers; all roads led to Aintree and were jammed solid; some scuffles developed in brimful taverns along the way; and pickpockets had a field day.

The fashionable wore tall hats with curved brims and short boots with loose 'trowsers'; some were dressed in frock coats, while others kept to knee breeches and hessian boots. Women, and there were a fair few, wore large, fan-shaped bonnets, shawls across their shoulders and 'skirts of majestic volume'.

Soon the crowds had filled the stands to overflowing, paying 7/- each for the privilege, unable to find more than oranges and hot gingerbread to eat as other provisions ran out. They were abuzz. Would the Irish horse Rust beat the English favourite Lottery, who could be backed at 5–1? Or would the fancied mare The Nun prove good enough on the day? Surely the best bet to clear the 5-foot stone wall in front of the stands would be another well-backed mare, Charity, for she was trained over stone walls in Gloucestershire. Would Tom Ferguson's three Irish horses, Rust, Daxon (which he was to ride himself) and Barkston, cope with the fly fences after their native banks and ditches?

There were only three really formidable fences on the course. Besides the wall, there was a dammed brook making 8 feet of water, faced by

a 3 foot 6 inch timber paling out of plough; this was called Brook no. 1 (but not for long...). Brook no. 2 had a small bank guarding a deep wide ditch and stout post and rails, with an overall spread of 9 feet and a considerable drop. The rest – a total of fifteen on the first circuit, with fourteen jumped again on the second round – were mostly little banks barely 2 feet high, gorsed on top and faced with small ditches. The last two fences were ordinary, upright sheep hurdles.

But the ground was as testing as the most difficult fences; it had been a fill-dyke February and there was plough and wheat to cross as well as turf, very tiring over a distance of 4 miles. Then, as now, it was not a course for the unfit or the faint-hearted.

By the time all the runners and riders had got themselves sorted out – The Nun, found to be 'too fat',

think of: he crawled into the deepest part of the brook to escape the flying hooves. Thus the fence entered history, and ever since has been known as 'Becher's Brook'. As for the captain, he is purported to have said that he never knew water tasted so foul without whisky in it, scrambled out, remounted and chased after the remainder, so hard that he soon regained the lead – only to fall again, after which Conrad galloped off loose, avoiding recapture and a possible further fall.

Meanwhile, Tom Ferguson and Daxon were setting a great pace, the Irishman unaware that another of his runners, Rust, had been trapped in a lane by a mob who, not wanting him to win, had virtually kidnapped him.

LEFT: Packed stands in the National's inaugural year. The race was a success as a spectacle from the start.

BELOW: This is how Capt Becher looked to artist T. H. Bird in the 1830s.

was reputedly given a severe pre-race gallop – and two hours later Lord Sefton called the seventeen horses into line. With a mighty roar from the crowd, he dropped his flag and they were off, skipping over the first small fences.

Daxon was the first to show, followed by Captain Becher on Conrad, but when they came to the first brook Captain Becher fell and, with sixteen other horses thundering towards it, he took the first evasive action he could

There was another surprise at the end of the first circuit, when the Cotswold horse Charity fell at the wall, which Lottery jumped superbly. The Nun seemed to fade at the second brook, and Dictator caught his knees in a fence, fell and was remounted, but he fell dead at the next fence. The race's first fatality caused the sort of outcry in the press which has occurred repeatedly up until the present time – Dark Ivy being the victim in 1987.

It was now becoming obvious that Lottery was going the best and, when Daxon fell, with The Nun and Paulina tiring, Lottery and Jem Mason sailed into the lead. They put in a mighty 33-foot leap at the last hurdle and won, as they liked, in a canter.

Only Sir George Mostyn's Seventy Four, whose rider was the great 'Black Tom' Olliver, got anywhere near the winner; while the Irish, ignoring the fact that it was the same for everyone, belligerently claimed that the fences had been unfair! Paulina was a poor third, True Blue fourth, The Nun fifth,

... he could trot faster than most could gallop.

Railroad sixth, and Pioneer seventh and last. Of the remainder, poor Rust, who had been abducted, was recorded as pulled up, while Dictator, Conrad, Cramp, Rambler, Daxon, Barkston, Cannon Ball, Jack and Charity all fell.

Lottery's time of 14 minutes 52 seconds is the slowest on record (although in a couple of the early years no time was recorded), but the race had included heavy plough and there is no doubt that he was a great horse. So great, in fact, that, in future races, conditions were stipulated specifically against him, the like of which were not to be seen until the mighty Arkle almost a century and a quarter later. There was one race 'open to all horses except Lottery' and another for which the entry fees were: '£40 Lottery, £5 maidens, £10 all others'.

For Lottery swept all before him after that historic first Grand National win: he won at Cheltenham, Stratford-on-Avon, Maidstone and Dunchurch, after which it was said he could trot faster than most could gallop.

Lottery uncharacteristically fell at the stone wall in the 1840 Grand National, possibly through trying to take on Mr Power on Valentine, who had laid a bet that he would be first over that obstacle. Lottery took a terrible fall, bringing down Columbine and The Nun, who landed in a heap on top of him. Yet his reputation was such that the following year, after he had won the Cheltenham Steeplechase, the

BELOW: Another view of the wall, with one intrepid rider 'hailing a cab'.

Lottery beats Seventy Four to win the first Grand National.

Grand National conditions stipulated that a winner of the Cheltenham race must carry an *18-pound* penalty. (The weight for the National was a level 12 stone for the race's first four runnings; thereafter it became a handicap.) So in 1841, when the wall was temporarily replaced by an artificial brook, the great Lottery was burdened with 13 stone 4 pounds – which remains a record – and Jem Mason, with good sense ahead of his time, pulled the horse up.

In the next National, the organisers again insisted that Lottery shoulder the 18-pound penalty for his Cheltenham win two years earlier; the public would not forsake their hero and backed him down to 5–1, but the weight proved too much and he was again pulled up. It seems poetic justice that the winner was another horse of John Elmore's, Gay Lad.

In 1843, when the race became a handicap and the stone wall was revived for one more year before it became banned for ever, Lottery ran

> 'I can say without fear of contradiction that he was the finest horseman in England – I have never ridden with him without envying the perfection of his style.'

once more. Now carrying 12 stone 6 pounds, on fast ground in contrast to the first year's deep, he was backed to 4–1 second favourite and was not disgraced in finishing seventh.

Lottery is known to have won his last race at Windsor in 1844, but accounts of his retirement vary: either he became a hack at Epsom then pulled a cart at Neasden, or he pulled a plough, or he retired to the hunting field.

For Jem Mason there was to be a painful illness of cancer of the throat, from which he died in 1866. The esteem in which he was still held was such that Tattersalls organised a Jem Mason subscription, to which many people felt honoured to contribute. He had numerous glowing obituaries, none more sincere than that of his long-time friend and rival, Tom Olliver, who had ridden hundreds of miles with him both racing and schooling across country: 'I can say without fear of contradiction that he was the finest horseman in England – I have never ridden with him without envying the perfection of his style.'

GEORGE STEVENS

1856–70: Rode most winners

George Stevens (1833–1871), the only jockey to have won five Nationals.

IF THERE WAS EVER a fine judge of pace and master of the tactical waiting race it was George Stevens, record five-times winning rider of the Grand National, the instigator of the maxim 'hunt round on the first circuit'.

A jockey of unusual caution – whose approach was just the reverse of the devil-may-care attitude that typifies many intrepid riders – he was rewarded with almost no injuries in a career spanning twenty years, only to be killed while riding his cob at home.

Born in 1833 on Cleeve Hill, overlooking what is now the premier National Hunt track at Cheltenham, it was at Aintree, home of the world's most famous steeplechase, that Stevens left his indelible mark.

His was a feat of horsemanship and jockeycraft unparalleled. Between 1856 and 1870 he won the National on Free Trader, on the sisters Emblem and Emblematic, and twice on The Colonel; and he unselfishly passed on his knowledge and advice to many budding young riders.

About the most rash thing Stevens ever did was run away from home to become a jockey. Although he was light and small enough to ride on the flat, it was the sight of steeplechasers in action in the natural amphitheatre of Cheltenham racecourse below his home that stirred the lad. He grew up at a time when the sport was having to

'hunt round on the first circuit.'

withstand pressures from such as Dean Close, founder of the school which bears his name in Cheltenham, who opposed racing on moral grounds.

Once in the saddle he displayed nothing but cool confidence.

In Tom Olliver, one of steeplechasing's first riding cracks, George found the best possible mentor, and he gleaned much valuable advice from him.

George Stevens calculated his riding

to the last degree in order to avoid interference. To see his frail form shivering with nerves before a race, one might have thought his career doomed, but in fact he was simply concentrating intensely on the task ahead. Once in the saddle he displayed nothing but cool confidence. He would invariably lay off the leaders on the first circuit and at Aintree would frequently drop himself out in last place.

In race after race those in the stands thought he must have left it too late. Time and again he would catch hold of his horse's head and come with a rattle to pass runners tired by the pace and distance; his timing seldom let him down.

George was eighteen years old when he achieved his first major success, winning the Grand Annual Steeplechase at Wolverhampton; and that year, 1852, he had his first ride in the Grand National, without success. The title 'Grand' had been prefixed to the National five years earlier in 1847, when its precise title became The Grand National Handicap Steeplechase.

From the start his style caused considerable comment. Never one to bustle a horse going into a fence, he remarked, 'More races are lost through a horse being interfered with than by falling of their own accord.'

George's home town of Cheltenham

The gentry in all their finery flocked to the early Grand National meetings.

took the small, delicate-looking man to their hearts. After his first National win on Free Trader in 1856, at the age of twenty-two, they lit a bonfire on Cleeve Hill and presented him with a watch. The horse's owner, Mr W. Barnett, also gave him a present of £500. Free Trader, a brown stallion by The Sea, carried only 9 stone 8 pounds and started at 25–1, in spite of having finished second the previous year, only two lengths behind Wanderer. It was the year Mr Topham was criticised for cutting the size of the fences.

George Stevens should really have won six Grand Nationals. He rode in the race without success in each of the four years after Free Trader, including 1858, when poor weather postponed it for three days and only 500 people attended. In 1861 he turned down no fewer than thirteen

rides in order to take the mount on Jealousy, whom he was sure would win. Then at the last minute an owner who paid George a retainer vetoed it, even though he did not offer an alternative ride. Stevens had to watch Jealousy win from the stands.

His 1862 mount was unplaced, but then came his splendid double on full sisters, the chestnuts Emblem and Emblematic, both of them rather weedy-looking flat-race cast-offs. Lord Coventry had bought the mares from Mr Halford, paying 300 guineas for Emblem as a three-year-old after thirteen runs on the flat with one win, and 250 guineas for Emblematic. They were not bred to be staying chasers; their class came from their sire, Derby-winner Teddington. Emblem was sent hunting in the Cotswolds to learn her new job, but she appeared to be decidedly lacking in aptitude. The plough

George Stevens on Emblem, Lord Coventry standing with him.

which was still much in evidence round Aintree would surely sap her of what little stamina she had. But that was without taking her jockey into the reckoning; for, over the first 4 miles of the 1863 National, she did not race at all.

Stevens simply hacked her quietly at the back, going the shortest way, while all sorts of disasters took place ahead of them, and did not produce her on the scene until the last hurdle. The crowds held their breath then as she jumped sideways, but the consummate horseman Stevens sat tight and the mare drew away for a 20-length victory. The residents of Cleeve Hill lit another bonfire that night.

They were to do so again the following year, when Stevens rode Emblematic. The popular press had been full of criticism about the small size of the course and the state of the Grand National in general, and had especially expressed surprise that a flat racehorse should be able to compete in a race intended for staying chasers.

Emblem Cottage, George Stevens' home on Cleeve Hill, Cheltenham.

In fact, Emblematic was more robustly made than her sister, with good shoulders and quarters, although also somewhat lacking in bone, and she relished the perfect ground and bright weather.

It was another race with plenty of mishaps among the twenty-five runners, and it climaxed in another masterly Stevens-produced win. What's more, the jockey won £300 from having backed her; Lord Coventry won £500 from his bet, which he gave to Stevens. On the proceeds, George built a new home on Cleeve Hill, calling it Emblem Cottage.

Both mares ran in 1865, Lord Coventry 'declaring to win' with Emblematic, as was the custom of the time when two or more runners were in the same ownership. Emblematic started favourite but she was carrying 18 pounds more than before and Stevens for once overplayed the waiting game, finishing third to Alcibiade. Emblem, burdened with 12 stone 4 pounds on her slender back, was pulled up.

If the mares' breeding had been in the purple, the case with Stevens's next

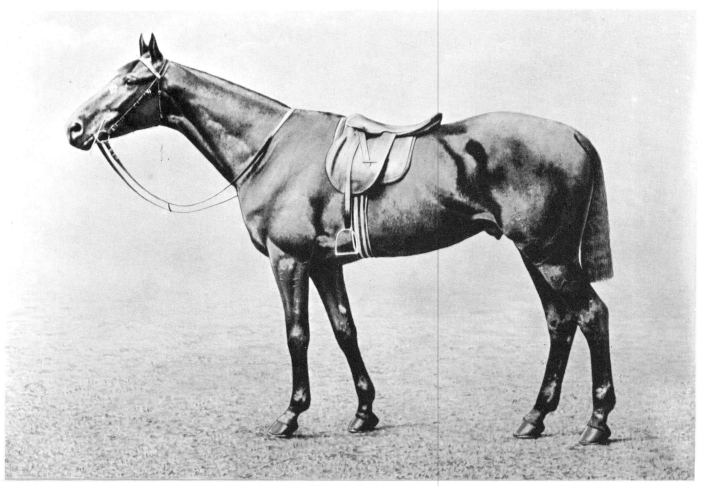

The Colonel.

National winner was just the reverse, for The Colonel was supposed to have Exmoor-pony blood on his sire's side and his dam was half-bred. Nevertheless he also had Stockwell blood in him. Stockwell had won two Classics, the 2000 Guineas and St Leger, suggesting he possessed both speed and stamina, and was a champion sire for over a decade.

The Colonel was bred near Ludlow by John Weyman, who co-owned him with Matthew Evans, an uncle of George Stevens's wife. Stevens helped to break in The Colonel, who was big and had powerful limbs – far more strongly built than the mares. He ran one year in Mr Weyman's name and the next in Mr Evans's.

As usual, Stevens had been offered several mounts in the 1869 National, and again he made the right choice in The Colonel. He was probably rather like Lester Piggott in painstakingly ferreting out the best prospect.

The race was almost a carbon copy of his previous wins: plenty of trouble up front as horses fell or refused or were brought down; behind them, riding a copybook waiting race, the incomparable Stevens, like a cat poised to pounce. The cheers for his cool riding, which had taken him into that winner's enclosure for a fourth time, were deafening. Again, his home town cheered to the echo, sang his praises, drank his health – and lit another victory bonfire.

When George Stevens, then thirty-seven, set out on The Colonel in 1870, he already had a record number of National wins under his belt, but of all his rides in the race this was to prove the most exciting. For, that year, there was one rider out to emulate him, to take a leaf out of his book. As Stevens and The Colonel lobbed quietly round in the rear on the first circuit, for once they were not alone: George Holman and The Doctor were there too. And when Stevens made his forward move, Holman followed suit, finding, as Stevens had so often before, a mount fresh and full of running beneath him.

The man who looked as if a puff of wind would blow him over had ridden nearly 100 winners in the toughest sport of all.

The consequence was one of the greatest finishes in the history of the race, as the pair, closely attended by the mare Primrose, raced neck and neck towards the last flight. There, Primrose pecked, but The Colonel and The Doctor, both as gallant as their names, fought it out stride for stride with the crowd roaring. In the end it was only Stevens's superior strength and experience which prevailed; riding like a man inspired, he coaxed The Colonel home by a neck, with Primrose only a length away in third.

When George Stevens rode his retirement race on The Colonel the next year, unplaced, the crowds broke into spontaneous applause for their hero as he returned. The man who looked as if a puff of wind would blow him over had ridden nearly 100 winners in the toughest sport of all, five of them in the Grand National itself. The toast of the town wherever he went, he could look forward to a well-earned retirement, coaching young riders and probably horses, too.

It was not to be. As he hacked home towards Emblem Cottage after meeting a few friends in The Rising Sun on 2 June, a gust of wind blew off his hat and, as a lad lifted it back to him, Stevens's horse took fright and bolted down Cleeve Hill. Nearing the foot of the steep hill, the horse stumbled over a drainpipe and Stevens was thrown into the gutter, crashing his head against a stone. Aghast local people gingerly carried him into a nearby farmhouse, but his skull was fractured and he died the next day without recovering consciousness.

A plaque marks the spot where he fell:

In memory of George Stevens, the rider of the winners of five Grand National steeplechases who, after riding for 20 years with no serious accident was here killed by a fall from his hack only three months after riding 'The Colonel' in the Grand National of 1871.

TOP: The Clown, the cob on which Stevens suffered his fatal accident.

ABOVE: The headstone marking the spot on Cleeve Hill where George Stevens was killed.

THE LAMB

1868, 1871: Dual grey winner

Lord Poulett owner of The Lamb, from a cartoon published in 1887.

ONLY TWO GREYS – The Lamb and Nicolaus Silver – have won the Grand National, and the horses had several other things in common: either could have won in the show-ring; their owners, although separated by ninety years, became related by marriage; and both horses died as a result of breaking a leg.

The Lamb, a stallion who won in 1868 and 1871, was literally a pony, standing only 14.3 h.h. when first broken, and although he grew a little more he was most probably the smallest winner.

Foaled in 1862 by Mr Henchy, a farmer in Co. Clare, The Lamb was by Zouave out of an unnamed mare by Arthur, who was himself second in the 1840 Grand National; Zouave was bred by Mr Courtenay, owner of Matthew, the first Irish winner of the National in 1847.

The Lamb had features similar to an Arab horse: an almost dish face; big, dark, liquid, wide-apart eyes; and a marked daintiness. Certainly he looked too frail and small to be a racehorse to the first person to whom he was offered, one Edward Studd, who had just won the 1866 Grand National with his Salamander. 'He's not fit to carry a man's boots,' the owner declared. (Mr Studd had to swallow his words some five years later when his horse Despatch led over the last in the National,

only to be beaten on the run-in by The Lamb.) The very prettiness of the horse earned him his name. Mr Henchy's son was a delicate lad and he liked the gentle foal so much that he named him The Lamb.

It was for a sickly child that The Lamb was finally bought, as a pony, by Dublin veterinary surgeon Joe Doyle for £30. It is believed that Doyle passed a half-share on to a William

'He's not fit to carry a man's boots.'

Long for £300. Mr Doyle's daughter suffered from consumption and it was considered necessary for her to pursue an activity in the fresh air.

Joe Doyle's granddaughter Noreen (Begley) became the third wife of Jeremy Vaughan, owner of the 1961 winner Nicolaus Silver; Mr Vaughan is a first cousin of Captain Tim Forster,

trainer of three National winners, Well To Do, Ben Nevis and Last Suspect.

Being a top vet, Joe Doyle had an eye for a horse and could see at once that the grey pony was a smart little number – too much so for his weak daughter, as it turned out, for he was constantly jumping out of his paddock. This was quite likely the result of too much food and not enough exercise, but anyway it was discovered he had a turn of foot and so he was leased to Lord Poulett to go into training.

The sixth earl, Lord Poulett had served in three regiments before settling in Waterloo, Hampshire, where he was Master of the Hambledon Hunt for nine seasons and became a founder member of the National Hunt Committee and a steward. He was also a keen yachtsman and a notable whip.

The Lamb's first runs were in Ireland, where he started well by winning the Kildare Hunt Plate at Punchestown by 4 lengths for the £285 prize. But he failed in his next two runs at Louth and he was sent to England, where he was trained for the National.

Helping Lord Poulett was his great friend, the gentleman rider George Ede, alias 'Mr Edwards', who lived with him and who rode 306 winners in fourteen years before his untimely death in the Grand Sefton of 1870 on a chance ride. Ede's other great passion was cricket and he was a joint founder of Hampshire Cricket Club and a re-nowned batsman.

By the time the 1868 National came round, it was clear that The Lamb was one of those little horses with a big heart, that intangible quality that can make all the difference between win-ning and losing on the racecourse. He had agility, too, and was soon vying for favouritism with Chimney Sweep and Moose.

1868 was very much an inter-national year, with challengers from France and Germany as well as

The Lamb was one of those little horses with a big heart.

Ireland, but the meeting did not get off to an auspicious start, for on the open-ing day there was one walk-over and one race in which all three runners refused the first fence! Nevertheless, Liverpool was bursting at its seams. The National was not thirty years old and, then as now, held tremendous sway with the public. A fierce wind blew down the elite's gambling tent and the police had their work cut out to move the crowd of roughs who swarmed round.

The Lamb was trained by Ben Land, who had transformed the pretty pony into a hard, fit, well-muscled race-horse. Land had formerly been a far-mer in Norfolk, where he kept his own pack of staghounds, and was an amateur rider, but he had turned to training of both horses and riders with great success. George Ede had been under his wing when still an Eton schoolboy; George would leave his school lessons for coaching in steeplechasing.

The success of that coaching was never more apparent than in the Na-tional of 1868. The race itself was full of incident, with several horses refusing and falling. One unfortunate casualty on the flat was Lord Poulett's Chimney Sweep, who struck a stone as he crossed the Melling Road, shattered a pastern and had to be destroyed.

The Lamb, meanwhile, was in the front rank and led Pearl Diver by half a

George Ede, sporting the fashionable moustache of the time.

length approaching the water. Here, Ede's prowess, quick thinking and cool head came into their own, for he was being harried by two loose horses, one on either side. He calmly hit one with his whip, changed hands, and hit the other before jumping the water per-fectly. It was an operation executed smoothly, quickly, neatly and efficient-ly – to the delight of those spectators sharp-eyed enough to have spotted it – and one that would be equally admired today in that relatively rare thing, a real horseman.

Going out into the country for the second time it was the previous year's winner, Alcibiade, who took over from The Lamb, Pearl Diver, Moose and Colonel Crosstree, and this quintet drew some hundred yards clear of the remainder. Then Pearl Diver and The Lamb broke clear, going into the last together. 'Now you'll see what the Diver will do with the pony,' said one watcher, but it was the gallant grey who squelched through the mud best for a victory, quoted variously as by a head or by 2 lengths.

The National is full of might-have-beens... The Lamb was entered again the following year but, by one of those irritating mistakes, his age was incorrectly supplied and his entry re-

fused. So, while The Colonel won the 1869 National, The Lamb was fourth in the Grand Sefton, a race patently too short for him.

That was to be his last race for two years; The Lamb suffered a wasting disease in his hindquarters, his muscles shrank to nothing, and in the end it was only rest and blistering which cured him.

Lord Poulett had a habit of getting the best connections for his horses. In the 1870–71 season, with George Ede having been killed in the 1870 Sefton, he had to find a new jockey. Chris Green, who rode two National winners on Abd-el-Kader and Half Caste, had taken over the training, although in fact Lord Poulett did much of it himself. After a dream, three months before the race, Lord Poulett dashed off a letter post haste to Tommy Pickernell, who rode as 'Mr Thomas', saying:

Let me know for certain whether you can ride for me at Liverpool on The Lamb. I dreamt twice last night . . . the first dream he was last and finished among the car-riages. The second . . . he won by four lengths and you rode him. I saw the cerise and blue sleeves and you as plain as I write this. Now, let me know as soon as you can and say nothing to anyone.

The little grey with a heart like a lion was undoubtedly one of the National's all-time greats.

28
1868

On his way to victory in 1868 is the grey, The Lamb.

As race day drew nearer, the enthusiastic earl had found it impossible to say nothing himself – and so, when trainloads of passengers disembarked at Liverpool and saw a lamb escape from a wagon in a siding and run down the platform, they all knew on which horse they would be placing their shillings! The incident added to the feeling of rejoicing that was already in the air following the wedding of Princess Louise to the Marquis of Lorne at a time when it was unheard of for a princess to be allowed to marry a subject of the crown.

It was The Lamb's first appearance of the season but that was nothing unusual in those days and reports of his well-being were so encouraging that money was heaped on him to the extent that he came out favourite, in spite of his two-year absence and the presence of other previous winners Alcibiade and The Colonel.

At the parade it was clear that The Lamb had thickened out and grown and, unusually for a grey, his coat shone. His appearance was a great credit to his new trainer and to the son of his former trainer, Ben Land junior, who found that it was all he could do to hold the horse as he led him round. (Ben Land himself was to die by cutting his own throat a year later.) The crowds pressed round as 'Mr Thomas' prepared to mount, watched by a relaxed Lord Poulett and his friend Tom Townley. Tommy Pickernell's experience was to stand him in good stead. Born in Cheltenham, he had ridden in Tasmania with such success that the natives there eventually got up a petition asking him to stop! He returned to England, where he was coached by 'Black Tom' Olliver and William Holman and rode under both rules all over Europe.

On a perfect spring day the horses paraded before a crowd of about 45,000, some of them enjoying the privilege of private boxes for the first time. The Colonel was burdened with 12 stone 13 pounds following his wins of the previous two years, and The Lamb carried 11 stone 4 pounds. Even so, many people expected The Colonel to become the first-ever triple winner – a record that, in the event, was not to be set for another 106 years.

The twenty-five runners set off at a scorching pace on ground described officially as 'perfect' and charged through a crowd of local boys who had failed to clear the course in time, scattering them in every direction and injuring not a few. The Lamb was close up and a pocket handkerchief could have covered fifteen at the water. There was still plough in two places, approaching Becher's and at the Canal Turn, where The Lamb lost his place both times. As he approached the Canal Turn for the second time he found two fallen horses in front of him, but neither he nor his jockey panicked and he jumped over them both with the agility of a cat.

Mr Thomas Pickernell, who was aboard The Lamb in 1871.

Back on turf The Lamb regained his position after being vigorously ridden and as they came back onto the racecourse the contest clearly lay between him and Mr Studd's Despatch. The two horses were absolutely together at the last hurdle but The Lamb met it in his stride and cleared it in splendid style to tremendous cheering from the crowd. Despatch threatened briefly on the flat, but it was The Lamb who found the faster turn of foot to run out a 2-length winner in the very fast time, bearing in mind the plough, of 9 minutes $3\frac{3}{4}$ seconds.

The crowd fever and hero hailing for such as Red Rum and Aldaniti in modern times is nothing new. For those extra-special winners it has always been part of the National scene: Cloister, for example, with his welter weight of 12 stone 7 pounds, and Manifesto, who shared in the cheers for the future king's winner, Ambush II, when defeated by him in 1900.

And so it was before any of these for The Lamb. It was a fantastically popular result. The Irish went wild and, it is said, horse, jockey and owner were 'carried bodily' into the winners' enclosure, where amidst the excited reception most of The Lamb's tail hairs were pulled out by souvenir hunters

and Lord Poulett had his gold watch pinched from his pocket (it was later retrieved). Tommy Pickernell, who rode in a total of eighteen Grand Nationals, said in later years that The Lamb was 'the finest fencer' and best horse he ever rode in his life.

Before the next year's National, Lord Poulett's lease on The Lamb ran out and the horse's original owner, Joe Doyle, sold him to a German, Baron Oppenheim, for the then huge sum of 1200 sovereigns. He was made to carry 12 stone 7 pounds in the race, which, despite his tremendous courage, was simply too much for such a small horse to cope with. Still he ran his heart out; yet again he avoided heaps of trouble, but close to home the weight proved too much and on the flat he relinquished third place to his old rival Despatch behind Casse Tete and Scarrington.

The National had again been The Lamb's first run of the season, but he was kept busy after it, running at two hunt meetings. In the first, at Abergavenny, only two weeks later and carrying 12 stone 10 pounds, he was unplaced but he then won at South Hampshire by 30 lengths.

His new owner took him to Germany and in September ran him in the Grosser Preis von Baden-Baden, when he was ridden by Count Nicholas Esterhazy. It was a race of nearly 3 miles and sixteen fences, including a 6-foot-high 'bullfinch'. The gallant 'pony' was winning easily when, just a hundred yards from the winning post, he hit a patch of bog-like ground and, in trying to extricate himself, broke a foreleg and had later to be destroyed.

The little grey with a heart like a lion had won four of his fifteen races and was undoubtedly one of the National's all-time greats.

THE BEASLEY FAMILY

1877–92: Part I, Four brothers

Tom, one of the four Beasley brothers who rode in the 1879 National.

OF ALL THE DISTING-UISHED families who have been connected with the National over the years, few can be more remarkable than the Beasleys. They can be traced back to the sixteenth century, originating from the west of Ireland, were reared on the Curragh, and have always been involved in racing.

Four amateur brothers, Tommy, Harry, Willie and Johnny, rode in the 1879 Grand National and over fifteen years, from 1877 to 1892, they rode four winners, six seconds and two thirds from thirty-four rides; in 1961 Harry's grandson, Bobby, rode another winner, Nicolaus Silver. The brothers were also involved in the only two objections in the history of the race.

Of them all, Harry was perhaps the most outstanding: after winning on Come Away in 1891, he continued steeplechasing until he was seventy-three years old, when he rode at Punchestown. Even that was not the end of his race-riding career, for he rode on the flat for the last time when he was eighty-two. It is said that he once booed his own son, Willie, for beating him by a short head in a 4½-mile chase at Punchestown; Harry was a mere seventy-two at the time.

As for Harry's training methods, they were unorthodox in the extreme. Come Away, who finally gave him a winning National ride, had very bad legs. It was said that, to avoid galloping him on ground hardened by frost, he used to take him out onto the Curragh at night, and gallop him by the light of storm lanterns before the frost had got into the ground. His usual mode of reaching the Curragh from his stables was to jump the rails dividing them.

His brother Tommy had a better National record but was unluckier in the end. He won the big race three times, was second twice, third once and fourth once. But eventually he was killed at the double of banks at Punchestown, and was buried beside it.

Willie was second once, but Johnny was never placed in the National and rode in the race less often than his brothers.

The Beasley National story began in 1877, when Sultana, ridden by 'Mr Beasley', was pulled up. The next year Tommy was second on Captain Grotton's Martha – and he was to win or place for six years in succession. In 1878 Tom lodged the first of only the two objections ever made in the race, alleging foul riding by Jack Jones on the winner, Shifnal. But it was quickly overruled and left a bad taste in the mouth then just as it would now.

Tom rode Martha again in 1879, the year when all four brothers rode, repeating his front-running tactics of the previous year, but the mare could give no more when challenged by Jackal and the winner, The Liberator, finishing third. None of the brothers fell. Willie, on Mr P. M. V. Savrin's Lord Marcus, and Harry, on Mr R. Stackpoole's Turco, both got round, to finish eighth and ninth respectively, and John pulled up on Victor II. Of eighteen starters on ground described as 'average', ten completed the course and only four fell.

Victor II, the only Beasley horse not to complete, was the shortest price of the four, at 100–8. Turco was 100–6, while Martha was on 50–1 in spite of her good run the previous year, and Lord Marcus was unquoted. (Jackal, who finished second, started at the unusual price of 1000–65.)

There was at the time a trainer called Harry Eyre Linde who made winning the Grand National his prime objective in life and built replica Aintree fences on his Curragh training grounds; it seems surprising that no more than a few trainers do so today, sending their horses straight to the National with only park-course experience behind them.

Certainly the practice was successful for Mr Linde, a sergeant in the Royal Irish Constabulary, and for the five-year-old Empress, named after the Empress of Austria, who used to hunt in Ireland. The public not unnaturally assumed that the big chestnut with just a little flat-racing experience would be a complete novice. But Mr Linde had

… the going was so heavy that the thirteen runners could only trot through the mangold fields.

schooled her so thoroughly, and the Irish backed her so heavily, that she started at 8–1 in the National of 1880. With Tommy Beasley in the saddle, she came through beaten horses after the second Valentine's to tackle The Lib-

Harry Beasley on Mr W. G. Jameson's 1891 winner Come Away.

erator. She was flying at the finish, jumped the last superbly and won by 2 lengths. The race was watched by a record crowd, the Prince of Wales among them, and both Harry Beasley on Woodbrook and Johnny on Victoria were among the ten to finish from just fourteen starters.

It was thought that the mare would go on to more victories, but the one apparent disadvantage of Linde's continual schooling was that it had a weakening effect on horses' legs and many broke down. So it was with Empress, and she never ran again, retiring instead to stud.

The ground was bottomless the following year; it had snowed all week and the going was so heavy that the thirteen runners could only trot through the mangold fields. Not surprisingly, a very slow time was recorded. It proved an easy win for Tom Beasley on Woodbrook. Only The Liberator, humping 12 stone 7 pounds, could live with him until falling at Valentine's, when the 1876 winner

Regal took up the challenge, but it was a short-lived one, Tom's horse winning in a canter. Woodbrook was sold to a German for £1300 but died at New-market within a year.

Tom was again on a Linde-trained horse the next year, but they were beaten by a Linde cast-off. Seaman had been sold to Lord Manners for £2000 and the whole of Ireland was laughing, for they knew the horse was unsound. Back at Newmarket, the local wags, seeing the horse's legs, also screwed the hurdle, but the amateur picked him up, held him together, and drove him on. From the bustle with which Tom Beasley suddenly set about Cyrus as Seaman appeared at his quarters, it would appear that he was well and truly caught napping. He was beaten by a short head.

So Lord Manners became the first peer to win the National and, like Dick Saunders exactly 100 years later, was successful in his only ride in the race. As for Seaman, his hind leg had broken

Clearing the water in 1883 is Tom Beasley, right, on the fourth-placed Zitella.

feared that his lordship had been outsmarted.

Lord Manners was a genuine amateur who had never ridden in the National before. In 1882 it was again snowing, the ground was heavy and several horses fell, including the favourite, Mohican, another Linde horse. Tom brought Cyrus through with a seemingly invincible, devastating run and, even as Lord Manners and Seaman appeared on the scene at the last hurdle, the race looked a foregone conclusion.

Seaman was a length behind; he

down irreparably and he never raced again – the third Linde or ex-Linde winner in a row never to do so, and none of them over seven years old.

In 1883 Tom was favourite on the Linde horse Zitella and Harry was riding Mohican. A number of the small, trappy fences had been improved but there was still some plough. Ten runners made it the smallest field in the National's history. It was Zoedone's turn for victory, for the horse appreciated the bigger fences which slowed down some of the faster runners, especially in the ground made heavy by rain. Zitella faded to finish

Harry, Tommy and Willie rode in 1887, seen here jumping the second fence.

fourth and Mohican fell.

The 1884 winner, Voluptuary, was bred at Hampton Court stud by Queen Victoria, was sold for less than £700 as a yearling, and reputedly ended his years on a revolving stage in Drury Lane, appearing nightly in *The Prodigal Daughter*. The six-year-old was ridden to victory by Mr E. P. Wilson, an outstanding amateur who rode in seventeen Grand Nationals in all.

It was a three-horse race going into the final flight, between Harry Beasley on Frigate, Roquefort and Voluptuary; Frigate just led but stumbled and was outpaced by the classically bred Voluptuary who ran very well.

Roquefort, an impressive third, had supposedly pulled a dog cart in the past, but he won the race the next year, 1885, giving Mr Wilson a second successive win, when the course was all grass and railed in for the first time; Frigate and Harry were second again. Poor Zoedone had evidently been poisoned; she fell at the practice hurdle with blood pouring from her nose, then ran lifelessly until taking a vertical dive at the second Becher's and falling in terrible pain. She recovered but never ran again; her owner, Count Kinsky, was heartbroken.

By 1890 the Grand National was taking the shape we know today, railed in, with big fences. W. B. Wollen's splendid picture captures all the drama.

It was certainly a very popular win for Frigate and a real case of try, try, try again...

The only good thing to come out of Zoedone's misfortune was that, from then on, security was considerably improved and a number of highly undesirable characters were weeded out of stables. It was a time of general improvement, and in 1888 the course was altered to its present shape and finished over two small fences within the flat racecourse.

When Willie was second on Frigate in 1888, after Harry had filled the same place on her in 1884 and 1885, the mare looked destined to be always the bridesmaid. But in 1889, this time with Tommy up, and having fallen at the first in 1886 and unseated in 1887, she finally came back the blushing bride – only to fall again in 1890.

Several fancied contenders fell in 1889, including both Voluptuary and Roquefort. Why Not was clear two out, but Tom Beasley kept Frigate going to such cheers that those who could not see thought one of the royal runners, Magic or Hettie, must have won. It was certainly a very popular win for Frigate and a real case of try, try, try again...

Harry Beasley was the only jockey ever to ride the 1891 winner Come Away, and the Irish backed the powerful seven-year-old down to 4–1 favourite.

Come Away, owned by Mr W. G. Jameson, trained and ridden by Harry Beasley, was a tall horse with strong quarters, a long, narrow neck and fine head. He was a high-class individual by Cambusland out of Larkaway and had won two Conynham Cups at Punchestown and a Valentine Chase. But he was difficult to keep sound – hence his midnight frolics on the Curragh – and he had been fired.

The 1891 National proved a contentious ride as well as a winning one for Harry. No fewer than four previous winners were in the race and when three of them, Ilex, the second favourite, Roquefort and Gamecock, jumped the water in line at halfway it looked like being a vintage National. The pace proved too much for the other previous winner, Voluptuary, while two future winners were also in the race: Why Not, who fell carrying joint-top weight of 12 stone 4 pounds, and Cloister. Ilex was a spent force, as was the Linde-trained Cruiser, giving Tom Beasley his last ride in the race (they finished sixth). Going to the last it was a close-fought battle between Cloister and Come Away. Captain Roddy Owen tried to squeeze Cloister through on the inside halfway up the run-in but, as he reached Come Away's quarters, Beasley edged his mount inwards and closed the gap. It was a rousing finish and, as Come Away lived up to his name to score by a length, he clocked the fastest time since The Lamb twenty years earlier.

But it was not over yet; against trainer Richard Marsh's wishes, Captain Owen lodged an objection. Marsh warned him that he might come off second-best again, and so it proved, the stewards taking the view that Beasley had acted within his rights and overruling the objection. Come Away's dodgy legs had finally given way and, although he was fired all round, he was another horse who never ran again.

Harry Beasley's last ride in the National the next year was a complete contrast, for Major Kearlsey's Billee Taylor bolted with him, careering right off the racecourse. But that was not the sort of performance Harry would be remembered for. He loved life and lived it to the full, dying peacefully in his sleep at the age of ninety-one. Now the portrait of Harry and Come Away hangs in pride of place above the sitting room of his grandson, Bobby.

THE BEASLEY FAMILY

1961: Part II, Bobby Beasley

Bobby Beasley, winning rider in 1961 on Nicolaus Silver.

BOBBY BEASLEY has been to hell and back since he won the 1961 Grand National on Nicolaus Silver.

The victory made him financially secure for, with his £2500 share of the prize money, he was able to buy himself a farm in Ireland – 'I could not be in the position I am today had it not been for that,' he says. But he has waged a lonely struggle that saw him in

> 'I would give up racing tomorrow if I could, but I would need a blood transfusion.'

the pits, physically and emotionally a wreck – from alcoholism.

It is now eighteen years since Bobby

touched a drop of alcohol. He has a second wife, Linda, a son, Scott, three and a half, and a neat little house on the edge of Marlborough overlooking the downs just a few miles from his stables with which he has re-started as a trainer. It has not been easy to pull himself back again. 'I would give up racing tomorrow if I could, but I would need a blood transfusion,' he says.

'I had no intention of being a jockey or getting involved.'

At the start, Bobby Beasley did not look like following the family tradition. Born in London, when his father, Harry (junior), was riding for Atty Pearse, he grew up in Ireland from the age of two, yet – strangely, given the country he was living in and the fact that his father trained on the Curragh (for Dorothy Paget through Charlie Rogers, who held the licence) – he did not learn to ride. During childhood, religion was drummed into Bobby, through Christian Brothers, convent education and Catholic family life.

'I had no intention of being a jockey or getting involved,' he recalls. 'My father tried to steer me towards university and more security than racing might bring, and I wanted to take a degree in agriculture. Then one summer when my grandmother, who was a big influence, was staying, she persuaded me to give it a whirl. I was fourteen and had never sat on a horse, but once I made the decision to give it a go, it became an obsession with me – and it's never gone, unfortunately!'

Bobby began by riding as an amateur for his father. Then, when he turned professional, he joined Paddy Slater's stable.

He rode in his first Grand National when he was nineteen, on a tiny mare called Sandy Jane. She stood only 15.2 h.h. but, Bobby says, 'I was young and naive and would nearly have paid to ride.' In fact, by paying his own fare over and staying in a bed and breakfast, it cost him a tenner (after his fee).

This was in the days before the fences were sloped and, Bobby says, the only time he could see over them was when he was in the air. Half way round the second circuit, he was trailing about four fences behind the leaders with many other runners pulling up all around them, but kept going to finish sixth, both horse and rider exhausted. Bobby remembers the trainer, Paddy Murphy from Kilkenny, saying to him, 'If you had laid up with them, how far would you have won by?' The mare's stomach was raw from where she had scraped through the fences and Bobby will always remember the sight of her companion goat licking her wounds. Sadly, Sandy Jane later died when foaling.

Bobby rode Anglo the year after that horse had won the National, but Anglo hated Aintree and after being stuck on the Chair he refused at, of all fences, the water!

He also rode Lizawake, in the year Paddy Farrell broke his back on Border Flight. 'There was a French jockey all over the place,' remembers Bobby, 'and I called to Paddy, "He's going to cause us trouble." Moments later he had knocked me off, then went into Paddy.' As for Lizawake, he jumped the rest of the course loose and finished three fences clear. He ended his days as a successful show-jumper.

It was while Bobby was still with Paddy Slater that his chance came to ride Nicolaus Silver in the Grand National.

A year before the 1961 National, he had seen Nicolaus Silver, then trained by Dan Kirwan, in a 3-mile chase at Naas and remembers thinking: what a smashing looking horse; what a pity he's so moderate.

Nicolaus Silver, a striking grey, was exceptionally well balanced and so good looking he could have won in the show-ring. He was also a very kind horse on whom, when he came to England, Mercy Rimell used to lead the string on non-work days.

Shortly after the Naas race, Nicolaus Silver came up for sale at Ballsbridge and some of Paddy Slater's owners tried to buy him, but were outbid by Fred Rimell on behalf of owner Jeremy Vaughan, himself a great character.

Tim Brookshaw rode the horse for his new stable, in a race at Windsor.

Above: John Frederick Herring's unfinished study of three steeplechase cracks in 1846. Brunette (left), Discount (centre) and Jem Mason on Lottery.

Left: Right from the start, the Grand National has been about jumping. Here, the inaugural winner Lottery shows how it should be done while beside him two come to grief.

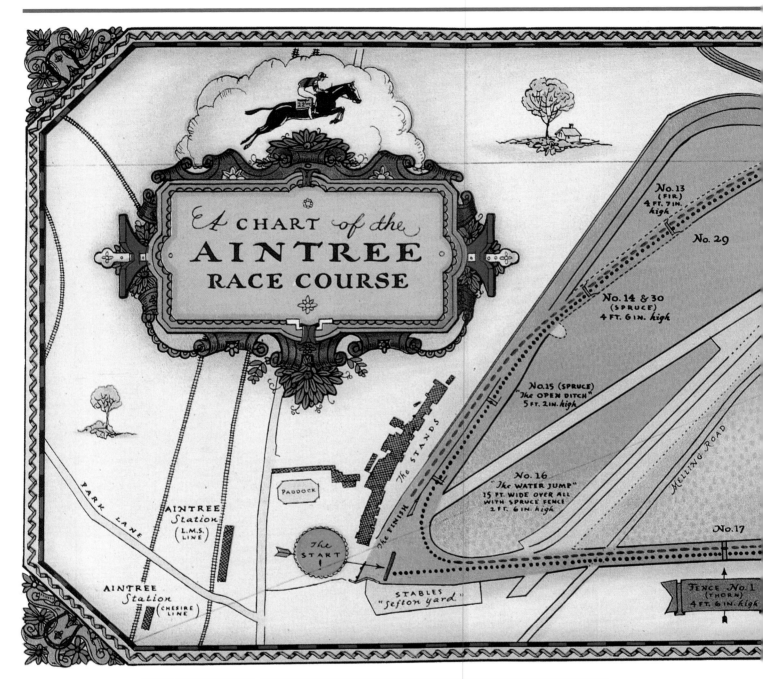

A CHART of the AINTREE RACE COURSE

No.13 (FIR) 4 FT. 7 IN. high

No. 29

No. 14 & 30 (SPRUCE) 4 FT. 6 IN. high

No.15 (SPRUCE) The OPEN DITCH 5 FT. 2 IN. high

MELLING ROAD

No. 16 "The WATER JUMP" 15 FT. WIDE OVER ALL WITH SPRUCE FENCE 2 FT. 6 IN. high

No.17

PARK LANE

AINTREE Station (L.M.S. LINE)

AINTREE Station (CHESIRE LINE)

PADDOCK

The STANDS

The FINISH

The START!

STABLES "Sefton yard"

FENCE No. 1 (THORN) 4 FT. 6 IN. high

Left: In the early years of the Grand National, most of the fences were small banks topped by 2 foot palings.

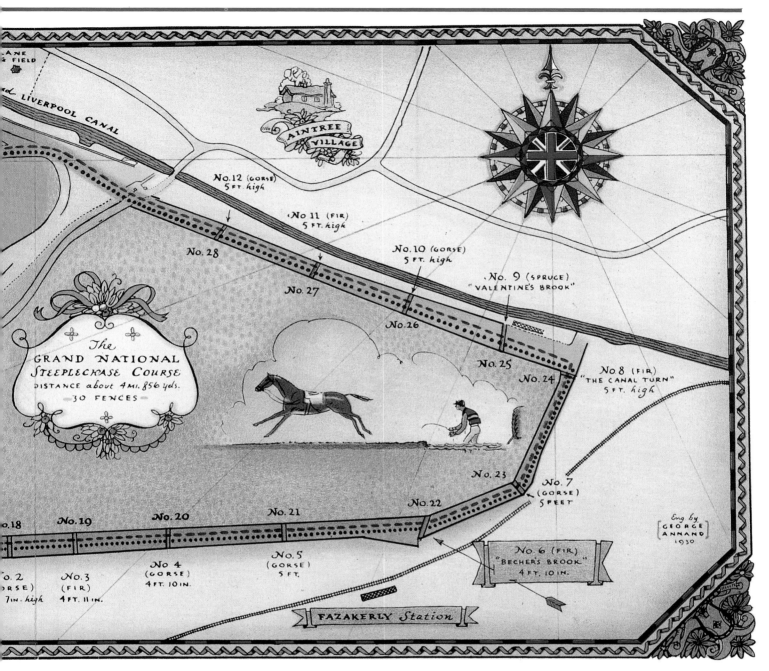

Above: An early map of the course.

Many grey horses are born black but The Lamb, one of only two greys ever to win the Grand National, is said to have become black in older age.

Above: Manifesto, perhaps the greatest Grand National horse of all.
Below: The Prince of Wales' Ambush II won this Grand National.

Above: Manifesto ran in the Grand National a record eight times.

INSPECTING THE BLACK
6ft 3 DROP (12ft if you drop in the ditch)
AT BECHER'S

Left: The most famous fence in the Grand National is Becher's Brook, and it never fails to draw the gapers.

Above: John Burke, Rag Trade's jockey. The pair won the 1976 National.

Left: BBC commentator David Coleman with John Burke and Rag Trade's trainer Fred Rimell.

Down but not out. Nicolaus Silver recovered from this mistake to win.

PREVIOUS PAGE: On their way to victory: Bobby Beasley and Nicolaus Silver.

But he thought he was too careful for Liverpool. So Bobby Beasley received a phone call from Fred Rimell offering him the ride. Bobby was retained by Paddy Slater, who had a runner, Clipador, in the race, but to his credit Slater let Bobby off it, saying he could probably earn more by riding the grey.

Bobby travelled to England twice to ride Nicolaus Silver in preparatory races. To begin with he found the horse stuffy, but then he seemed to come alive.

A pre-race scare nearly prevented Nicolaus Silver from getting to the course at all. Doping was rife at the time and there was a particular gang doing the rounds. The Rimells, aware of the danger, moved the horse from his normal box and swapped him with another grey in the yard, High Spot. High Spot, in Nicolaus Silver's usual box, was 'got at' and was so affected that he never ran again.

Even then, Nicolaus Silver nearly did not make it. When he arrived at Liverpool on the Friday before the National, it was found he had been 'pricked' by the blacksmith when having his racing plates put on. He spent all of Friday night with his foot in a poultice, drawing the abscess, and happily on Saturday morning was found to be sound.

1961 was the year the Russians had two runners in the National. 'I remember the lads laughing and wondering how those "pit ponies" had got in,'

Bobby recalls. 'They had long coats and tails and unplaited manes; the jockeys were brave to ride them, but they probably were forced to be.'

Bobby enjoyed a nearly trouble-free ride on Nicolaus Silver, heeding his idol Bryan Marshall's advice to 'let down your jerks, go round the inside, and take your time'.

'His only mistake was when I asked him too far off Becher's,' says Bobby. 'I can still feel the reverberation now, and the horse's effort to get up – his nose was on the ground. I remember thinking then that if I had a horse I thought a lot of I'd hate to run it in the National, but when you are young, and have the will to win, you can't afford to get involved emotionally with the horses. But even now, I still remember the tremendous effort that horse made to recover.'

A good many horses came to grief, including both the Russians. Going to Valentine's last time the field was led by the previous year's winner, Merryman, with Wyndburgh and the next year's winner, Kilmore, close up, and Nicolaus Silver improving until, with two fences left to jump, he had taken over the lead.

Nicolaus Silver attacked his fences with enthusiasm and, in Bobby Beasley's words, his 5-length victory was achieved entirely on merit. Bobby also praises Fred Rimell for the impro-

Three Russian horses came over in 1961. Two ran but neither completed.

vement he wrought in the horse – 'at least 21 pounds'.

Bobby came across Nicolaus Silver again when the horse was hunting in Sussex: 'I begged the girl who had him to let me have him in retirement, but the next thing I knew he had broken a hind leg galloping through a gateway and was put down.'

After his win in the Grand National Bobby joined Fred Winter, but sadly this was also the time when his sickness set in.

'The first drink I ever had was in Ireland after winning the Galway Plate,' Bobby remembers. 'I was young and green, and the hard-drinking men I was with persuaded me it was time I stopped drinking Club orange and "grew up and became a man". I got silly on champagne, and that was the start of it.'

> ## Nicolaus Silver, a striking grey, was exceptionally well balanced and so good looking he could have won in the show-ring.

He adds, 'People do not look on alcoholism as an illness; they can see cancer as an illness, or if a pop star kicks heroin the papers praise him, but not someone with a drink problem. People take the attitude that all such a person needs is a kick up the backside and plenty of hard work.

'It was dreadful when I had to leave Fred Winter; he was marvellous to me and told me my job would still be there when I came out of hospital, but I felt too ashamed.'

In fact, Bobby returned to Ireland and, in an attempt to beat the booze, took up racing again, with truly remarkable results. In 1974 he won the Cheltenham Gold Cup, no less, on the young and brilliant Captain Christy.

By this time he had been divorced in England and was very much a lapsed Roman Catholic who had had his 'adolescent fling' late in life – a man who had built up something, then set

The striking grey head of Nicolaus Silver.

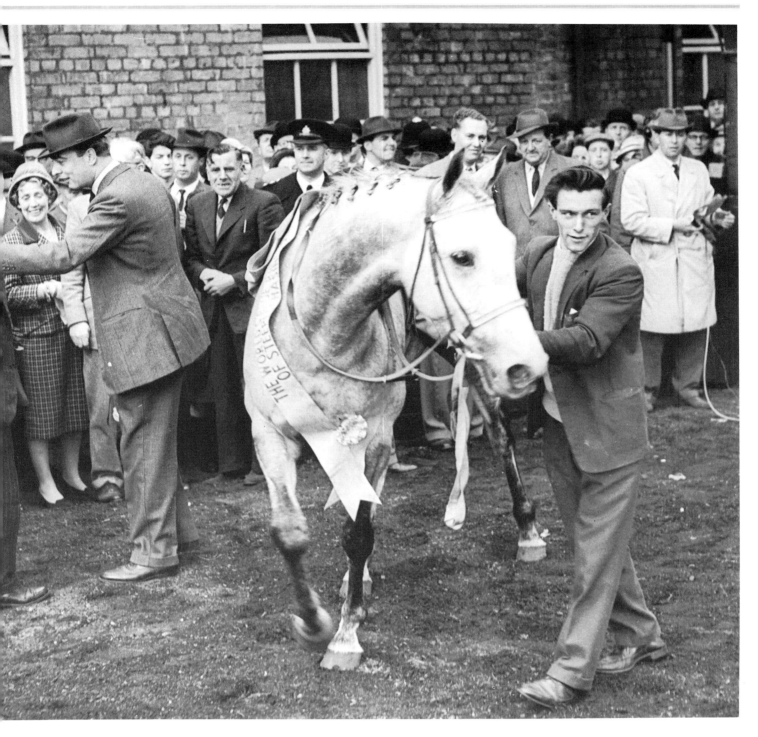

Winner's enclosure: behind Nicolaus Silver is owner Jeremy Vaughan and trainer Fred Rimell (second from right).

'Winning on Christy was almost a bigger kick than the Grand National because it meant I had kicked the booze.'

about destroying it all.

'Winning on Christy was almost a bigger kick than the Grand National because it meant I had kicked the booze,' he says. 'But it has been a long hard haul to be accepted again,' he adds, drawing on yet another cigarette and drinking black coffee – relics of his years of wasting to do the weight. 'I have the scars and I still feel an outsider...'

CLOISTER

1893: Largest winning margin

Mr C. C. Duff, later Sir Charles Assheton-Smith, owner of Cloister, the 1893 winner.

OF ALL THE WINNERS in the Grand National's 150-year history, Cloister can lay claim to being the most dazzling. On a swelteringly hot March day in 1893 he led from start to finish in an unbelievable display of boldness, jumping and weight-carrying.

There were both past and future winners in the line-up but Cloister made it look a one-horse race as he powered to a record 40-length victory, carrying a record 12 stone 7 pounds, and in a time of 9 minutes 32⅖ seconds – a record that stood for forty years.

Three records in one go – which was all the more remarkable because Cloister was born at decidedly the bottom end of the scale, with a sire and dam both described as 'useless'. Bred in Ireland by Lord Fingall, Cloister's sire, Ascetic, later proved himself beyond doubt by also getting the 1903 and 1906 winners, Drumcree and Ascetic's Silver. But in mid-career he earned his keep by being taken to collect the post each day from the village after failing as a racehorse. Cloister's dam, Grace II, not only failed on the racecourse but was described as a hopeless hunter as well.

Their dark bay offspring, however, grew into a super stamp of horse, epitomising all that is best in the staying chaser. One has only to look at W. A. Rouch's portrait of Cloister in either D. H. Munroe's book *The Grand National*, or *The Grand National* by Clive Graham and Bill Curling, to visualise

But how many 'ifs' and 'might have beens' are there in the history of the great race?

his devouring stride and great jumping power, for he stood well 'over the ground' and possessed good bone, splendid sloping shoulders, sensible head carriage and big quarters with a 'jumping bump' from which he held a well-sprung tail. By maturity, he stood 16.3 h.h., and given his size it is not surprising that when he was sold by Irish dealer James Daley he was still somewhat backward. The kind, well-mannered, intelligent horse changed hands several times as a youngster, so that by the time he ran in his first National, in 1891, he was listed as 'aged'. He was in fact seven years old, considered almost universally today as too young for the race, but up until 1887 no horse *over* that age is listed in the admittedly somewhat scanty records as having won.

When Cloister made his first National appearance he was owned by Lord Dudley and trained by Richard Marsh, who was later to train for two kings, Edward VII and George V. On that clear day, there were no great expectations of him, his recently side-lined stable companion Royal Meath being reputedly far his superior. Come Away, the Irish horse, started favourite in a field of twenty-one, and Cloister, his stable's second string, was unconsidered at 20–1. He must have had some assessable form, however, for he carried 11 stone 7 pounds.

It proved a remarkable race between two of the era's finest jockeys, Harry Beasley on Come Away and Captain Roddy Owen on Cloister. It is

Cloister pounded rhythmically on, dust flying behind his heels.

too simplistic to say that Captain Owen was outjockeyed, for he was described as a 'fearless and peerless' horseman and 'the finest of all soldier riders'. As the pair fought out the finish, Owen tried to squeeze Cloister through a gap between his rival and the rails. Harry Beasley, nearing the end of a long and distinguished professional career, would not have it, and 'closed the door' by moving his horse across, effectively boxing in Cloister, and came away to win by a length.

Against trainer Richard Marsh's advice, the furious Captain Owen insisted on an objection, and the two jockeys came perilously close to a punch-up, while the Irish looked like lynching Captain Owen should he be awarded the race. But the stewards ruled that the winner's manoeuvre had been fair play and overruled the objection.

Come Away had broken down badly, and the winning margin was a narrow one. *If* Captain Owen had taken Cloister round Come Away's outside for a clear run, he surely might have won... But how many 'ifs' and 'might have beens' are there in the history of the great race?

By the following year Cloister had matured considerably and had also changed hands. He was now owned by Mr Charles Duff – later to become Sir Charles Assheton-Smith and to own two more winners, Jerry M and Covercoat in 1912 and 1913 – and trained by Arthur Yates.

Roddy Owen would have given anything to ride Cloister again in the 1892 Grand National. The horse had run well all season and even with a weight of 12 stone 3 pounds he was favourite – although no horse carrying over 12 stone had ever won. But with the new stable came a new jockey for Cloister, another amateur, Mr J. C. Dormer. Captain Owen had to make do with the scrawny Father O'Flynn, a 470-guinea purchase with a reputation for refusing. Five years earlier the horse had won a two-year-old selling race at Aintree – shades of Red Rum!

However, the thirty-six-year-old Owen was determined to win a National before going off to fight abroad. (He was to die of cholera or food poisoning serving with Kitchener in Egypt four years later.) Using all his strength on Father O'Flynn, and taking full advantage of his 26-pound weight pull with the front-running Cloister, he emerged from the fog which shrouded much of the course that year to kick on for a surprising 20-length victory.

So Cloister had now been runner-up twice. Could he make it third-time lucky, even carrying 12 stone 7 pounds, having failed under less weight the previous year? His supporters thought so, and in 1893, at nine years old and in his prime, he again started favourite.

Cloister's amateur rider, Mr Dormer, was now out of action, having had the misfortune to lose an eye in a horrible fall at Sandown, and so the horse had yet another pilot, stable jockey William Dollery.

The race was on 24 March that year, during a freak spring heatwave. The ground at Aintree, always well drained and fast drying, was described officially as 'very hard and dry'. As the crowds began to pour into the course, by foot from Liverpool, in horse-drawn conveyances or by steam train, they could sense they were in for a scorcher. They weren't to know that the race would be a scorcher too.

There was a keen sense of anticipation in the packed stands, while Cloister's owner, Charles Duff, strutted about proudly in his suit and bowler hat, sporting a handlebar moustache and monocle, a pair of binoculars slung over his shoulder and resting on his ample belly. The runners jumped the practice flight of hurdles in front of the stands and cantered on down to the start.

At first, William Dollery, the professional, tried to be master of Cloister's performance, attempting to hold him up and present him at the first couple of fences, but the jockey quickly let the horse settle in his own inimitable style: head low, as he ate up the ground, gripped hold of the bit and surged forward – a packed powerhouse doing what he loved best, galloping and jumping.

There may have been other runners alongside or fractionally ahead of Cloister at the first fence; after that, he never saw another horse. He flicked over the fences as if they were toys, his long, lolloping stride devouring the ground effortlessly for every yard of the $4\frac{1}{2}$ miles.

There were fifteen runners in the race, but fourteen of them might just as well not have been there. Cloister pounded rhythmically on, dust flying behind his heels, the rest well strung out behind him by the end of the first circuit. He took the water in his stride, flicked over the hurdles and set out on a glorious second circuit: a procession led by the king, his minions trailing.

It was no longer a matter of who would win but by how far he would do it. Down the daunting stretch towards Becher's Cloister galloped; the big drop fence and brook might just as well have been another hurdle and he swept on, his lead increasing all the time.

All Dollery could hear was the beat of his magnificent partner's hooves and, as they headed back towards the racecourse proper, the rising crescendo of the ecstatic crowd. Two fences from home Cloister was still gaining on his rivals, good winners many of them, but outclassed, outgalloped, outjumped and totally eclipsed now.

When the post came, Cloister's nearest rival, Aesop, was a full 40 lengths adrift; Cloister had had no other horse to spur him on for over 4 miles but on the fast, dry ground he had clocked an astonishing record time. And he had shouldered his 12 stone 7 pound burden as if it were a feather weight.

It was the greatest single Aintree performance up to that time, if not of all time. Those fortunate enough to witness it talked about it for the rest of their lives – and the memory brought tears to their eyes.

Nothing like Cloister's achievement had been seen before, nor has been since, nearly 100 years later. The great era of Manifesto was shortly to follow; Golden Miller, five times winner of steeplechasing's blue riband, the Cheltenham Gold Cup, added the 1934 National to that class sequence;

Crisp came the closest to a Cloister-like victory but tired; Red Rum is a living Liverpool legend who was as clever as they come; and the little grey hero The Lamb had already stamped his name in the National record book: any of these might have been judged better than Cloister, but none won quite like him.

Nor was Cloister's a moderate year. True, it was in the days of much smaller fields than currently, but it included the previous year's winner, Father O'Flynn, who finished sixth, and the next year's, Why Not, who was third.

Further success looked assured for Cloister, but the fates – or possibly some underhand dealings – contrived to put him out of the next two Na-

In 1893 Cloister led virtually from start to finish to win by a record 40 lengths.

A portrait of Cloister, Dollery up.

tionals. Intrigue may have been involved – unless it was a figment of Charles Duff's somewhat neurotic imagination; certainly there were some mysteries which remained unravelled.

When Cloister was beaten at Sandown by Horizon only a few weeks after his Aintree win, most people, his trainer included, put it down to the race's having been too close to the National. But there may have been a greater significance in that dull performance.

Cloister went mysteriously lame shortly before both the next two years' Nationals, when already a well-backed favourite, and Mr Duff was convinced that his horse had been nobbled. But with hindsight his trainer believed that Cloister must have strained himself internally, perhaps in his kidneys, during his epic National run, which would account for his poor showing so soon afterwards and which, Arthur Yates thought, only recurred when the horse was under the greatest strain during preparation for the next two Nationals.

This may well have been the answer. But it did not explain how he came to win the 1894 Sefton Chase at Liverpool apparently without suffering any ill. And it did not explain why the bookmakers suddenly lengthened Cloister's odds before those next two Nationals, almost before his owner and trainer themselves knew that anything was amiss.

The public were full of confidence about Cloister's 1894 National attempt, even though the horse was handicapped at 12 stone 11 pounds. He had won the Sefton, he was working magnificently, and his odds were amazingly cramped for a National at 6–4. Suddenly his odds shot out to 6–1. On that same day he returned from schooling at Sandown slightly lame. The vet was called and Cloister recovered, but the moment he was schooled again the trouble recurred. Pain in his sciatic nerve was diagnosed, and he was withdrawn a few days before the race.

If that caused consternation and suspicion among Cloister's supporters, it was nothing compared with the outcry that followed his almost identical withdrawal the following year, despite rigorous efforts on the part of Charles Duff to guard him.

In his attempts to thwart skulduggery, if indeed there was any, Mr Duff moved Cloister to Harry Escott's stables on the South Downs at Lewes, Sussex, and installed plain-clothes detectives nearby to keep watch. At first there was no cause for anxiety. The horse was fit, his preparation was proceeding well, and he was established favourite again.

For one of his last pieces of serious work before the race, Mr Escott sent Cloister on a gallop over fences. He ran and jumped perfectly for a mile, his old brilliant self, then suddenly, without warning, he collapsed onto the ground with his tongue hanging out, in much the same way as Devon Loch was to do so sensationally 50 yards from winning the 1956 National. As Cloister staggered to his feet it was obvious he was in pain, and he was scratched from the race. Again, his odds had lengthened before it was seemingly possible for the bookmakers to have heard of this latest mishap . . . Charles Duff was convinced there had been foul play, either from within the stables or even on the part of one of the detectives.

So, while Wild Man From Borneo won the 1895 National, in which Manifesto finished fourth on the first of his eight runs in it, the mystery surrounding Cloister remained, never to be conclusively solved.

MANIFESTO

1895–1904: Most runs

Manifesto is arguably the most consistent National horse of all time.

BEFORE RED RUM devotees suffer apoplexy, and bearing in mind that statistics can be interpreted differently, consider the following. Red Rum: five runs, three wins, two seconds, from the age of eight to twelve years. Manifesto: eight runs, two wins, three thirds, one fourth, one fall, one unplaced, from the age of seven to sixteen years.

Red Rum holds the course speed record and record number of wins. Manifesto jointly holds the record winning weight (12 stone 7 pounds), and the record weight for a place (12 stone 13 pounds); and was probably also the oldest runner, at sixteen years – even then he had to carry 12 stone 1 pound.

Comparisons done, let's look at Manifesto himself. He was a well-made, beautifully proportioned bright bay with black points, a class head, with intelligent eyes set off by a white star and broken snip, a good shoulder and powerful quarters, which were to help him carry the big weights he was allotted.

By Man of War, a supposedly savage stallion, Manifesto was bred in Ireland by solicitor and hobby farmer Mr Harry Dyas, out of his appropriately named mare Vae Victis (Latin for 'woe to the vanquished') at Navan in County Meath.

Although many early National win-

ners, where recorded, were young (five-year-olds won four times up to 1880 and few were over seven years old until the end of the 1880s) Mr Dyas was, to his credit, content to be patient with his horses. Manifesto was a gawky, unfurnished youngster and, after falling in a chase and winning a hurdle in England at the age of four, he returned to Ireland to be given more time to fill out. He ran only twice as a five-year-old, winning a race at Derby, and again only twice at six.

Manifesto took to the mighty fences like a duck to water ...

When Manifesto was seven, Mr Dyas deemed him mature enough for a fuller programme. The horse won the Lancashire Chase and from then on the public began to sit up and look at him. Even in his first National, and despite his inexperience, he was set to carry 11 stone 2 pounds.

Fog hung so densely over the flat expanse of Aintree on National day in 1895 that spectators could hardly see anything of the race, and the nineteen jockeys themselves could see each fence – now all upright furze ones – only as it loomed eerily, black and large, out of the mist.

Manifesto took to the mighty fences like a duck to water and, under Terry Kavanagh, made much of the running until tiring and finishing fourth to Wild Man from Borneo.

That promise came to nought the next year. Some records state that Manifesto fell at the first and brought down Redhill; others that it was Redhill who brought down Manifesto; another, perhaps more likely, that the pair collided. Certainly there was confusion at the first fence as jockeys jostled for position.

Whatever the truth of it, Manifesto and his jockey, Gourley, were out of the race. Twenty-eight runners made it the biggest field for twenty-three years; the bottom weight had been reduced to 9 stone 7 pounds; and the prize money had jumped dramatically from £1500 to £2500 plus entrance stakes. It was won by amateur David Campbell on The Soarer.

The following year, 1897, saw a record attendance, and a bit of style had been added to proceedings by the introduction of paddock name-cloths for each horse. The Prince of Wales's emblem had been embroidered on the corner of the cloth carried by his horse, Ambush II. It was the year of Queen Victoria's Golden Jubilee, and the spectators were in buoyant mood.

Manifesto, a tough and courageous horse.

Mr Dyas, whose gambling prowess was such that bookies apparently quaked in their shoes when they saw him arrive with his loaded satchel, had put Manifesto into training with Willie McAuliffe at Eveleigh and engaged Terry Kavanagh to ride again. It was said that Kavanagh, if told to make a certain weight, would do so by hook or by crook, even if it meant humping sacks of potatoes by day and sleeping in a manure heap at night! There was no need for such drastic action in order for him to ride Manifesto, who, having run before Christmas for the first time – when, unquoted by the bookmakers, he finished unplaced – had been allotted 12 stone 7 pounds.

The same stable's Gentle Ida, 'a slashing great mare', was fancied even more than Manifesto, but she was withdrawn at the last minute and Manifesto and Terry Kavanagh started 6–1 favourites.

The Soarer was in the race again but he fell and fractured his skull at Valentine's and when Timon, leader for much of the way, fell at the penultimate, Manifesto, up with the leaders throughout, was left clear and stormed away to a 20-length victory.

He ran twice more that season, falling in the Lancashire Chase but winning the 3½-mile Grand International at Sandown, the forerunner of the Whitbread Gold Cup, carrying 12 stone 5 pounds. After a winning reappearance at Gatwick the following February, carrying 12 stone 10 pounds and giving *37 pounds* to the runner-up, he looked the closest thing to a certainty for Liverpool.

Manifesto was then sold to Mr Bulteel, who had made a fortune on the Stock Exchange and was anxious to own a National winner. The price was the then huge sum of £4000

J. H. Thornely's magnificent picture of the water jump in 1897, with the winner, Manifesto.

(the same figure was exchanged in a similar bid thirty years later, in 1927, for Jack Horner, winner in 1926). Mr Bulteel, however, suffered the sort of bad luck familiar to so many owners before and since when his magnificent new purchase was injured after getting loose. His stable lad, in a careless moment, had left Manifesto's box inse-

It was not until the following January, happily fully recovered from the consequence of his escapade, that Manifesto ran again. He was unplaced in a hurdle race carrying 13 stone, then came second in another hurdle on 12 stone 7 pounds.

That winter was exceptionally harsh. Everywhere there was frozen or

and his pilot, George Williamson, saw 'one of his legs sticking straight up over my head; the toe of my boot was on the ground and both irons gone. I left everything to the horse and he recovered himself and I picked up the reins and went on.' In such calm and modest words, Williamson described (in *Winter Kings*) his fine feat of horsemanship and Manifesto's ability to find a 'fifth leg'.

Manifesto was carrying 12 stone 7 pounds – 18 pounds more than when he had won previously – and, this time, stable connections thought that Gentle Ida, who had meanwhile been sold for

George Williamson, who rode Manifesto to his second victory, seen in the royal colours.

... Manifesto's ability to find a 'fifth leg'.

an even bigger sum than Manifesto himself, would have the beating of him, being in receipt of 14 pounds. Mr Dyas did not think it possible for any horse, even Manifesto, to give her a stone, and she started favourite, with her stable companion 5–1 second favourite.

But Gentle Ida fell heavily at Valentine's the leader Pistache fell at the Chair and Manifesto made a brilliant recovery at the Canal. Manifesto was pulling Williamson's arms out and there beside him, taking him on at his fences, was riderless Gentle Ida, as if out to prove herself. To all but Williamson himself, it looked a frightening duel as Manifesto responded with bolder and bolder jumping. After Valentine's for the second time, Williamson made his move, hitting the front shortly before the home turn which started the enthusiastic crowds cheering, and came home to a fine 5-length victory with his ears pricked, over Ford of Fyne, receiving 25 pounds, and Elliman, receiving 24 pounds. It was to be Manifesto's last win.

curely latched. The horse pushed it open and – freedom! With a week to go before the big race, fit, blooming and raring to go, he galloped off across the surrounding countryside, misjudged a 5-foot gate and rapped a fetlock so badly that he was out of action for several months. The erring stable lad, scared stiff by what he had done, did a scarper and went to work for another stable under an assumed name.

snow-covered ground over such a long period that even Aintree itself looked threatened. When National day finally came, conditions remained so dodgy that hay was placed both sides of each fence, and this nearly proved Manifesto's undoing.

All the hay was supposed to have been cleared away before the race, but a patch was left by mistake at the Canal Turn. Manifesto slipped on it,

Of all the gallant failures in the history of the race, few can rank greater than Manifesto's in 1900 and 1902. His performance then could be described as even braver than those which brought him his two wins.

By the turn of the century Manifesto was the undisputed champion chaser of his day and excelled nowhere more

In 1899 Manifesto won again. Here he is seen warmly wrapped up in the paddock.

than at Liverpool. He had the cocky stature of a king who knows he reigns over all, and Aintree was his kingdom, as it was to be over seventy years later for Red Rum. In 1900 the handicapper allotted him a weight of 12 stone 13 pounds, forcing him to give 48 pounds to some horses. Only Arkle once had to give 49 pounds, but not in the National.

Covert Hack, the only faller on the first circuit, brought down the favourite Hidden Mystery at the water when loose. Turning for home, the Prince of Wales's Ambush II led from Barsac – yet who should be stealthily creeping up on them but Manifesto. The crowd drew breath: their hero *could* do it. He drew alongside the royal horse at the second last and stride for stride, neck for neck, they galloped towards the last fence. It was a battle royal indeed and the roar of the spectators rose to an unprecedented crescendo – its like not to be heard again until just before Devon Loch's debacle in 1956. Ambush touched down first, but here was Manifesto, fighting his way back; for a moment he appeared to be in front – or was he? It had been a final all-out effort and, with barely 100 yards to go, the people's hero conceded to youth and the crippling weight. As Williamson eased him, Barsac stole second place, and hats came off for a royal victory.

For an age of strict etiquette and formality, the scenes that followed were astonishing. Grown men cried at the defeat of Manifesto. A scribe of the time commented, 'There are some things

about which it appears sacrilege to write in commonplace black and white.'

In 1902 Manifesto was fourteen years old; heavy rain had turned the ground to a quagmire; the old boy was set to carry 12 stone 8 pounds through it.

Manifesto was the undisputed champion chaser of his day.

Ridden by Ernie Piggott, Lester's grandfather, Manifesto made a supreme effort. Shannon Lass's forward move three out was matched by Manifesto; but it was a 50–1 six-year-old called Matthew, carrying only 9 stone 12 pounds, who jumped the last with her. Then suddenly the crowd was

Grown men cried at the defeat of Manifesto.

looking at a potential miracle: Manifesto was coming up from behind with a stupendous run. Fifty yards from the line, the impossible still looked possible, but again that gruelling run-in proved just too long; the mud was just too deep; the weight was just too much; the courage was still there, but it was not enough. He was beaten 3 lengths and 3 lengths by Shannon Lass, receiving 35 pounds, and Matthew, receiving 38 pounds.

Still it was not the end of the line. In 1903 Manifesto was no longer top weight, Ambush bearing that with 12 stone 7 pounds, but the fifteen-year-old Manifesto nonetheless carried 12 stone 3. Williamson was in the saddle again, and he started at 25–1.

Manifesto was never going to win it, but in an incident-packed race he showed all his old resolution, to hold off Kirkland by a head and secure third place. There were greater cheers for him than for the winner, Drumcree, Ambush having fallen at the last.

Incredibly, in 1904, at sixteen years old, Manifesto received weight from only one horse, Ambush (who fell at the third). Now quite the old man of chasing, he was treated as a star by the spectators, who crowded round him during his early morning work and admired his vigour, sprightliness and unblemished legs. A leading flat-jockey of the time even asked to be allowed to sit on him. There was no one who seriously thought Manifesto could win but many believed he might place and backed him to do so. He started at 20–1 and was this time ridden by H. Piggott. But the advancing years had caught up with the horse and Manifesto, sure-footed to the end, was outpaced, to finish unplaced behind Moifaa.

What a truly amazing horse he was, as tough and courageous, sound and genuine as they come. His Grand National record reads: fourth, fell or brought down, first, first, third, third, third, unplaced. It speaks for itself.

MOIFAA

1904: New Zealand winner

THE MOST ROMANTIC of all Grand National stories belongs to Moifaa, the New Zealand horse reputedly shipwrecked and marooned on his journey over. He was labelled the ugliest winner, poor chap, but then the old adage 'Handsome is as handsome does' has always rung true, and pictures of him don't portray him as particularly bad-looking.

In 1904 Moifaa may have looked to English eyes a horse of 'incredible ugliness', with the head and shoulders 'of a camel', but he powered his way to the front and there he stayed; nothing could live with him and he left a litter of fallen idols in his wake.

New Zealand, far more so than its larger neighbour Australia, is ideally

Moifaa, in a portrait that belies his 'ugliest winner' tag.

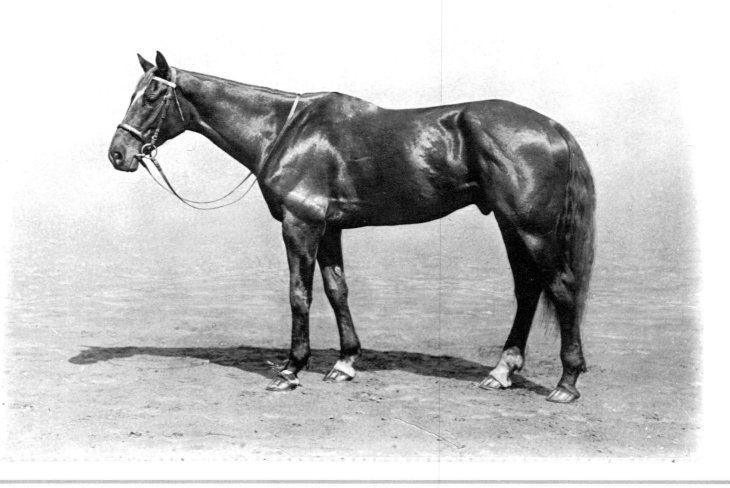

Mr Spencer Gollan who shipped Moifaa over to England for the Grand National.

suited for producing the thoroughbred. It has a temperate climate and lush, fertile grass rich in minerals, with the optimum amount of rainfall and warmth.

The horse was almost certainly not indigenous to the Antipodes but imported from both England and South Africa, the first recorded shipment into Australia being in 1788.

The Australian Race Committee was set up in 1840 with the objectives of breeding for strength, endurance and maximum speed. When New Zealand acquired its own racing organisation fifty years later it followed the same maxim, with the result that both countries successfully bred horses with these qualities not only for flat racing and steeplechasing but also for the immensely popular sports of trotting and pacing.

It was easy for the British and Irish to dismiss horses from down under out of hand as small fry. In the 1970s, though, it became fashionable, largely through the successes of top jockey-turned-trainer Stan Mellor, to import a good many New Zealand horses who, in spite of being at a six-month disadvantage in age owing to the different seasons on the southern hemisphere, held their own with honour here.

If the rumour that went the rounds in America after his victory was true, he was lucky to have reached Aintree at all. It was detailed in D. H. Munroe's 1931 history of the Grand National:

There is a sort of Robinson Crusoe tale current in America with regard to Moifaa which seems to be unknown in England but it makes a splendid legend.

According to this story, Moifaa was ship-wrecked off the Irish coast at the end of his journey from New Zealand and was given up for lost. Some fishermen, however, while about their business on an early morning a few days later, discovered the horse parading back and forth on the strand of a small island on which he had taken refuge and ferried him ashore.

Refreshed by his icy swim in the waters of the North Atlantic, he is reputed to have entered into training with a vim and eventually strolled round the Aintree course to win the National.

In view of this story there is humour in the fact that Moifaa's sire was a horse called Natator (swimmer).

... a horse of 'incredible ugliness', with the head and shoulders 'of a camel'.

This story should perhaps rank in the 'truth is stranger than fiction' category and be given at least some credence.

When Moifaa arrived in England, by whatever means, he had already conquered all-comers in his native country. As the 1904 National approached, his connections, like those of Americans Battleship, Jay Trump and Ben Nevis in years to come, had decided that the moment was ripe for him to take on the ultimate test against the world's best steeplechasers. They had nothing left to prove in their home country. Moifaa had won nine of his thirteen New Zealand races, including a £500 3½-mile race in June 1901 in which he carried 13 stone, giving 3 stone to his nearest rival. He was probably the Antipodes' first star chaser, for racing had only begun in any organised fashion in New Zealand in the 1890s, barely ten years before Moifaa's departure for England. Indeed, the very first racing in New Zealand is said to have taken place on the beach of Wellington Harbour in January 1840 by a group of British settlers.

A brown gelding, Moifaa was eight years old when he arrived in England. He was not immediately impressive. It must have taken time for horses to acclimatise, to say nothing of coping with the disadvantage of the six months' calendar difference.

Moifaa was the third New Zealand horse in the space of six years to sail to England for a crack at the National. All three, Levanter, Liberator and Moifaa, had won the principal steeplechase in New Zealand, the Great Northern Steeplechase at Ellerslie, North Island, founded 103 years ago.

Liberator was a top-class horse on both sides of the world but failed to reach Aintree. Then Levanter paved the way for Moifaa by running fifth in the 1900 National and fourth in 1901.

Moifaa himself won the Great Northern in 1901, after which he was bought from Alfred and Emily Ellingham of Hastings, Hawke's Bay, by wealthy pioneer, jump-racing enthusiast and all-round athlete Spencer Gollan, expressly to aim at Aintree. (Gollan died in 1934 after being hit by a bus in London.)

'Riding off' the unwanted attentions of a loose horse at the Canal Turn.

Ellerslie, flanked now by a motorway and with an ultra-modern grandstand under construction, has two flat racecourses and a particularly testing steeplechase course which certainly showed Moifaa's stamina. It slopes away from the oval flat course, up a steep hill at the far end which is climbed twice. It was also essential for Moifaa to jump well, for the fences included posts and rails, and an unusual double in front of the stands.

Moifaa failed in his first three races in England, and one can imagine cynics muttering disparagingly about their 'poor relations' on the other side of the world not being up to standard. But, when it came to Aintree, the big fences, heightened in 1904 as if on cue, suited the massive New Zealander down to the ground.

Moifaa, trained by Mr O. 'Jim' Hickey and ridden by Arthur Birch, was a 25–1 shot and carried 10 stone 7 pounds. The twenty-six runners included past winners Manifesto, now sixteen years old, and King Edward VII's horse Ambush II, as well as future winner Kirkland, fourth the previous year.

In all the preliminaries, Moifaa towered above everything else, and it was impossible not to notice him, with his giant head and high withers; everything about him was big.

Moifaa's domination in the paddock continued in the race. Birch was little more than a helmsman, able to steer but incapable of holding back the big horse as he bulldozed his way through the fences. Behind him horse after horse fell like novices; Kirkland was the only one able to stay anywhere near him, briefly heading him once.

Railoff was the first to go, falling at the first; Ambush and Deerslayer fell at the third; Cushendon and Inquisitor at

Moifaa storms to victory in the 1904 race from Kirkland and The Gunner.

the fourth. The thorn fence before Becher's saw the worst carnage: Patlander, Hill of Bree, Comfit, Kiora and Loch Lomond all fell, Loch Lomond breaking his neck. At Becher's itself, Biology came down; Honeymoon fell two fences before the water, May King

'… a great machine at high pressure over fences who would jump any fence he saw.'

and Old Town having dropped out of proceedings somewhere along the way.

Moifaa was in command as the survivors stormed past the grandstand. Only midway through the race half of the twenty-six runners were out of it. The riderless Ambush knocked out Detail at the ditch before Valentine's, and Pride of Mabestown fell two from

home. It was left to Kirkland to follow Moifaa to the post, a respectful 8 lengths behind the black colours with white sleeves and red cap.

The victory was so impressive that the King, looking for a replacement for the ageing Ambush II, who did not run in the race again, arranged for Lord Marcus Beresford to buy the winner on his behalf. Lord Beresford described Moifaa as 'a great machine at high pressure over fences who would jump any fence he saw'.

Moifaa duly ran in the King's colours the following year and started favourite, but 1905 proved to be Kirkland's turn and Moifaa himself fell at Becher's. It was his last attempt in the race for, like many another big horse, he went wrong in his wind and was given away as a hunter. This sport I'll wager he enjoyed, although he must have given a hairy ride to whoever was mounted on his back!

RUBIO

1908: American-bred winner

Major F. Douglas-Pennant's Rubio (H. B. Bletsoe up), winner in 1908.

WHEN AN AMERICAN turn-of-the-century entrepreneur exported a number of young horses from his Californian stud to England, his fingers were well and truly burned and he did not repeat the experiment.

Yet somewhere among that group of failures was a future Grand National winner who was first to become famous for pulling a hotel bus between shafts. His name was Rubio.

The American was Mr J. B. Haggin of the Rancho del Pasto Stud, Sacramento, and in July 1899 he dispatched eighty-seven yearlings to Newmarket. It was rather like sending coals to

Newcastle, and many of the youngsters made little more than knacker money.

Rubio was bought by a Northamptonshire farmer and dealer, Septimus Clarke, for 15 guineas. Although Rubio was American bred, his sire, Star Ruby, had been bred at the Eaton Stud, Cheshire, by the Duke of Westminster, while the dam's sire, Sir Modred, had been imported to America from Australia, where he had been a top performer. Mr Haggin bought Star Ruby for 1000 guineas and won some nine races with him, including one over 4 miles. Star Ruby did not race in the top bracket but he became a successful sire in America and was usually well up in the list of sires of winners.

As a dealer, Septimus Clarke had a knack of showing off his horses where they would be seen to best advantage by potential customers. He was successful with Rubio in the show-ring and took him hunting with the Grafton, where he caught the eye of Major Frank Douglas-Pennant of Sholebroke Lodge, Whittlebury. The major bought him as a four-year-old for 95 guineas and soon discovered out hunting that, while everyone else was galloping, Rubio was just cantering. Realising he might have a racehorse on his hands, Douglas-Pennant sent him to Leicester Repository sales; when Rubio failed to reach his reserve of 60 guineas he put the five-year-old into training with Bryan Bletsoe senior at Denton, Northamptonshire.

Rubio was soon fulfilling his potential, for he won the Grafton Hunt Plate at the Grafton Hunt Steeplechases on Easter Monday 1903. He followed this by winning the Winchester Steeplechase at Portsmouth Park, then made it a hat-trick in the Kimberley Steeplechase at the Nottingham Hunt meeting.

But Rubio then broke down badly. On the advice of Buckingham vet Mr W. Hazleton, he was lent to the proprietor of the Pomfret Arms, Towcester, now called the Saracens Head, to work between shafts.

The specific intention of the exercise was to strengthen and harden Rubio's legs by making him pull the hotel bus which ferried guests between the hotel and the railway station. This he did for two months, followed by more road work at Sholebroke with Major Douglas-Pennant's hunters, so that by the autumn of 1906 he was back in training, this time with Mr W. H.

More at Danebury, Stockbridge.

So, although it is true that Rubio had pulled a bus, the reputation that he developed as a 'cab horse' turned good could hardly be described as accurate.

He ran once that autumn, finishing third at Kempton Park, and in 1907 he was beaten by a head at Hurst Park and won at Newbury. He fell at Gatwick, but at Towcester, carrying 12 stone, he won easily.

The following season, after some goodish form, he was entered for the Grand National of 1908, but he was not particularly fancied. Indeed, his stable companion, the good-looking mare Mattie Macgregor, was more so.

Mattie Macgregor was owned by Frank Douglas-Pennant's father-in-law. She and Rubio were both trained by Mr Withington, who had taken over the Stockbridge stables, where his head lad was W. Costello, in whose name the licence was held.

W. Bissill, the stable jockey, was given the choice of the two horses for the Grand National. In order for him to make his decision, a 4-mile trial gallop was held at Aynho, near Banbury where Bletsoe trained. Rubio had suspect legs, while the mare had shown good form in Ireland. At the end of the gallop, the jockeys rode up to the trainer, who asked Bissill to make his choice: it was to be Mattie Macgregor. H. B. (Bryan) Bletsoe was then fairly inexperienced, but he was offered the ride on Rubio and jumped at the chance.

Hardly had the jockeys got out of earshot than Withington said to Mr Charlie Brown, over whose land part of the gallop had been held, 'Bissill has chosen the wrong horse!'

The following description of the race day itself is taken from a delightful commemorative booklet, *The Romance of Rubio's National*, written for friends one Christmas by the late Martin Clarke, grandson of Septimus, the original buyer of Rubio:

The day of the National dawned fine and the large number of racegoers who had taken up their temporary quarters in the busy city realised that, as far as the weather was concerned, the Grand National Day of 1908 would be an undoubted success. With the elements favourable and a great interest prevailing (due to the King's horse Flaxman being entered amongst others) the turnstiles were soon very busy and in the end recorded a larger gate entry than ever before.

The stands were packed and it was hardly possible to move about in the spacious ring. The sun was in evidence during the greater portion of the time that racing was in progress. With a slight breeze, the course was kept free of mist and the onlookers had a good view from start to finish.

The only familiar figure missing was the Earl of Derby. The demand for tickets for the county enclosure was so extensive that the management entertained fears that the company would never be accommodated.

Movement was so difficult that punters had to bring all their powers into play to reach a bookmaker.

A note in the racecard informed racegoers that:

The Empire Theatre, Leicester Square, London, hold the exclusive rights for the Bioscope of the Grand National, and will show nightly pictures depicting the race from start to finish.

There were twenty runners, with Kirkland 13–2 favourite and Tom West and Springbok well fancied; Mattie Macgregor was 25–1, the King's Flaxman 33–1. Rubio was among the

66–1 outsiders for the 3000-sovereign race.

It was noted that both of Withington's horses looked extremely well in the paddock

But the King's horse seemed a little too much on his toes and was sweating freely. His tail was well plaited but with a horse known to suffer leg trouble the augurs were not good for the bruising race that was about to begin.

The first to leave the paddock was Tom West, trained by Bryan Bletsoe's father, Bernard, and within a few minutes the runners were cantering over the then still customary practice flight of hurdles.

At 3.03 p.m., starter Mr Coventry had the runners off to a perfect start, but there was plenty of grief to come. Three runners fell at the first, and seven in all were out of it by the end of the first circuit.

Rubio's jockey, Bryan Bletsoe, remembers the race as follows:

'When I got on Rubio, he was watching everything and he was very sensible and quiet. I was disappointed I could not get the inside place, which Tom West took from me, but Rubio jumped the first few fences beautifully. When we got to the Canal fence I was lying fourth, Newey, Anthony and Murphy in front (on Roman Law, Flaxman and Tom West).

'Rubio jumped very quick and gained several lengths on the turn. I did not see any of the falls in the front first time round because I was in front of them.

'Rubio hit the first fence on the racecourse very hard. That was where Rollason came down and I thought to myself "you must not do that any more" so I steadied him down and losing my place a little to give him his second wind.

'He took off lengths too soon at the water, and I thought that it was impossible for him to get over, but he took it

The 1908 paddock scene, with the ladies resplendent in the dress of the time.

nicely. He must have jumped an enormous distance.

'I looked at Newey at the last fence in the country the second time round and when he fell directly afterwards I said to myself, "that is another out of the way!" I thought after that Tom West was my danger, but he fell at the fence after Becher's, hitting it hard shooting Murphy over his head.

'Flaxman then seemed the one I had to beat, but I heard him hit the fence next to the Canal and I knew that I had him beaten. I was in front then, with Mattie Macgregor close beside me, and that is how we came onto the racecourse.

'Rubio was going very well, and he kept jumping away from Mattie. I knew three fences from home that I had only to stand up to win. He was not tiring at all. He could have gone another two miles. He jumped the last fence perfectly and pulled up fresh and unless he had been very fit could not have done what he did."

So the stable companions finished first and second, but there were very few cheers for the winner. Few seemed to have backed him. Flaxman was just beaten for third place by The Lawyer III, who later that night, after eating up his food, dropped down dead. Flaxman may have been unlucky, for Algernon Anthony, his jockey, broke a stirrup leather at the first fence in the country second time round, and Anthony performed some miracles to stay in the saddle, but effectively his chance had gone.

Rubio's performance was well praised by the hacks of the time but Kirkland, the favourite, who ended up last of the seven finishers, and who towered over his rivals, was described 'as powerful as Pickford's vanners and seemed to race like an old man'.

It was a proud Major Douglas-Pennant who, with his wife, received the magnificent trophy (it is

Over the Water Jump in 1908 come, left to right, Johnstown Lad, Flaxman, Mattie Macgregor, Tom West, Roman Law, Extravagance and Rubio.

now on display at the Royal Green Jackets Museum, Winchester), and the owner was duly grateful to his young jockey, writing to him the same day:

Dear Bryan,

I must write you a few lines, though I am only just home, to again tell you how delighted I was with your performance today. If you were to ride the race a dozen times again, you could never ride a prettier, fairer or more patient race.

How few have ever done what you did in winning it at the first attempt. In due course I intend to send you a cheque for £300 which to some extent, I hope, will show my appreciation of your riding today. I only wish that I had been guided a bit by what your father kept telling me, and that I had backed him to win me a bit.

'I was sorry about Tom West's bad luck and fear that Murphy from all accounts must be badly hurt.

Yours very gratefully,
F. Douglas-Pennant

It would appear from this that Douglas-Pennant had had no wager, although his family believes he had £5 (on odds of 66–1). Septimus Clarke betted the same amount – and with his winnings bought his brother Stanley his first motorbike, to commute home at weekends from his job in Manchester!

It would also appear that Bryan Bletsoe, grateful to Bissill for having made the wrong choice of horse to ride, sent his fellow jockey a present, for Bissill wrote him a thank you letter and

said it would remind him 'of the nice ride we had together at Liverpool'.

Bissill attempted to make amends the following year when he did ride Rubio but, starting at 20–1, he fell. In fact, the horse's racing days were numbered. The following year, for the benefit of his local admirers, he ran at Towcester (where Major Douglas-Pennant was a steward and became a patron), but without success, and he ended his days in retirement at Sholebroke.

In his eighties, on the death of a cousin, Major Douglas-Pennant inherited the title of Lord Penhryn; he was the fifth baron. He went on to make a record himself, being named in *The Guinness Book of Records* as the first-known peer of the land to become a

centenarian. On his 100th birthday he was interviewed by Jack de Manio of the *Today* radio programme. His youngest daughter, the Hon. Susan Douglas-Pennant, has inherited a love

Grudon's feet were enterprisingly filled with butter to stop the snow balling.

of racing. She remembers her father as 'fair but firm, a real stickler for time and something of a martinet'.

There is a delightful little poem which nicely sums up Rubio's win, by 'Ararana' (W.W.R.) in a booklet called *Racing and Sporting Rhymes*, published by Perkins and Co. in the 1920s.

The crowd scene at the Canal Bridge in 1908.

What's won the National?
Well what do you think?
Why Rubio's won it
Come let's have a drink.

But you didn't back it?
No, I didn't do that;
Tom West was my choice
For the price of a hat.

But Tommy slipped up
At a fence in the muck
Which shot Murphy off,
So he came in with the ruck.

But who was the rider?
Ah! that's why I drink,
So here's to young Bletsoe
Always fit as a pink.

He drinks not, he smokes not,
He always is cool,
His hands are as light
As the silk on the spool.

He sits in his saddle,
Firm as a rock,
He jumps a big country,
On the flat he's a jock.

You can read in the 'Sportsman'
How he ne'er lost his place,
Though he nursed the old
    Yankee
And thus won the race.

The price was a record,
Over sixty to one,
The layers looked happy,
When the paying was done.

From a long-established Northamptonshire family, one of six boys and three girls, precious little ever worried Bryan Bletsoe, who is said to have remarked casually after his Grand National win, 'I'm glad I didn't fall off'.

Apprenticed near Oakham, he was a good judge of pace and had wonderful hands. 'When we had a horse we could do nothing with, he would just get on it and ride it perfectly,' his nephew Bernard Bletsoe says. Bernard also believes that his uncle rode the winners of the Irish, Scottish, Welsh and South African Nationals as well as that at Aintree.

'My uncle was not a great worker and was usually hard up but he was very generous,' Bernard says. 'If we wanted anything as kids, like gramophone records, he would get it for us.' (When he was training at East Ilsley after retiring as a jockey, Bryan often seemed to find himself with owners who could not pay their bills, and who usually left him a bad horse to pay off the debt.

Bryan Bletsoe was an officer in the Northamptonshire Yeomanry during the First World War and served in Egypt. He took a job with the BBC at Bedford during the Second World War. He retired to Easton Maudit, near Northampton, having married doctor's daughter Irene Nash fairly late in life, and died about ten years ago leaving no children. But he left the Bletsoe colours to his nephew Bernard, whose wife Phyllis has a useful horse, Odye Hills, carrying them still.

Bernard Bletsoe senior, father of Bryan and grandfather of Bernard junior, had bred, owned and trained Grudon to win the 1901 Grand National. It was the year when the going was recorded as 'very deep – course white with snow', and the weather as 'blinding snowstorm'. Grudon's feet were enterprisingly filled with butter to stop the snow balling, and his connections were rewarded by the sight of their horse galloping safely to an easy win as others slipped out of contention all around him.

Now Phyllis Bletsoe hopes she can become the third Bletsoe to win the Grand National, perhaps with Odye Hills.

LUTTEUR III

1909: French winner

Lutteur III, Georges Parfrement up, the last five-year-old to win.

THE FRENCH GRAND NATIONAL at Auteuil is exceptionally challenging. Its figure-of-eight track has an assortment of fences the like of which are not seen anywhere else. They include a stone wall, water jump with white rails, huge ditches, very wide and high brush fences, a bank, and even a bullfinch where the top several feet of thin birch has to be jumped through by the horses. It is no wonder that so few foreigners have ever been successful at Auteuil, the exception being the amazing Mandarin in 1962. With his bit dangling broken and useless under his head and his jockey Fred Winter ill, Mandarin mustered his final reserves of strength to win by a head.

Few French horses have ever attempted the even more daunting Aintree Grand National, but one who did so, brilliantly, was Lutteur III, the 1909 winner, owned, like Mandarin fifty years later, by a member of the Hennessy family of brandy fame.

Lutteur was a failure on the flat who had seen a fence for the first time in his life only eighteen months before the Grand National in which he

As a two-year-old, Lutteur was too slow and immature to win anything.

had trouble with his hocks and fetlocks and, not surprisingly, M. Hennessy was all for selling him. But his trainer, M. Georges Batchelor, pleaded with the owner to put Lutteur by until he was ready to go 'over a country', and he persuaded M. Hennessy to let him keep the horse as his trainer's hack.

When he returned to the track, Lutteur had matured and developed, but

chelor had his sights set on Aintree, but an accident at Auteuil nearly put paid to those dreams. Lutteur was out of action for the summer but was back to his best by the autumn. The following spring he was shipped to England for his final National preparation. He was stabled at Lewes with Harry Escott, who had already trained Cloister during that great horse's 'cloak and dag-

Owner, M. James Hennessy.

Trainer Harry Escott gives instructions to jockey Georges Parfrement.

triumphed – at the tender age of five. He was a wishy-washy chestnut, generally considered a bad colour, but he was a full horse and well put together and, like so many other National winners, was beautifully balanced.

By St Damien (who was by St Simon), Lutteur was bred by M. Gaston Dreyfus with some good strong blood on both sides of his pedigree. M. Dreyfus sold him for 610 guineas to James Hennessy, whose family was to have such a long and happy association with English steeplechasing.

As a two-year-old, Lutteur was too slow and immature to win anything; he

in his initial run he finished last in a hurdle race at Enghiem – it seemed that the stable's patience had not paid off. Then, to the surprise and delight of all concerned, he won a steeplechase on the same course and suddenly there was no stopping him. He proved a natural over fences and before long he had won five steeplechases at Auteuil and was beaten a neck in another. At only four years old, he had become the talking horse of all French steeplechasing.

The chestnut's performances were so startling that already M. Bat-

ger' spell, and had a month or more in which to acclimatise and have an English run.

There were many, M. Hennessy included, who in later years considered Lutteur's first English run his finest race of all. Just five years old, he went to the Champion Steeplechase at Hurst Park on 10 March to take on older and more experienced horses on level terms over strange fences. The way in which he slaughtered a high-class field, including Leinster and Mount Prospect's Fortune, considered England's most brilliant chasers of the time, left spectators gasping.

Now all England, as well as his compatriots, was talking about this French phenomenon. Frenchmen flocked to Liverpool and plenty of money was laid on Lutteur, making him joint favourite with Shady Girl, and reasonably handicapped on 10 stone 11 pounds.

A twenty-one-year-old jockey of Yorkshire descent, Georges Parfrement, had the ride. He had already ridden Lutteur at Hurst Park, but this

… if Lutteur jumped the first safely, he had little to fear.

time, having eyed up the Aintree fences and their big drops, he had lengthened his stirrup leathers considerably. He felt that, if Lutteur jumped the first safely, he had little to fear.

It was a perfect day and the international flavour added to the tingling atmosphere as the thirty-two runners paraded. The portents for Lutteur were good, for his stable companion, Enthusiastic, had won the opening race, and Lutteur himself looked a picture; his spring coat was blooming and Georges Parfrement was soon to show he had a wise head on young shoulders. Only M. Hennessy himself could not be present, business having called him back to France.

The previous year's first and second, Rubio and Mattie Macgregor, were both in the field again. Parfrement, willing to concede ground in favour of the safer outside berth, lined up wide and at the second attempt the starter had them under way. By the end of the first circuit, as they jumped the water, Lutteur was still well in arrears, but Parfrement had not let out a notch of rein yet; when he did so, the response was immediate, for Lutteur cruised smoothly through his field with contemptuous ease, with a mile to go.

Rubio had fallen before the water, Mattie Macgregor refused, Ascetic's Silver, winner in 1906, broke down, and Shady Girl was knocked out of it — so, as Lutteur threaded his way

Parfrement took Lutteur III on the wide outside (top left of picture) and so avoided any pile-up. Gilbert Holiday's drawing shows the fall at the water of the previous year's winner Rubio.

Nip and tuck the pair battled up the run-in, the five-year-old gaining a short-head verdict.

through, the main dangers had gone. His worst moment came at the second Becher's, when a loose horse cannoned into him, but Parfrement held him together skilfully. At the second Canal Turn he was disputing the head affairs with Judas and the pair drew clear of the remainder. To the spectators it was clear that, bar a fall, Lutteur had the race at his mercy, for he was only toying with Judas. Lutteur was not the easiest of mounts but Parfrement rode a peach of a race on him, using his head and calm judgement to win cleverly by 2 lengths. Lutteur was the only five-year-old to win this century, and one of only three entire horses, with Grudon, 1901, and Battleship, 1938. They returned to a hero's reception; half the runners had completed the course and there were no serious falls.

The story was different when Lutteur returned to Liverpool two years later, 7–2 favourite and carrying 12 stone 3 pounds, for there was a chapter of accidents. Some of the fences had been reduced in size, but it was raining hard and the ground was very heavy.

After two false starts, many galloped off far too fast in that long run to the first fence, as happens today. Some observers claimed that the trouble was caused by the new-fangled fashion of the professional jockeys' 'forward seat', and there was even one writer who unflatteringly commented that 'Half the professional jockeys funk the journey from the start.'

In the event, the 1911 race went to an amateur, Jack Anthony, then relatively unknown but later to become renowned for his prowess around Aintree. That day he managed to avoid fallen and loose horses galore with Glenside and kept the outsider on his feet to come home alone. Lutteur, who this time had jumped off much faster and was up in the front rank, was baulked badly and got stuck on top of the fence after Becher's (since 1967 known as Foinavon's). Remounted horses were left to fill the places: Rathnally, Shady Girl and Foolhardy.

It was three years before Lutteur reappeared at Liverpool, following tendon trouble. He was then ten years old, and it was five years since his famous victory, but he was set to carry more weight than ever before, 12 stone 6 pounds, and started second favourite at 10–1. France was also represented by Trianon 11, but it was to be Sunloch's year.

In the two years which Lutteur had missed, both races had been won by Sir Charles Assheton-Smith, the former Mr Duff, owner of Cloister, who thus joined the select band of triple-winning owners. His 1912 winner, Jerry M, joined the few winners to carry 12 stone 7 pounds, ridden by Lester Piggott's grandfather Ernie; and in 1913 his Covertcoat won.

In 1914 the fences had been reduced further in size and all twenty runners negotiated the first five safely. But, as Sunloch set sail in front, at one time 40 lengths clear, the more experienced jockeys fell into the trap of waiting for him to come back to them – and he did not. By the time the French pair went after him in earnest, he was gone beyond recall. Lutteur, ridden by A. Carter, finished third behind his compatriot but not even a mistake at the last could stop the owner-trained winner, who was carrying only 9 stone 7 pounds.

So Lutteur's third and final effort had been thwarted, though he had run a commendable race five injury-filled years after his victory. Over forty years later, his owner's family was to have an indirect effect on the Grand National when they followed the initiative of another brewing family, that of Colonel W. H. Whitbread, in sponsoring a prestige 3-mile chase. Appropriately, Mme Peggy Hennessy's Mandarin won its inaugural running.

With the introduction of the 'Whitbread' in the spring of 1957 and the 'Hennessy' in the autumn of the same year, staying chasers were no longer aimed exclusively at the National, and the injection of extra cash brought a new lease of life to the sport in general. In time, the National was to join the sponsorship bandwagon too, and return to the top of the prize-money league.

Lutteur III was the first French-owned, bred, ridden and mainly trained horse to win the Grand National, but in 1862 Huntsman won for his French owner, Vicomte de Namur, and French jockey, H. Lamplugh. Lamplugh had been second in 1859 on Jean du Quesne.

Alcibiade became the first French-bred horse to win, in 1865, as well as being the first successful five-year-old. His was a real old-fashioned coup and it was remarkable in that it was the young horse's first-ever run in a steeplechase. His connections had schooled him thoroughly in secret and tried him well against an older, more experienced horse, and it was Alcibiade who always came out the better. In the race, the closing stages developed into a thrilling duel between him and Hall Court, ahead of the favourite Emblematic. Nip and tuck the pair battled up the run-in, the five-year-old gaining a short-head verdict. It was one of the most thrilling finishes in the history of the National.

GREGALACH

1929: Biggest field

Mrs M. A. Gemmell's Gregalach, R. Everett up.

THE VICTORY of a ten-year-old tubed maiden called Tipperary Tim in 1928, when thirty-five of the record forty-two runners fell, and only the remounted Billy Barton finished behind the winner, led to changes in conditions the following year to try and ensure a smaller and better qualified field.

The starting fee for each horse was increased to £100, and two forfeit stages at which the horses could be withdrawn were introduced, to try and deter owners of 'no-hopers' from taking part. But two other factors influenced matters: the very fact that a 'no-hoper' had won the previous year encouraged owners of such horses to believe that there was always a chance; and the prize money had been increased out of all proportion with previous years.

The race was worth some £13,000 to the winner, of which £5,000 was put up by the executive and the rest came from the sweepstake on the entrance fees. Ten years earlier, just after the First World War, the race had been worth £3,590, and ten years before that it was worth £2,500, having been £510 in its inaugural year back in 1839. In 1929 there were still many races worth

The 100–1 outsider Gregalach comes in surrounded by the crowd.

only £150 to the winner, but a horse could earn that amount by finishing fourth in the National.

So, instead of the desired reduction in the field, just the reverse occurred. In 1929 a staggering sixty-six horses went to post, some of them barely capable of raising a canter.

In fact, much of 1928's debacle had been caused not by the number of runners (they were fully aware of the unusual situation and went so steadily that all of them safely negotiated the first fence), but by one runner bringing down virtually the whole field, as was to happen in Foinavon's year of 1967. Ironically, it was the classiest horse in the field who was responsible. Easter Hero, who was to win the next two Cheltenham Gold Cups, swerved and

ran along the ditch in front of the Canal Turn before being straddled on top of the fence. It is believed that thirty-five horses were knocked out of the race in one fell swoop.

Easter Hero was again in the mammoth field of 1929, carrying 12 stone 7 pounds. Since his mishap the previous year, the open ditch at the Canal Turn had been filled in and done away with. Nevertheless its 90-degree angle ensured that it still offered a unique test in the steeplechasing world.

Among Easter Hero's sixty-five opponents was a seven-year-old gelding called Gregalach, the third string of Tom Leader, whose Sprig had won two years previously and was in the race again along with Mount Etna, Sandy Hook and Bright's Bay.

Anticipation hangs in the air over Aintree early on Grand National morning. Here jockey Andy Turnell, trainer Michael Scudamore and lad discuss prospects.

*1968, and the galloping grandad Tim Durant on his way to becoming the
oldest rider, at 68, to complete the course.*

**Right: Peter Biegel captures the
1967 Grand National. At Becher's
Brook (top), the riderless
blinkered Popham Down safely
leads the way but at the next he
swerved in front of the fence and
knocked most of the runners out of
the race at a single stroke.**

"Starting down over Beechers"

and

The hest !!

Below: The same fence taken from a different angle. Crisp took to the daunting fences like the proverbial duck to water.

Left: Crisp and Richard Pitman were well ahead at Becher's Brook second time round in the record-breaking National of 1973.

The love of life exudes with every breath from Red Rum down on the Southport dunes.

Above: Perfection – Red Rum poised over Becher's in perfect balance on his way to his second Grand National Victory in 1974.

Left: Noel Le Mare – dapper, neat, sporting. Red Rum fulfilled the octogenarian's lifelong National dream an incredible three times.

Red Rum captured on Southport sands with all four feet off the ground, his reflection caught in the water, in perfect symmetry.

Above: Here's to victory! Brian Fletcher's triumphant wave matches the crowd's exultation of Red Rum's second great win.

Left: Donald 'Ginger' McCain and his wife Beryl enjoy an eve-of-National party at their Southport yard in 1976.

A bright chestnut with a white star, he was a fine, upstanding horse, powerfully built, rangy, with good bone and plenty of scope.

But, although Gregalach's price was 100–1, he was not a complete no-hoper like Tipperary Tim, as his future record would prove. His form was good enough already for him to be handicapped at 11 stone 4 pounds. It was partly that, with so many other runners to consider, his claims had not struck a chord with punters looking for their annual flutter.

Gregalach was fashionably bred; like Easter Hero, he was by My Prince, and had the looks to match. A bright chestnut with a white star, he was a fine, upstanding horse, powerfully built, rangy, with good bone and plenty of scope. Mrs M. A. Gemmell had bought him for 5000 guineas from Mr T. K. Laidlaw, who in turn had bought him from his Irish breeder, Michael Finlay. Gregalach's long price could also be attributed to the fact that his stable was known to prefer at least two of their four other runners to him, and that his jockey, Australian Robert Elliott, a former naval officer, was comparatively inexperienced, having begun race-riding quite recently as an amateur.

The day of the race dawned dry and sunny and there was an influx of enthusiastic American supporters who had crossed the Atlantic by liner to cheer on their representative, Billy Barton, who they felt sure would make amends for his bad luck the previous year. Then owned by Mr Howard Bruce, grandfather of Charles Fenwick, who was successful in 1980 on Ben Nevis, Billy Barton had fallen in the lead at the last fence, leaving Tipperary Tim to come home alone.

The huge number of runners and their attendants crammed into the paddock like sardines, praying none would be kicked, while ringside spectators could barely wade through all the names listed on their racecards. Most of them had eyes for only one, their Easter Hero, and it looked like being a one-horse race, too, as he set off at the head of the pack from flag fall. Mercifully, all sixty-six horses safely negotiated the first fence. Easter Hero's rider, Jack Moloney, was attempting to keep out of the way of the rubbish, but he was mindful of what had happened the previous year, for, as he approached the Canal Turn, he eased back to let others give Easter Hero a lead at his bogey fence, fearing that the horse would remember his last experience there.

Easter Hero was in trouble. The glowing chestnut Gregalach was upsides and gaining on him.

Not a bit of it. Easter Hero jumped it with ease and soon resumed his rightful place at the head of affairs, like a general leading his troops to battle, and with his ears pricked. Following him at a respectful distance in about seventh place, also with his ears pricked, was Gregalach, whose tangerine colours almost matched his bright chestnut coat.

Others fell by the wayside, including Tipperary Tim, and as Easter Hero led over the water the packed stands responded with spontaneous applause; just nineteen of the sixty-six runners were left, with a complete circuit still to go.

Again, Moloney took a safety precaution at the Canal Turn, allowing Richmond II and Shady Hook to lead him over it briefly, then on he swept majestically. It looked like being Easter Hero first and the rest nowhere.

Suddenly there was an ominous shortening of the favourite's stride. Easter Hero was in trouble. The glowing chestnut Gregalach was upsides and gaining on him. To the disbelief of the watching crowd, it became clear that the favourite could *not* shake off the outsider. A few moments later Gregalach had swept by and he drew away to win by 6 lengths.

Moloney, to his eternal credit, did not pick up his whip. 'If he slowed down, you knew he had given all,' he said later. He set a fine example to others of his profession.

Richmond II stayed on to finish third, with Melleray's Belle fourth. Altogether, fifty-six horses failed to finish, tenth and last place going to a remounter, Camperdown.

Easter Hero's defeat was one of the Grand National's hard-luck stories, for it turned out that he had spread a front plate, which had twisted into an S shape and was cutting into the protective boot of his other foreleg with every stride from the moment he suddenly faltered.

It was the sort of outcome which set the tongues wagging. The 'if only', the 'might have been', the 'who would have won if' brigade were in full voice. But it was a meritorious win for Gregalach, his rider Bob Everett, trainer Tom Leader and owner Mrs Gemmell; just because the crowds had been unable to recognise the combination from the massive card should not detract from their achievement. They were the ones who got things right on the day.

The sight of those sixty-six horses thundering towards the first fence of the 1929 National must have been one of the race's most enduring spectacles. It cannot be repeated since the introduction in 1984 of a statutory maximum of forty runners, following a reduction from 60 to 50 in 1979. Any horses declared over that number are eliminated by a process of the lowest weighted coming out first, so there is no danger of excluding the best horses.

There were other years of big fields between 1929 and 1984, notably fifty-seven in 1947, when the race was won by Caughoo.

It is hardly surprising that so many want to compete as huge prize money and prestige are at stake. There has been greatly increased interest in the race since it was saved for posterity by donations from the Levy Board, Seagrams and the public in 1983 after years of uncertainty when Aintree seemed likely to be sold for building land. The trustees, Lord Derby, Dick Francis and Liverpool Football Club chairman John Smith, formed Aintree Racecourse Co. Ltd to run the course on a 999-year management agreement.

For the record, those sixty-six runners in 1929 were: Gregalach, Easter Hero, Richmond II, Melleray's Belle, May King, Grakle, DDB, Delarue, Kilbairn, Camperdown, Sprig, Bright's Boy, Koko, Great Span, Trump Card, Mount Etna, Knight of the Wilderness, Billy Barton, Lloydie, The Ace II, Ardeen, Carfax, Ballystockart, Stort, Lordi, Master Billie, Le Touquet, Skrun Prince, Overdraft, Rampant, Tipperary Tim, Darracq, KCB, Ardoon's Pride, Sandy Hook, Herbert's Choice, Dwarf of the Forest, Drinmond, Uncle Ben, Beechmartin, Ruddyman, Hawker, Gay Don II, Denburgh, Sultan of Wicken, Kilbrain, Ballyhanwood, Soldier's Joy, Irina, Duke of Florence, Harewood, Mabestown's Pride, Rathory, Cloringo, Merrivale II, Miss Balscadden, Odd Cat, Best Home, Big Wonder, Fleet Prince, Kwango, More Din, Stage Management, Theorem, Toy Bell and Wild Edgar.

Gregalach's trainer, Tom Leader, came from a renowned Newmarket family, although his father, Tom senior, first trained in Wroughton, Wiltshire. When he moved to Newmarket, he named his home Wroughton House. It was a very tall, narrow house, with three floors and four bedrooms, but as new children were born – there were five boys and three girls altogether – so an extra stable from the yard alongside would be incorporated into the house.

It was natural that the children should become interested in horses, and evidently horses took an interest in them too, for whenever they played a game of tennis the horses' heads could be seen over their stable doors moving from side to side watching the progress of the ball.

Most of the children went into flat-race training – Colledge (known as Col), Fred and Jack (known as Har-

Sixty-six horses start the 1929 race, a record never to be broken.

vey) all trained on the flat. Some also had and rode their own point-to-pointers, while Tom went into National Hunt, and Steve, who did not marry or train, was accountant to all of them. One of the sisters, Ethel, married the trainer Jack Jarvis.

The brothers came through the First World War without loss and there was a great family atmosphere at their home, which Tom junior fostered when he eventually took over Wroughton House. He was a freemason, a Worshipful Master of the Newmarket Lodge, as well as being a lay preacher; and in adult life all five brothers continued to meet up to attend 8.00 a.m. Holy Communion in Newmarket.

Tom was also an outgoing character who, according to his nephew Hugh, could be the despair of his wife, Ethel. The couple had three sons, including Ted, who rode Sprig to victory in the 1927 National, the year of the first radio commentary of the race, but in 1929 he elected to ride Mount Etna.

The weather before the 1929 National was so bad that it was not easy to prepare the runners. Arthur Goodwill, now seventy-eight years old, was then a stableman at Tom Leader's, and recalls Gregalach having to trot round a straw ring in the yard and on the front lawn to keep fit. Arthur went on to ride for Tom Leader, then trained himself until he retired in 1980; his daughter, Linda, was one of the first successful lady riders on the flat.

Gregalach's victory marked the second successive 100–1 winner – at that time the only two in the race's history – but Gregalach went on to prove it had

In 1931 Gregalach proved his 1929 victory was no fluke when he was second to Grakle.

been no fluke, showing good form the next season, including finishing second to Gib, who won eight races in a row. But then he ran mystifyingly last at Hurst Park and damaging rumours started to fly round the racing world. The upshot was that Gregalach was moved to the stables of H. Waldron. He had a bad splint, was reported as being a doubtful starter, and was taken out of the betting for the next National.

On the morning of the race itself, however, he worked well and so took his place in the line-up along with forty others, carrying 12 stone. He was close up with the leaders at the Canal Turn but was baulked and put out of the race shortly afterwards. His rider that year was again Bob Everett, but in 1931 it was Easter Hero's former jockey, Jack Moloney, with Mr Woodland as the trainer.

Easter Hero was reported to be recovered from lameness and Gregalach to be back to his best form. But then Gregalach ran three 'miserable' races in a row and, as there was no obvious physical cause, it was assumed that he had some form of internal trouble. Not surprisingly, punters' interest in him waned, until shortly before the 'off', when his odds went to 25–1.

It was a beautiful sunny day with perfect ground, and Gregalach, again bearing 12 stone, soon showed that he really was back to his best. Both the top-weighted Easter Hero (12 stone 7 pounds) and Gib (12 stone 5 pounds) fell, as did the Czechoslovakian horse Gyi Lovam!, who had won the Grande Pardubice at home.

Altogether, twenty-five of the forty-three starters fell, but none got in the way of Gregalach as he led at the water and set off foot-perfect on the second circuit. Indeed, his jumping was almost too good, and his extravagant leap at the second Canal Turn must have cost him the race for it landed him so far out that he was forced to run wide round the right-angled turn, while three horses passed him on his inside, with Grakle close behind them . . .

Going to the last, it was a battle royal between these two. Grakle led by half a length; Moloney picked up his whip and Gregalach responded; they drew alongside; but Grakle had the inside and, inch by inch, he drew away for a 1½-length victory in one of the fastest recorded times. The previous year's winner, Shaun Goilin, on 12 stone 4 pounds, was sixth of twelve finishers.

REYNOLDSTOWN

1935 and 1936: Dual winner this century

WHEN MAJOR NOEL FURLONG travelled to Ireland in the early 1930s it was with the specific intention of buying himself a future Grand National winner. The horse he procured was an excitable, jet-black youngster named after his birthplace, Reynoldstown – and the horse was to fulfil the major's ambition not once but twice.

Noel Furlong had left his native Ireland a decade earlier because of the Troubles. Protestants' houses were being set on fire and there were fears that his son would be kidnapped. The fact that Noel had married a Roman Catholic was an added problem. His son, Frank, aged about eight, was sent ahead to London by boat and train with the coachman and told to wait at the Cavalry Club until his father arrived.

Shortly afterwards, in 1920, Noel Furlong paid his first visit to the Grand National, travelling by train. He found himself next to father and son, Jack and Algernon Anthony, trainer and amateur rider, who won that year's race with Troytown. Always a keen hunting and point-to-pointing man in Leicestershire, and before that in Fermoy, County Cork, this chance meeting fired Noel Furlong's enthusiasm for racing, and he wondered if he could achieve the same distinction with his own son in due course.

Frank himself did not show much interest in horses until, at eighteen, on the spur of the moment, he followed hounds on a carthorse. His interest was furthered in the army, when he became great friends with Fulke Walwyn (the pair set up training together before the war) and Frank caught the racing bug.

> ## 'I have found it more satisfactory to work him without a noseband, I cannot say why.'

His grandmother relinquished her home-bred side-saddle hunter, Robin O'Tiptoe for him to point-to-point and, although very amateurish, he went on to win the 4-mile National Hunt Chase at the Cheltenham Festival of 1932. The following year he made a successful first foray into the Grand National, finishing second on Robin O'Tiptoe's half-brother, Really True.

The exploits of his son further fostered the racing ambitions of Major Furlong, who set off on a horse-hunting trail that led to Ireland and Reynoldstown, a youngster by My Prince who was the 'in' stallion of the day, having already sired the Grand

National and Cheltenham Gold Cup winners, Gregalach and Easter Hero.

In the village of Reynoldstown, just north of Dublin, lived Dick Ball who, apart from Reynoldstown, also bred the classic winner, Ballymoss.

Reynoldstown was very highly strung and wild, but his breeding was right (although only in the half-bred book) and Major Furlong bought him for £1500, a lot of money in those days, and arranged for his transport home. Major Furlong's granddaughter, Griselda Houghton-Brown, still has Dick Ball's account:

> The man's fare and travelling expenses, £4; transport to boat, 43 miles, £2.3/-; insurance for £1000, £3.15/-; freight to Tilton, Leics, £6.19/-; total £16.17/-.

In addition, there was a contingency of £200 to be paid for the first race valued at £400 or more that Reyoldstown won. In a letter, Mr Ball said, 'He has eaten three years of good oats,' and added, 'I have found it more satisfactory to work him without a noseband, I cannot say why.' He was still without a noseband four years later, when he won the Grand National.

It was not all plain sailing for Reynoldstown on the path to Grand National fame. In many ways, his exceptionally nervous temperament made him his own worst enemy, and at times his jumping left a lot to be de-

Reynoldstown 'took on' the fences, tackling them with enthusiasm and respect.

Dual Grand National winner Reynoldstown with his owner/trainer Major Noel Furlong and his first successful rider, Frank Furlong.

sired. He 'buried' Frank Furlong in a novice chase at Cheltenham and, once in England, he was only ever ridden by Noel and Frank Furlong and Fulke Walwyn. Even during the horse's retirement, the young Griselda would not venture into his box.

But the occasion and atmosphere of the Grand National brought out the best in Reynoldstown and he 'took on' the fences, tackling them with both enthusiasm and respect.

The 1935 National was a splendid family affair, for Major Furlong both owned and trained his black horse, and his son, Frank, rode him. This was in the heady heyday of Golden Miller, who, until then, had done nothing to blot his copybook: just the reverse, in fact; he had then won the Cheltenham Gold Cup in the preceding four years, and had won the Grand National the previous year. With such form, there appeared no

A train is used as a grandstand to watch near Becher's Brook.

The Prince of Wales was at the races in 1935, seen here in the paddock.

***Greeting home the victor, Reynoldstown (Frank Furlong up).**

reason why he should not win again, even with 12 stone 7 pounds on his back, and he started at 2–1.

Sadly, it transpired that Golden Miller would have none of the pace again, and it was his great Gold Cup rival, Thomond II, who took on Reynoldstown. On the second circuit the pair drew clear from Becher's, where Reynoldstown and Frank Furlong survived a bad peck. The two horses rose as one at the last, Reynoldstown distinctive with his workmanlike face and no noseband, Thomond with his white star and the striped sleeves of his jockey, Billy Speck. But the amateur Frank Furlong, already with a second in the race on his only previous ride, found himself drawing clear on the run-in, and Thomond, who had had a hard race against Golden Miller at Cheltenham, faded into third place.

For the Furlongs, it was a fantastic family achievement – and a remarkably quick return on their investment in a potential Grand National winner. They left the course in high spirits on their way to the traditional revelries in Liverpool – and Frank promptly bumped into a car in front of him in the queue to get out. The irate driver jumped out and confronted him. 'Who do you think you are – have you won the bloody Grand National or something?' he stormed. 'Well, yes, actually I have,' came Frank's reply.

There was a tremendous party at the Adelphi Hotel, with Fulke Walwyn in

'Reynoldstown made a terrible mistake at Valentine's. He was nearly on the floor and that cost him ten lengths.'

great form, and a certain amount of damage was done, including to a painting, for which Frank had to pay the repair bill.

The following year, when they were again celebrating victory, Frank spotted the same picture, said, 'That's mine!' – and threw a bottle at it . . .

There are those who claim that Reynoldstown's second Grand National was due to luck. 1936 was the year when Anthony Mildmay's reins broke on Davy Jones when they were leading at the second last. Most books record that they were heading for certain victory.

Golden Miller was again in the field and once more he started as favourite, jointly with Avenger, but it was a rank outsider, the tubed Davy Jones, who stole most of the limelight.

Golden Miller went at the first and, although he was remounted, he refused persistently at the ditch after Valentine's, hating the whole experience. Two fallers left Davy Jones in the lead with over a circuit to go. At the Chair he landed a length ahead of Double Crossed, with Avenger, Emancipator, Reynoldstown and Blue Prince all in the air together. Poor Avenger broke his neck at the next fence, and at Becher's second time round Davy Jones had half a length advantage over Reynoldstown (who was carrying 12 stone 2 pounds).

His jockey Fulke Walwyn, later to become five times champion trainer, with horses for Her Majesty Queen Elizabeth the Queen Mother in his care, takes up the story:

'Reynoldstown was always going well. We were just behind the leader at the Chair then drew upsides with Davy Jones, and we jumped Becher's and the

Canal Turn together. Reynoldstown made a terrible mistake at Valentine's. He was nearly on the floor and that cost him ten lengths.'

No one else was in the reckoning and Fulke was steadily making up the lost ground on that long sweeping turn towards the second last: 'I was nearly upsides again and, when Anthony Mildmay's reins broke, I had to check Reynoldstown to let him out. I saw the reins on the ground and I saw Anthony hit him on the head but he couldn't stop him running out. Then all I had to do was jump the last. I think we would have won anyway.'

And who is to dispute the man on top? It was something Fulke, ever the gentleman, said little about at the time, not wishing to compound Mildmay's disappointment.

Reynoldstown nevertheless went down in the records as a dual Grand National winner with plenty of honour.

Fulke Walwyn rode Reynoldstown in 1936 because Frank Furlong had put on considerable weight in the intervening year; he had also accepted a gift of £1000 from his father for winning the 1935 race and, as an honourable gentleman, immediately said that his acceptance of the money made him a professional, so he gave up his amateur status. Fulke did exactly the same thing a year later, in consequence of his win on Reynoldstown.

After the 1936 victory, the Furlongs received a telegram from Edward, Prince of Wales, whom they knew from the hunting fields of Leicestershire. It read: 'Hearty congratulations once more and I backed Reynoldstown again. Edward RI.' (Apparently, the prince used to drive round Hyde Park

In 1936 Reynoldstown did it again this time ridden by Fulke Walwyn.
He is seen jumping Becher's second time round, just behind Davy Jones.

'Then all I had to do was jump the last. I think we would have won anyway.'

during the race, so that he could listen to it on the car radio.)

While a long and luxurious retirement lay ahead for Reynoldstown, and for Noel Furlong too, Frank's life was all too short. War was looming, and he joined the Fleet Air

It was quite impossible to turn out Reynoldstown in a paddock, for he would simply jump out.

Arm as a pilot. It was he who located the *Bismarck* and repeatedly radioed its position until he ran out of fuel and was forced to ditch in thick fog. Remarkably, as he paddled his life raft, Frank was picked up by an off-course Allied boat, but that was the end of his good luck, for he was killed later in the war. He left behind a widow, who went her own way, and a baby daughter, Griselda, who was brought up by her grandparents, Major and Mrs Furlong. When she was a year old, Griselda moved from Leicestershire to Marston St Lawrence near Banbury. Not long before his death, Major Furlong at the age of eighty-five was able to give her away when she married farmer Peter Houghton-Brown. Fulke Walwyn's sister, Jane, was her bridesmaid.

At Marston, Reynoldstown, ever excitable and highly strung, was cared for as if he was still a racehorse by his devoted groom, Mac – two pensioners together. It was quite impossible to turn out Reynoldstown in a paddock, for he would simply jump out; instead, he was led out daily for a buck and a kick at the end of a lead rope, and groomed, rugged and generally made a fuss of. To the young Griselda, he was ferocious, gnashing his teeth, and 'ready to eat' her.

At the age of twenty-four, Reynoldstown cut his foot on an old bottle, contracted tetanus and had to be put down. He was buried in the grounds near the stables and, by an amazing coincidence, was to be joined there in later years by another Grand National winner, Well To Do. Marston House was sold in 1958 to Mr John Sumner, whose wife, Heather, had owned Well To Do until her death a year before his National victory of 1972.

In common with Reynoldstown, to whom he was related, Well To Do was exceptionally highly strung and used to sweat up freely, but winning the National transformed him. He revelled in the adulation and became much calmer, allowing people to make a fuss of him, in contrast with his predecessor.

Like Reynoldstown, he was trained by his owner, Captain Tim Forster – 'as good a friend and as straight a trainer as one could have', in John Sumner's words – for in her will Heather Sumner had left the pick of her horses to her lifelong trainer.

Captain Forster was only persuaded to enter Well To Do for the Grand National at such a late stage that his decision had to be communicated by telegram.

In the race itself, the chestnut was beautifully ridden round the inside by Graham Thorner, who found him a natural jumper, well balanced and capable of seeing a stride and placing himself accurately going into a fence even when under pressure: attributes which he shared with many a Grand National winner, notably Red Rum.

Bought as an unbroken three-year-old, Well To Do was so wild that it took three men to catch him. Mrs Sumner hunted him for a season before he went into racing, and it was to the hunting field that he retired with John Sumner, having won only one more race after the Grand National – appropriately, the race named in his honour at his local track of Towcester. Well To Do hunted with the local Bicester pack and also went spring hunting in the West Country with the Devon and Somerset Staghounds, which the old horse loved. He ended his days grazing peacefully in the paddocks of Marston, where Reynoldstown could never be let loose, and was put down and buried in the grounds in 1985, at the age of twenty-three.

BRUCE HOBBS

1938: Youngest winning rider

Bruce Hobbs, who at 17, was the youngest rider to win the National.

FOR BRUCE HOBBS there is only one day in the year: Grand National day. It is fifty years since he became the youngest ever jockey to win the National, by the closest of margins, on one of the smallest horses to achieve victory in the race, Battleship, who was also the last stallion to win.

'The National's the greatest spectacle in the world.'

Despite a highly successful career as one of Newmarket's leading flat

trainers, Bruce Hobbs, a tall and well-preserved sixty-seven, is probably remembered more for that win than for anything else, and he wouldn't wish it any other way. 'The National's the greatest spectacle in the world,' he says. 'If they alter the fences they might just as well run it at Sandown. There is no other atmosphere like it and since

> Battleship, a chestnut, stood only 15.1½ h.h., but was a 'big little horse' to ride and 'a charming character, you could do anything with him', in spite of his full-horse status.

being saved and under the present management it has had its vitality renewed.'

Descended from four generations of Leicestershire hunting stock, with up to fifty thoroughbred hunters stabled at a time at his father's Melton Mowbray yard, Bruce grew up in the cream of hunting country; he was given his hunt buttons at the tender age of nine. He was not only a fearless rider across country but had the showman's knack too, as he demonstrated with the virtually unbeaten 14.2 h.h. show pony Lady Marvel. He was also one of the original members of the Quorn branch of the Pony Club.

Bruce Hobbs was born in America, where his father, Reginald, was for a time master of the horse to Singer Sewing Machine heir Ambrose Clark, but when he was two years old his family came to England in order for his father to set up the Melton yard for Mr Clark.

When Ambrose Clark found he had less time for commuting from America for his English hunting, he transferred his interest to racing, installing Reg Hobbs in Lambourn. He also introduced several American owners to the yard, one of whom was the 'dowager' of the American racing scene, Mrs Marion Du Pont Scott, wife of film actor Randolph, who donated the original trophy for the Carolina Cup in 1930.

For the young Bruce, racing was a natural progression from the world of ponies and hunting and he had his first ride in a hurdle race at the age of fourteen, and first win at fifteen in a hurdle at Wolverhampton.

At the end of 1936, on his sixteenth birthday, Bruce turned professional, and at the age of seventeen he finished third in the jockeys' table, as well as becoming the youngest ever rider to win the National.

Bruce did not achieve victory at the first attempt. In 1937 he rode Flying Minutes for Mrs Ambrose Clark. He was going well enough to think that he might place when the horse made a mistake at the last ditch four from home – 'And I fell off,' says Bruce. 'I was sixteen and full of enthusiasm without too many nerves. I was a hunting man and the loose horses were the biggest trouble.' He also rode Flying Minutes in the Sefton Chase over the National course and was beaten by a short head.

The next year, when Bruce was well established and making his name as a professional, there was a choice of four Grand National horses in the home yard: Flying Minutes, Bagatelle, What Have You and Battleship. Bruce, not surprisingly, chose Flying Minutes, but at the eleventh hour the horse broke down.

The chance of riding the second favourite, the George Beeby-trained Delachance, then emerged, for his usual jockey, Fulke Walwyn, was injured. But a week before the race Fulke had recovered sufficiently to take the ride after all. So the diminutive American stallion Battleship became Bruce's

Battleship, one of the smallest horses ever to win the National, with Bruce Hobbs, in 1938.

third choice, and that only for financial reasons. 'Purely because I was offered more money to ride him – although he was also the best of the remainder,' he comments with a wry smile.

Battleship, a chestnut, stood only 15.1½ h.h., but was a 'big little horse' to ride and 'a charming character, you could do anything with him', in spite of his full-horse status. By Man O'War, America's legendary 'racing machine', winner of twenty of his twenty-one races, out of Quarantaine, who won the French Oaks, he had the class to help him overcome his small size. He had had a successful career in America, winning from 4½ furlongs to 4¼ miles, thus taking in a slightly broader width than Red Rum, whose shortest race distance was the English minimum of 5 furlongs.

Battleship won the American Grand National of 1934 at Belmont Park but broke down, and when he arrived in England in 1936 he had been fired. His owner, Mrs Scott, who lived at Montpelier, Virginia, once the home of President Madison, fourth president of the United States, was nevertheless keen for him to run in the 1937 Grand National – something Reg Hobbs managed to forestall.

Mrs Scott had her way the following year, however, by which time Battleship had won several English races and had been beaten by only threequarters of a length in the National Hunt Chase at the Cheltenham Festival, wearing blinkers for the first time. Bruce had been unable to ride him at Cheltenham, having broken his nose in the Champion Hurdle and therefore being out of commission.

'I've won the National!'

Battleship was eleven years old when he ran at Aintree that sunny but cold day in March 1938 when overnight rain had made the going good. The only attribute that gained him a mention in previews was his size; dubbed the 'American pony', he started at odds of 40–1 and again wore blinkers.

Bruce Hobbs enjoyed a superb ride on the little horse. 'He jumped those big fences beautifully although he landed very steeply over Becher's; remember, he was a stallion and didn't want to hurt himself,' recalls Bruce, who wisely had had his reins lengthened by 6 inches so that he could slip to the buckle in true hunting style over the big drop fences.

As the leaders cleared Becher's for the second time and began to race in earnest, it was clearly a four-horse race between Royal Danieli, Workman, Delachance and Battleship, with the previous year's winner, Royal Mail, unable to cope on 12 stone 7 pounds.

Battleship just led and had the inside, three horses stretched out perfectly in the air together, yet from the stands it still looked as if the race lay between the other three. Instead, it turned into something of a David and Goliath contest on the long journey home as the big, long-striding, impressive Irish horse Royal Danieli led little Battleship.

At the third last fence, just before they crossed the Melling Road to come back onto the racecourse proper, Battleship made a major mistake and all but crumpled on landing. 'It won me the race, I'm sure!' says Bruce. 'He had to come from behind and he was running too freely at that stage; if he'd gone clear he would have given up, thinking his task was done, but the mistake stopped him in his tracks.'

To the watching crowds it looked as though Battleship's chance had gone, and that Workman (who was to win the next year) would follow the big-striding Royal Danieli home. But young Bruce, who had learned to sit tight in the hunting field, held the little stallion together, rallied him, passed Workman, who hit the second last hard, and set off after the big horse.

At the last fence he still had 3 lengths to make up and, when a loose horse carried him wide over to the stands side, the task indeed looked forlorn. But Battleship had plenty of battle in him and just got up.

I've won the National! was Bruce's first thought as he flashed past the line.

It was in the days before the photo finish, but the jockeys concerned usually have a good idea of who has won . . . After agonising minutes the judges' verdict was announced: Battleship by a head! It was a great result for the bookmakers and the band of American supporters, but not for the majority of punters, especially not for the usually vociferous Irish, who were stunned into silence. As for Mrs Scott, she was too overcome with excitement to lead her horse in.

Battleship returned to America to a hero's welcome as the first American-bred and -owned winner of the Grand National, and spent his retirement at Montpelier, living to a ripe old age, blind in one eye but in good heart at thirty.

Bruce Hobbs's promising career was to be cut brutally short. The following season, 1938–39, he broke his back in a selling hurdle at Cheltenham, at a flight by the winning post which was permanently removed after the accident. He was out of action for six months and had just returned with a winner at Buckfastleigh on his initial ride, giving Fulke Walwyn his first as a trainer, when war broke out.

So Bruce, the youngest Grand National hero, joined up at Bath on 3 September 1939 and became simply Trooper Hobbs 327184. He joined the North Somerset Yeomanry, because one of the stable's owners was in it and because it meant he could be with

horses. In March 1940 he went to Palestine with the horses and was commissioned into the Queen's Own Yorkshire Dragoons – 'a marvellous bunch who I still keep in touch with'.

Bruce saw much active service and was awarded the Military Cross. But, like other good jockeys, when he returned he had put on too much weight and, after a short battle with the scales, he gave it up, put an advert in the *Racing Calendar* – and began a valuable five-year period as private National Hunt trainer to Mr and Mrs John Rogerson, whose daughter, Valda Embiricos, owns the 1981 National winner, Aldaniti, and is a cousin of Jim Joel.

From there Bruce moved on to become assistant trainer to George Beeby at Compton, Berkshire. Then, through an introduction by royal jockey Harry Carr, he began his long association with Newmarket, joining Captain Sir Cecil Boyd-Rochfort as assistant for eight educational years.

'They're off'. The start of the 1938 race in front of stands packed to capacity.

'I relive it every year.'

Battleship, at Becher's, just ahead of Royal Danieli and Workman.

A short spell at Gibsons, the New-market saddlers, was followed by another as assistant to Jack Clayton, after which he became private trainer to Radio Rentals and racehorse magnate Sir David Robinson. Although that job ended in the sack after two years, Bruce had nothing but admiration for the man: 'I am a horseman and he was a businessman and the two just didn't gel, but the experience stood me in good stead and was a stepping stone for me.'

Subsequently a consortium of owners, Sir David Wills, Jocelyn Hambro, the late Mr T. F. Blackwell and the late Major Jim Phillips, formed Palace House Stables and installed Bruce Hobbs as trainer: 'They put me on my feet and it was the start of a very rewarding twenty years.'

Bruce retired in 1985 but today finds himself as involved as ever in new challenges within the racing world he loves. He was made a member of the Jockey Club in 1986 and is a member of the disciplinary committee, work which takes up some three days a week. He is also a director of the National Stud, along with chairman Chris Collins, David Gibson and Peter Willett. He loves shooting and cricket, umpiring for the Newmarket Racing XI and enjoys three grandchildren.

Although Bruce Hobbs trained the winner of the Irish Derby, Tyrnavos, had eleven places in Classics, and has trained horses such as Hotfoot, Jacinth, City of Truth and Catherine Wheel, there has been one thrill in his life to beat them all: that day in 1938 when he and Battleship got up on the line to win the National. 'I relive it every year,' he confesses.

DEVON LOCH

1956: Unluckiest loser

'… And this is Devon Loch.'

THE PONY CLUB MEMBERS looked suitably awed as the kind bay horse turned his handsome head inquisitively towards his young visitors. This was the high spot of the Pony Club's visit to Mr Peter Cazalet's famous stables at Fairlawne, Shipbourne, near Tonbridge in Kent, for they had all heard of Devon Loch, the horse who didn't win the Grand National.

The Queen Mother waves good luck to her horse Devon Loch as he leaves the paddock before the 1956 National.

In later years, one girl who had been on the trip particularly remembered the horse being swathed in bandages; another the lovely old-fashioned stable, with its brick floor and curved iron railings atop the wooden partitions.

The whole place left a lasting im-

'The Queen Mother's first thought was for the misfortune of both Peter Cazalet and Dick Francis.'

pression: the magnificent originally William and Mary house set back from the road, surrounded by daffodils in spring, a ha-ha dividing it from the field in front; the spotless Victorian square yard well away to one side, with its clock tower, and tack room reeking of newly polished leather, the saddles and bridles hanging line upon line. Everywhere there was an aura of smartness and pride in the work – no casual manners or sloppy jeans in sight.

This was the stable whence Devon Loch set off to become the most famous Grand National loser of all time – the royal horse owned by the most popular National Hunt supporter in the land, HM Queen Elizabeth the Queen Mother. He was the horse who sailed round 4 miles 806 yards of the Grand National with the race at his mercy, the thirty fences safely behind him, only to sprawl suddenly for no apparent reason just 50 yards from the winning post.

At least seven theories have been put forward as to what caused the dramatic, baffling collapse on that fine March day in 1956: the noise of the crowd's cheering a royal winner frightened him; he tried to 'jump' the outside of the water jump; he had eaten too much glucose and got cramp; he was suffering from lack of oxygen; he had a heart attack; he had a weak hind leg which gave way at the crucial moment; he hit a 'false' patch of soft ground.

The only thing that is certain is that the cause will never be established beyond doubt. On that bitter-sweet day, when so many hopes and dreams were shattered, and so many of the nation's people came to feel somehow cheated, the Queen Mother remained a shining example to all. She showed

concern only for her horse, for the lads who looked after him, for her trainer Peter Cazalet, thwarted for a third time through sheer bad luck, and most of all for her jockey, Dick Francis. The one person for whom she shed no tear was herself; there was never a sign of self-pity. She bore what that great leveller, the racing game, had to offer with magnanimity.

'The Queen Mother's first thought was for the misfortune of both Peter Cazalet and Dick Francis,' says her private secretary of the last thirty-three years, Sir Martin Gilliat. And when Fred Rimell and Dave Dick, whose ESB had been left victorious, were taken to meet the Queen Mother, they were 'practically in tears, they were so sad for her'. Sir Martin adds, 'It is impossible to know what happened; the Queen Mother is open to ideas, but the general consensus seems to be that it was the volume of noise from the cheering, this comes over and over again; the water-jump theory seems to have been rather ruled out.'

It was fitting that the Queen Mother should have chosen Peter Cazalet to train her horses, for it would have been hard to find a more immaculate yard than Fairlawne, with training standards to match.

Cazalet was a perfectionist and in his head lad, Scottish born Jim Fairgrieve, a strict disciplinarian, he had the ideal man in charge. The stable that began with two horses and Jim and ended with forty-nine horses and twenty lads, was run like a regimental barracks, firmly but fairly. Some lads, hearing of more lenient yards when away at the races, would leave, but it was surprising how often they returned, and those with any trace of ability were given every help to further

'It is impossible to know what happened; the Queen Mother is open to ideas.'

their careers. Jim would often boast that he had the best lads in the country.

When the Queen Mother visited, she wouldn't see so much as a hayseed out of place. Once, on a pre-royal-visit inspection, Peter Cazalet found the horses duly polished, the stables scrubbed, the yard washed down. 'Jim,' he called, 'there are some cobwebs behind that piece of gutterpipe.' By the time the Queen Mother called, the cobwebs were gone.

Jim Fairgrieve had served with the Royal Army Veterinary Corps in the East in the last war but was invalided out with recurrent malaria. He worked with stallions at Newmarket, and then moved to Burroughs and Wellcome, who had taken over Fairlawne during the war and were developing various equine vaccines.

One day at Fairlawne Jim saw young Edward Cazalet riding his pony. 'How can I stop my pony being so fat?' Edward inquired. Jim inspected the animal for a moment, then replied, 'She's in foal.' Not long afterwards, on a cold and frosty autumn morning, the foal was born; Jim picked it up and carried it in his arms to a box. Peter Cazalet was home on leave and the two men met for the first time.

When Peter Cazalet started training after the war, Jim Fairgrieve remained in situ. And he stayed there to the end, from the first day in 1946 when they had two unbroken horses and went on to end their first season with fifteen winners to the sad day twenty-seven years later when Peter Cazalet died and the stable was dispersed.

It was in 1951 that Peter Cazalet bought Devon Loch, as a five-year-old, in Ireland. By Devonian (by Hyperion) out of Coolaleen (who was bred by clergyman Charles Daly), Devon Loch himself was bred by Willie Moloney in County Cork. Moloney usually bred for the flat, but it was clear that this immature colt was more of a chaser type, so he sold him to Colonel Stephen Hill-Dillon in Navan for 550 guineas as a yearling.

Colonel Hill-Dillon was patient with the horse, first running him in a flat race at Leopardstown for five-year-old maidens, then winning a 'bumpers'. After that he sold him to Cazalet with a £1000 contingency should he win the Cheltenham Gold Cup, or £2000 for the Grand National.

Devon Loch's arrival at Fairlawne nearly ended in disaster, for he broke loose when Jim was lunging him one day. He galloped hell for leather across the field, jumped a set of rails into the next one, luckily in the opposite direction from the road – and was caught without a scratch on him.

After a promising start in England, in which he was twice second over hurdles and second on his chasing debut behind the next Gold Cup winner Mont Tremblant, Devon Loch sustained a touch of leg trouble, was fired, and was then rested for two years. It was clear that he was a high-class chaser in the making and was worth waiting with. He also had the ideal temperament, and was much loved by all who came into contact with him, being quiet and a good 'doer'.

Jim Fairgrieve remembers that the horse's hindquarters did not match up with his front, for he had a poor 'second thigh'. Alex King, who was a lad at the Cazalet stables at the time, remembers that there was nearly always a bandage on his near hind joint when Marshall 'Mick' Taylor was schooling him. He believes that a weakness there made him slightly lopsided and could have affected his balance at the crucial moment before his collapse.

When Devon Loch returned to racing, Dick Francis was stable jockey, and Bryan Marshall was also riding regularly; Bryan predicted quite early in the horse's career that he would win the National.

Devon Loch won good races at Hurst Park and Sandown, was third at Cheltenham and fell in the Mildmay. The following season, 1955–56, he won his first race over 3 miles at Lingfield, won again at Sandown, was fifth in the King George at Kempton on Boxing Day, and was third in the Mildmay Memorial at Sandown. Significantly, perhaps, Bryan Marshall twice felt him falter in a race before finding a second wind. A hard winter caused some hold-up in work, but Devon Loch was second in the National Hunt Chase at Cheltenham, and then all sights were set on Aintree, the stable by this time full of hope.

Jim Fairgrieve, for one, had been backing him steadily through the winter, a couple of pounds a week at ever-reducing prices. Stable lad John Hole accompanied Devon Loch to Aintree and Alex King was in charge of the Queen Mother's other runner, M'as-tu-vu. They even planned how they would celebrate that evening, so sure were they that Devon Loch would win.

Jim spent the night before the race in the Cumberland Hotel, London, ready to catch the race train to Liverpool early the next morning. He was telling everyone that Devon Loch would win – he coupled him with every runner in the second leg of the Tote double, which was a flat race – but something kept nagging at the back of his mind. It was, he says, like a premonition, and it

… his jumping got better and better, making those massive fences look like hurdles.

gave him a sleepless night.

The royal party also travelled by train, a special one. The race was held on a Saturday, as it has been ever since 1949, having been changed from a Friday at the request of the Labour government.

The number of runners – twenty-nine – was not as large as on some occasions but the crowd was enormous. Two previous winners, Early Mist and Royal Tan, were in the field, as well as a future one, Sundew, but Must was favourite. Others who were well fancied were Carey's Cottage, ESB, Gentle Moya and Devon Loch. M'as-tu-vu, well backed the previous year when he fell on the final circuit after disputing the lead, was out at 40–1 this time.

Four runners fell at the first fence amid groans from the watching punters, as both Must and Early Mist had gone. M'as-tu-vu was in the lead and Devon Loch, middle placed to begin with, was jumping so well that he gained lengths at every fence.

For his jockey, Dick Francis, it was literally a dream ride. His only really anxious moment came two fences after the Canal Turn, when Domata and Derek Ancil came to grief and Devon Loch had to twist himself in mid-air like a cat to side-step him. From then on his jumping got better and better, making those massive fences look like hurdles. He treated the Chair as if it were a brush fence and when the water flicked beneath him he was lying sixth or seventh, still gaining in the air each time.

Sundew, lying second, fell at the second Becher's; Armorial III was leading, closely attended by Royal Tan, ESB, Eagle Lodge, Key Royal and Devon Loch. Gentle Moya blundered his way out of it, but Devon Loch avoided mishap and as he went into the Canal Turn for the second time he had only Armorial in front of him.

Dick Francis was in the incredible and enviable position of having actually to steady his mount in the Grand National with a mile to go. 'Never had I felt such power in reserve, such confidence in my mount, such calm in my mind,' he wrote later in his autobiography *Sport of Queens*. To be in that position in any race is a marvellous feeling; for it to happen in the Grand National a matchless experience.

Armorial fell at the fence after Valentine's and Eagle Lodge took over briefly until Devon Loch went on three from home, Dick Francis having time to note that those around him were already being hard-ridden – and he was still sitting with a double handful!

They galloped back onto the racecourse, strong and powerful, only two fences left, and those Devon Loch jumped as freshly as the first. ESB was close by, but he was a beaten horse; Devon Loch was only toying with him and, as they landed safely over the last, the royal horse moved up a gear and Dave Dick, seeing his chance gone, settled for second place.

The crowds were well and truly cheering in anticipation of one of the most popular wins in the history of the race, as Devon Loch opened up more of a gap and reached the elbow. The roar of the crowd was deafening, a tumultuous crescendo reaching far down the course to that bay horse who was winning for the Queen Mother. And then he was down, sprawled flat on the ground; it had not been a fall in the normal sense, but he was lying there spreadeagled like a floppy puppy. One moment he was winning the race, the next he was on the ground; there was nothing in between, no fleeting image of danger lurking, no stumble before the fall, no indication of imminent disaster – just collapse, as total as it was unforewarned.

All over bar the shouting – Devon Loch lands ahead of ESB over the last. Did the shouting cause his downfall?

'Never had I felt such
power in reserve, such
confidence in my
mount, such calm in
my mind.'

***The moment of truth. Members of the Royal Family gasp in dismay,
while others wave their hats aloft to salute a Royal victory.***

At that moment a graphic photograph was taken of the royal party and other spectators on top of the County Stand. Some are cheering delightedly; others have their mouths open in a big 'Oh', their eyes full of disbelief. Three quarters of the men have already raised their hats from their heads in salute of a royal victory.

Devon Loch got up again after his collapse more or less in one movement, with his rider still in the plate; Dick Francis's first instinct was to get going again and still be first past the post. But Devon Loch stood there stock still, as if incapable of engaging his hind legs into gear. It lasted only a few moments, but that was enough. Dick Francis dismounted, the most miserably disappointed, dejected, disconsolate man in England.

John Hole led Devon Loch back to the stables. The St John Ambulance Brigade came to Dick Francis's rescue;

although unhurt physically, he readily accepted their lift back, thereby avoiding the crowd's inquiring gaze.

Everywhere there was incredulity. Jim Fairgrieve had started pushing his way down from his part of the stand when he heard 'this awful gasp' and looked up to see the disaster occur. Alex King and John Hole, already planning how they would celebrate that night, just could not believe what their eyes were telling them. John, prepared moments before for the proudest moment of his life, leading in the winner of the Grand National, took him instead to the stables.

Within ten minutes, the Queen Mother herself was at the stables. The horse was thoroughly examined by a vet, who could find nothing wrong. His heart, lungs, legs and back were all sound and the horse was not unduly distressed after his exertions.

The sad demise was to open up a floodgate of conjecture. The only per-

The Grand National's biggest mystery captured on film.

And then he was
down, sprawled flat on
the ground.

Dick Francis dismounted, the most miserably disappointed, dejected, disconsolate man in England.

son convinced he knows what happened is the man who was riding him at the time: Dick Francis. He believes that it was the noise from, as he puts it, 249,999 people out there cheering for Devon Loch. In his autobiography, Dick Francis writes:

I have never in my life heard such a noise. It rolled and lapped around us, buffeting and glorious, the enthusiastic expression of love for the Royal Family and delight in seeing the Royal horse win. The tremendous noise was growing in volume with every second, and was being almost funnelled down from the stands on to the course.

I remember how startled I was when I first heard the cheers for M'as-tu-vu at Lingfield, and they were a whisper compared with the enveloping roar at Liverpool.

He concludes that the noise which was uplifting and magnificent to him may have been exceedingly frightening to Devon Loch.

Others have theories, though few claim they know the answer for sure. Some in the press speculated that Devon Loch saw the wing of the water jump to one side, thought he was going to be jumping it again, and took off in a 'phantom' leap. But slow-motion study of the film of the race would appear to refute this. Equally, if it was a heart condition, why didn't it show up afterwards? A vet thought that an infestation of red worms in early life might have caused bad circulation in his hindquarters.

Jim Fairgrieves believes that a hind leg touched the ground toe-first, instead of the full foot, causing the leg to slip backwards – a bit like slipping backwards when walking up a steep hill. 'But I've seen the film so many times, stopped and started, and I still don't really know,' he admits.

Alex King believes the collapse could have been caused by cramp resulting from a surfeit of glucose: 'We used to buy glucose for the horses by the crateful from Boots, but the late Professor Pugh had had some problems with athletes getting cramp from excess glucose. I don't know for sure what he discovered, but there was never a barrel of glucose at Fairlawne again after Devon Loch.'

Dave Dick is convinced that the cause was lack of oxygen. He had seen the horse's tongue hanging out almost black as he galloped alongside him on ESB. He believes that, as the horse recovered, and regained his supply of oxygen and normal breathing, so no ill effects remained to be seen on examination.

A police officer said there was a dark patch on the course which on inspection proved to be wet caused by a leaking stop cock near the water jump: could Devon Loch's fall have been caused by this patch of false ground?

Another possibly significant point is the time of the race. ESB finished only one second outside Golden Miller's record, so Devon Loch must have been easily on target to beat the course record himself.

Devon Loch never again showed any sign of abnormality and in fact went on to win again twice, a hurdle and a match against Early Mist. But one can imagine Peter Cazalet venting his pent-up frustration when a photographer, paying a rare visit to the stables, asked him to arrange for Devon Loch 'to repeat what he did at

A helping hand is offered, but no one could help Dick Francis then.

Liverpool' for him to picture! 'My father had taken it all extremely well until then,' says Edward Cazalet, 'but that man had to leave fairly quickly!'

Eventually the horse suffered a recurrence of tendon trouble and was given away to Sir Noel Murless as his hack, although it was Murless's daughter Julie, now Mrs Henry Cecil, who mostly rode him, for he could be a 'bit of a monkey' and whip round on Newmarket Heath. 'He was a marvellous old character,' she reveals, 'and rather fun to ride.'

In time Devon Loch returned to Sandringham where, in 1962, he was put down.

After the race, Dick Francis disappeared to his brother's at Bangor-on-Dee for the night to be out of the limelight. He went on to become a world famous best-selling author of racing thrillers, as if inspired by what the fates had doled out to him. He now lives in Florida, having taken with him memories of a remarkable ride, a bizarre ending, and his most treasured memento, an inscribed silver ashtray from the Queen Mother.

While the Queen Mother would still like to win the Grand National if the right horse came along, it is no longer a burning ambition of hers. Of all the many incidents in the history of the Grand National, none has been debated more than the disaster that befell Devon Loch. What irony it would be should the noise theory be true, that the very popularity of the horse who was winning should have caused it not to win.

As the Queen Mother said of the incident, speaking on a television programme about her horses in April 1987, 'That's racing.'

FRED RIMELL

1956–76: Trained most winners

WHEN FRED RIMELL saw the first of his record-breaking four Grand National winners gallop to victory, he threw his arms up in despair. His widow, Mercy, remembers that day in 1956 as if it were yesterday. As ESB strode past the post, Fred exclaimed, 'Good God, I have won, what a terrible thing to happen.'

For it was the year in which the Queen Mother's Devon Loch collapsed on the run-in, 50 yards from the winning post, with the race at his mercy. Most spectators were already hailing a royal victory. Their happy roar rose to a mighty crescendo, then dwindled to a heart-rending groan of bewilderment.

But although ESB won by default, and the circumstances of the win deprived his connections of the infinite pleasure a Grand National victory should bring, he was himself a class horse – and he put Fred Rimell on his record-breaking trail.

Racing and a love of all things rural came naturally to Fred, whose outgoing, affable personality was a big plus both as jockey and trainer, for he put owners at ease, and never had a bad word for anyone. In the words of Dave Dick, Fred was 'rather a special person in every way, a very good trainer and a nice person. And if he said a horse jumped, then you knew it did.'

Originally from a hop-growing, farming family in the Vale of Evesham, Fred's father, Tom, ran away to Newmarket at the age of fourteen. He became head lad to Fred Butters, and in one season they produced forty-eight individual two-year-old winners, before Tom returned to Worcestershire and started training at Kinnersley, where the stable still thrives.

'Good God, I have won, what a terrible thing to happen.'

Tom himself trained the 1932 Grand National winner, Forbra – by chance really. Owned by a bookmaker, Mr W. Parsonage, Forbra unexpectedly won a novice chase at Taunton, which in those days put him out of novice races once the current races were used up, unlike today when novice winners can continue for the whole season. 'That little win put him out of novices, so they went for the National instead,' Mercy Rimell says, 'and he won.' He was only seven years old at the time, and was ridden by Tim Hamey at odds of 50–1.

Fred revelled in the racing upbringing and loved hunting from an early age with the Croome, often whipping in. It was a marvellous grounding, and gave him a big advantage in later life both as jockey and

trainer. He also enjoyed shooting and fishing and, in Mercy's words, 'just loved life and lived it to the full'.

Fred Rimell told a marvellous story in his and Mercy's autobiography, *Aintree Iron*, of how, as a young man in the hunting field wishing to impress the young Miss Cockburn, he headed for a big brook with hounds in full cry. He fell in, his horse galloped off, then, putting a new twist on tradition, a 'knight in shining armour' came to the rescue in the shape of Mercy Cockburn. He hopped on behind her, but her horse, unused to the extra burden, went faster and faster, jumping everything in the way until they caught up with the rest of the field. It was certainly an exhilarating ride – and the start of a long and happy relationship.

Mercy was only seventeen when she married Fred in 1937, and is a knowledgeable and fearless horsewoman in her own right. After a successful show-pony career, she had won her first point-to-point at the age of fourteen, before there was a minimum age limit, has always ridden out with the string and, until Fred's illness, also loved her hunting. 'I missed it greatly at first, but you can't do everything. You either do one thing properly or mess about' – and Mercy is certainly not a person to 'mess about', having taken over the training licence in 1981.

Fred and Mercy's daughter, Scarlett Knipe, also won a race at the age of fourteen, the Newmarket Town Plate, and her first point-to-point at the then minimum age of eighteen, going on to become a top-ranking rider in the sixties and seventies. The Rimells' son, Guy, also won a point-to-point at sixteen and a hunter chase at eighteen, though he later turned his back on racing and now lives in Spain. But with great pride Mercy now watches Guy's daughter, Katie, who lives with her, point-to-point successfully, showing great style and flourish. She finished second in the Cheltenham Foxhunters in 1987 at 50–1 on Three Counties, and then won the prestigious Horse and Hound Cup at Stratford, the climax of a splendid season. Katie's younger brother, Mark, is hoping to ride for England in the junior three-day-event team and then he, too, is likely to start his racing career on Three Counties.

Had the war not intervened, Fred Rimell would have been remembered as much as a great jockey as a trainer; even so, he rode thirty-four winners as a professional on the flat, winning his first race at the age of twelve, when apprenticed to his father, and was champion National Hunt jockey three times, although he never rode a winner at Aintree. But his career after the war was short-lived: riding in the Cheltenham Gold Cup of 1945 on Coloured School Boy, he broke his neck for the second time and never rode again. He was encased in stiff plaster wrapped around his head and reaching down to his navel for three long months. Mercy recalls, 'It was horrendous,' a favourite word of hers. His hair grew to shoulder length and the first thing he did on leaving St Thomas's Hospital was to walk straight to a barber, afterwards feeling marvellous to be free and clean again.

Kinnersley in Worcestershire, only a mile or two from the River Severn and close by the M5, is a hamlet of black and white houses, an agricultural community with lush green fields, and home to some of the best National Hunt horses in England. Old favourites such as Comedy of Errors and Connaught Ranger roam there in contented retirement. It was there that

A delightful Bernard Parkin cartoon of Fred Rimell.

'ESB was a hell of a good jumper but did not stay a yard over three miles.'

Dave Dick pats ESB as he passes the post clear after Devon Loch's mystery fall in 1956.

Fred Rimell started training in 1945, and by the year of ESB he had already achieved notable successes.

ESB's owner, Mrs Leonard Carver, was a lifelong friend of Mercy Rimell. A former Master of the Warwickshire Hunt, Mrs Carver had, as Stella Pierce, been the outstanding lady show-jumper of her time, winning the Daily Mail Cup three years in succession at Olympia.

It is easy to forget, with so much attention focused on Devon Loch's misfortune, that ESB was himself a good class horse of Gold Cup calibre. In fact he won six races in the 1955–56 season alone and, after his Grand National win, in which he carried 11 stone 3 pounds, joined that select band of

horses to run well in the Whitbread, being beaten only half a length.

A good-looking horse, ESB was found as a three-year-old by Mercy Rimell's mother, Mrs Banham, in County Limerick. A show producer of distinction, Mrs Banham was looking for a show horse and, in ESB, nearly found the article, had he not slightly turned a foot. ESB was out of a mare called English Summer, and was by Bidar, hence his name.

Dave Dick, who rode ESB in the National, had won a race on him at Manchester and was booked well in advance for the big race. 'ESB was a hell of a good jumper but did not stay a yard over three miles,' Dave Dick recalls. 'His jumping and that bit of class

got him further in the National and I was just hanging on as long as I could. We were almost knocked over at Valentine's but even so he was still going better than Devon Loch going to the last, but once over it Devon Loch sprinted away from me. I thought: that's it, we're going to be second, and didn't knock him about.'

But, approaching the last, Dick had noticed Devon Loch's tongue hanging out completely black. Even so, he naturally did not expect what followed and when Devon Loch collapsed he says he nearly tripped over him. 'Both Dave Dick and Fred believed that the royal horse ran out of oxygen and collapsed like a marathon runner,' Mrs Rimell says.

Mrs L. Carver and her husband lead in ESB with trainer Fred Rimell just behind.

After the race, Dave Dick was taken to the Royal Box and introduced to the Queen Mother, who congratulated him and asked his thoughts on her horse's demise. 'I was delighted, madam,' he blurted out tactlessly and immediately wished the ground would open up and swallow him up in his embarrassment. In later years Dave met Her Majesty many times, riding several winners for her.

Dave Dick is a forthright, fun-loving character who seldom minces his words, and was always ready to smile at the misfortunes his profession could dole out. His was the era of big Grand National parties at the Adelphi Hotel in Liverpool, at which he was to the forefront of any pranks. His contem-poraries included Michael Scudamore, Tim Brookshaw, Terry Biddlecombe, Fred Winter, Bryan Marshall – great jockeys all of them, but, with the re-freshing generosity of an older gener-ation towards the younger, Dave Dick believes that John Francome was the greatest of them all.

Ask him how many winners he rode and Dave Dick booms, 'I haven't the foggiest idea.' But he did ride in the National thirteen times, failing to com-plete on only four occasions. He was apprenticed to his father at Epsom and rode on the flat for George Lambton when he could tip the scales at 7 stone 12 pounds. But once the war had intervened – he served in Scotland dealing with pack mules and ended up in Palestine with Tony Grantham and Frenchie Nicholson's father-in-law – he was always battling with his weight.

A broken knee forced Dave Dick's retirement in the mid-sixties and he became a bloodstock agent in London; this lifestyle was such an anathema to him that it was a wonder he lasted the year he did. Subsequently, he became manager of a stud in Compton, Berk-shire, married, had two children, took up golf, and retired in 1986.

ESB spent a peaceful retirement in the Carvers' beautiful, parklike grounds at Lapworth in Warwickshire, living until almost thirty years old. Mrs Carver herself died in the early 1980s. 'They were owners who really under-stood horses,' Mrs Rimell says warmly.

Grand National success rather turned the head of their next owner, a young man called Jeremy Vaughan. His father, Douglas, had 100 horses in training, including First of the Dandies, who was just beaten in 1948 by Sheila's Cottage in a desperate duel, and it became Jeremy's ambition to go one better than his father.

In the Ballsbridge catalogue of 1960, Mercy Rimell earmarked two possible horses for him. One was the executor's sale of Nicolaus Silver; omitted from his details was the fact that the horse was qualified for the Grand National, a sure sales point. 'I think I was the only person there that knew,' Mrs Rimell says, 'having looked it up.' Mr Vaughan had a 2000-guinea limit on a purchase price. Fred Rimell noticed

too much money for a bad horse,' came the offputting reply. 'The whole secret was that Nicolaus Silver loved the top of the ground,' Mercy says, 'and in Ireland he was always getting bottomless going.'

Jeremy Vaughan was in Spain when Nicolaus Silver showed his ability on a brilliant pre-race gallop, and Fred wired a cable to him suggesting he invest ante-post on the National. He backed him down from 66–1 to 28–1 and won a small fortune when the grey strode to victory under Bobby Beasley (see chapter 5 for a description of the race).

In later years, Jeremy Vaughan was to marry the granddaughter of Joe Doyle, dual Grand National-winning owner with The Lamb.

Fred Rimell's second National winner, Nicolaus Silver, led by owner Jeremy Vaughan, threads his way to the winner's enclosure.

1970 and Gay Trip (right) puts in a neat jump over the water, ridden by Pat Taaffe.

that Ivor Herbert was present at the sale and commented, 'That's our rival.' And so it proved, Ivor being the underbidder, but only after the Rimells had gone over their limit and secured the beautiful grey for 2500 guineas.

Afterwards they strolled into the bar, where they bumped into Nicolaus Silver's erstwhile trainer, Paddy Slater. 'What have I done, then, Paddy?' Fred asked. 'You have given

When Noreen Begley was taken to Annabel's night club with some friends who were trying to help her get over a divorce, she was not much struck with the London scene; the Jaguar cars and the Chelsea set she found boring and a far cry from her horsey, country life. 'Never mind, darling,' said her friends. 'Look, there's a horsey man over there who won the Grand National.' The pair met and danced and, somewhat the worse for drink, started vying with each other about their respective claims to fame, obviously neither believing a word the other said. So he had won the Grand National; so her grandfather had won it twice ... On it went. Jeremy did not much like to be outdone, and when they went their separate ways, both checked out the other's story and found it was true!

Noreen became the third Mrs Vaughan and although they now live apart, she running a stud and country house hotel in West Wales, and he a drink and drugs clinic in Jamaica, she visits several weeks each year with their young son, Julian. Described as 'a bit of a character and a hell of a nice guy', Jeremy had a 'bit of a problem' for many years, possibly stemming

'You have given too much money for a bad horse.'

from that National victory. 'Everyone who has won wants to buy you a drink,' says Noreen. 'Jeremy was young, fun and good-looking, as were the Rimells; he was generous, too. He had three girlfriends at the time and he bought them each a diamond brooch in the shape of a horse.'

Nicolaus Silver came even closer than ESB to winning the Whitbread, then called the Queen Elizabeth Chase, going under by a hard-fought head to Gold Cup winner Pas Seul.

Gay Trip should have won the Grand National twice, states Mercy Rimell unequivocally. Whereas their other 'might have been', Andy Pandy, fell at the second Becher's when well clear and running stunningly, Gay Trip himself made no such mistake. But, Mrs Rimell says, 'For some reason I will never understand, Terry Biddlecombe, normally such a good rider, took him the longest way round the whole race in 1972 and was only beaten two lengths by Well To Do giving him two stones.'

The video of the race shows that Gay Trip had been on the inside for the early part of the race, but was on the outer jumping Becher's. He came under pressure before the last but found another turn of foot in the rain

Pat Taaffe, at forty the oldest professional jockey in the race ...

and was making ground on the run-in, the commentator noting his outside berth with the remark 'He's trying to get the better ground.'

Gay Trip was another very nice horse and a pleasure to have in the yard, not least because his owner, Tony Chambers, was a good friend of the Rimells. He was Master of the Croome Hunt and also rode a bit as an amateur. He decided that he would like a decent horse in training, and Pat Taaffe told Fred Rimell of Gay Trip when they met at some London function. When they went over to Ireland to see him, Gay Trip had been blistered and was turned out. However, they returned a month later, liked what they saw, and bought him.

Although not quite as attractive as ESB or Nicolaus Silver, Gay Trip was a neat bay who stood barely 16 h.h. and was a 'typical Vulgan'. He was well named, for he was a gay spark, always trotting when others were walking, always cantering when he should have been trotting, but never with a nasty thought in his head. He had a devoted lad throughout his career called John Pullen, nicknamed 'Bromyard' since the days when, as a fifteen-year-old, he had used to walk from his Bromyard home to Kinnersley, a distance of about 15 miles. He stayed with the Rimells until after the birth of his third child.

A comparatively small field of twenty-eight went to post on good ground for Gay Trip's National in 1970. As they ran down that great line of fences approaching Becher's for the second time, Gay Trip was in third place and still running away with Pat Taaffe. He jumped Becher's beautifully. After Valentine's there were only eight runners left, the favourite, Two Springs, having fallen at the third. The eight were all in a bunch – the race seemingly could have gone to any of them. But Pat Taaffe, at forty the oldest

Fred Rimell and owner Mr A. Chambers lead in Gay Trip.

'I don't think anyone but John Burke would have won the Grand National on Rag Trade.'

professional jockey in the race, had Gay Trip beautifully poised on the inside, and the eight-year-old strode away to a fine win, carrying 11 stone 5 pounds, to beat two bottom weights, Vulture and Miss Hunter, by 20 lengths and half a length. In 1971 he fell at the first fence.

Mercy Rimell's praise for John Burke's riding of their fourth Grand National winner, Rag Trade, is fulsome, as was Fred's, who declared that the ex-amateur 'rode a blinder'.

Not her favourite horse, not least because he did not belong to her favourite owner, Rag Trade was described by Mercy as 'a big, ignorant brute', a far cry indeed from the elegance of the previous three. And no less a jockey than John Francome, who rode Rag Trade in the Grand National the year before the horse joined Fred Rimell, was equally damning, declining to ride him again after calling him 'a horrible horse and a horrible ride'.

Rag Trade, a big, heavy-topped chestnut by Menelek, bred by Mr I. Williams, was bought as a nine-year-old at Doncaster Sales by the hairdresser 'Teasy Weasy' Raymond for the then huge sum of 18,000 guineas. Fred Rimell had ridden once or twice for Mr Raymond before the war, and so when the owner rang up to say, 'I've bought a horse to win the National,' Fred not unnaturally agreed to take him. 'Teasy Weasy' brought two partners into the horse with him, Bill Lawrie and Herbert Keen from Kent, but, although these two paid equal portions of the bills, when it came to publicity all the credit for owning the horse tended to go to Mr Raymond.

Things were not always easy with the big horse, but he achieved the notable feat of winning the Welsh Grand National in the same season as

Aintree, following the Midlands Grand National the year before, when trained by Arthur Pitt.

At the time John Burke was on a crest: twenty-three years old, he had been married just over a year and had a baby daughter; he had won the Welsh Grand National and the Midlands Grand National as well as the Cheltenham Gold Cup on Royal Frolic; and he had ended the previous season with his best-ever tally of thirty-two wins. 'I don't think anyone but John Burke would have won the Grand National on Rag Trade,' Mercy asserts. 'He had the most beautiful hands of all the riders I have ever seen; he had a lot of sympathy for the horse and was a wonderful horseman.'

'A horrible horse and a horrible ride.'

John Burke himself says, 'Rag Trade was no flying machine but he was spot-on for the Grand National. He couldn't normally get within 20 lengths of Comedy of Errors [champion hurdler], even when just cantering, but two days before the race he was transformed.' He adds, 'whatever Fred ran in the National had a chance, he was a great trainer. He was one of the old masters, hard but fair, and his record speaks for itself.'

There were thirty-two runners in 1976 and Barona was 7–1 favourite, but with the ground firm there were many who felt Red Rum could now win for a record-breaking third time, the heavy ground and dual Cheltenham Gold Cup winner L'Escargot having conspired to beat him in 1975. But, well though 'Rummy' ran, the big ten-

Fred Rimell – trained four winners: ESB, Nicolaus Silver, Gay Trip and Rag Trade.

year-old Rag Trade could hardly feel the 10 stone 12 pounds on his back and responded willingly to John Burke's persuasion. He was always in contention, and from three out it was clear he was going to play a principal part in the finale. Red Rum still led over the last, but Rag Trade found an extra turn of foot to overhaul him and win by 2 lengths, with the mare Eyecatcher 8 lengths back in third.

All the success proved too much for the young jockey and John Burke went back to Ireland for a spell, before returning to England as a freelance jockey, then an assistant trainer. He still lives in Kinnersley, rides out when he can for Mercy, and is hoping to get a job with the Jockey Club.

The future did not hold out much for Rag Trade. The subject of a dispute between his owners, he suffered the ignominy of being sold at Ascot Sales, where one partner bought out the other for a mere 5000 guineas. He was sent to G. B. Fairbairn at Newcastle-upon-Tyne to train and ran in the following year's Grand National; but by then the big, heavy horse's legs were very dodgy and he broke down so badly that he had to be put down.

In 1977 Fred and Mercy Rimell celebrated their ruby wedding anniversary, and in *Aintree Iron* they reflected that they could 'look back on a partnership that is stronger than ever'. Their love, which had begun at first sight, endured forty-four years until Fred's death in 1981. They were a fine example of integrity and high standards not only in racing but to the world at large. Now the reins are competently held by Mrs Rimell, rightly proud of her granddaughter's prowess on the racecourse and with one outstanding ambition herself: to win the National as a trainer in her own right.

MICHAEL SCUDAMORE

1951–66: Most consecutive rides

Michael Scudamore, pictured in 1966, his last year in the saddle.

THE FIRST TIME Michael Scudamore rode in the Grand National, he looked up at the packed stands and thought: I hope it's twenty years before I'm up there watching this. As it turned out, he missed fulfilling that hope by a mere four years.

Racing is a three-generation affair with the Scudamore family, and a fourth generation is biding its time in the wings. It all began with a horse called Sawfish, bought by Michael's father, Geoffrey, in Hereford market for £5, with 10/- back for luck. In time he was sold on for about £200 to Wilfred Tate, for whom Geoffrey Scudamore won several hunter chases on the horse. Later, Michael was to have his first ride for Mr Tate, and now his son, Peter Scudamore, rides for Mr Tate's son, Martin. All three Scudamores also rode point-to-point winners for Charlie Knipe, father of Herefordshire stud owner, Robin.

But for the war, Geoffrey, who was in the air force, might have ridden Sawfish in the Grand National; as it was, he won a Becher Chase on him.

Michael grew up in the attractive Herefordshire village of Hoarwithy, at which point the River Wye is

> The resultant cavalry charge led to carnage at the first fence, when eleven fell or were brought down, among them young Michael.

wide and tranquil; and since 1957 he has lived not a stone's throw up a tributary valley, where he owns 80 acres and a black and white timber-framed farmhouse typical of the area, looking out onto his twenty-box yard and farm buildings. The lane to the farm is narrow and sunken, not unlike those in Devon, and wild daffodils bloom along the banks in spring.

Michael's grandfather did not race – 'it was not considered a gentleman's job' – but he was a great showing man with good hands, and he was very proud of his great-grandson Peter when he shared the National Hunt jockeys' title with John Francome in 1981–82.

Michael never wanted to do anything other than race; Peter was the same; and now Peter's two young sons, Thomas and Michael, are equally keen.

Michael's first ride in a race was for Charlie Knipe, at the age of fourteen in a local point-to-point, and he finished a long way behind. The following year he 'mostly fell or ran out' but in his third season he started to get into the swing of things and achieved his first winner – even though he'd fallen at the second last and remounted! Chepstow 1949 saw his first winner under rules.

In a memorable career Michael Scudamore rode to thirteen victories on the mighty Crudwell, including that horse's fiftieth win; he was second in the jockeys' table to Fred Winter; and he won virtually every major jumping prize except the Champion Hurdle: the Gold Cup on Linwell, the Welsh Grand National on Creola 11, the Triumph Hurdle on Square Dance, the King George VI Chase on Rose Park, the Mildmay on MacJoy, and the Topham on Barberyn – as well as the Grand National on Oxo.

To Michael, the Grand National *was* racing, and Aintree never ceased to have a particular hold over him. 'I loved walking through the big green gates on arrival and thinking: I've got here. I could always smell the gas works. Then I'd start thinking: I'll be lucky if I get round once. I used to stay at a little hotel called Hunts, which was just up the road from the Adelphi, on which all the Grand National socialising centred, and I'd go there and meet lots of people. I was nearly always wasting, but could never find a decent Turkish bath – there were only a few anywhere in the country then. Then I found one at Southport and stayed at the Royal there ever since.'

Stocky and thick-set like his father ('Peter takes after his mother, long and lean'), Michael learned to keep his weight to within 4 pounds of his minimum: 'The wasting didn't affect my strength. You get used to it, and know how far you can go.'

When he set out to ride East A'Calling for Charlie Knipe in the Grand National of 1951, it was with all the enthusiasm and confidence of a nineteen-year-old on the threshold of life. The horse had been second in the Becher Chase over the Grand National obstacles, and Michael's hopes were high. But they were dashed at the very first fence. A small piece of plough remained until 1951, where the Tophams grew potatoes, between the start and the Melling Road. It was thought to slow horses down on the charge to the first fence, and in 1951, the first year without it, there were 11 fallers at the first.

It was the year when a false start should have been called, many of the riders being turned the wrong way when the starter let them go. The resultant cavalry charge led to carnage at the first fence, when eleven fell or were brought down, among them young Michael. The picture taken afterwards of him standing with some of his colleagues says it all: the utmost

Michael Scudamore, far right, utterly despondent after falling at the first in 1951.

In 1952 he partnered Legal Joy (right) into second place behind Teal, seen here jumping the last fence.

'I've got to go home to feed the chickens.'

in despondency. 'It was the most disappointing day of my life,' he says simply, thirty-six years later... Altogether, twenty-five horses fell in the race, seven were brought down and only three finished, one a remounter; it was won by Nickel Coin.

By the following year, 1952, Michael had joined the ranks of professional jockeys, and his mount was Legal Joy. He was second jockey to Fred Rimell, under Tim Molony, who was riding Roimond. For Michael, the ride on Dorothy Paget's Legal Joy, secured by Fred Rimell, proved to be complete compensation for the previous year: the horse barely put a foot wrong and gave him a tremendous thrill, finishing second to Teal.

Michael recalls, 'Landing over Becher's was like landing in the middle of an arena, there were so many people there; it's the same at the start with the big roar; there's not so much between fences, then you can hear the commentary after Valentine's, where you seem to draw breath a bit. In those days the Chair didn't seem to cause so many problems, I don't know why, and people weren't perturbed about it.'

Michael was following Teal and Freebooter over the Canal Turn, where Freebooter fell, leaving him and Legal Joy second: 'Teal was always holding me – still it was a tremendous thrill.'

In 1953, Michael rode Ordnance for Fred Rimell and was enjoying a smashing ride on him, leading or disputing, until falling at halfway. Neither was hurt.

Hopes were high in 1954, when Michael was offered the ride by Frenchie Nicholson on Lord Sefton's Irish Lizard. Third the previous year with Bob Turnell, having been virtually stopped by a loose horse, Irish Lizard was nearly favourite, but he again found two too good for him: Royal Tan (whose jockey, Bryan Marshall, was winning for the second successive year, following his victory on Early Mist the year before) and Tudor Line.

Irish Lizard was something of an Aintree specialist but also a law unto himself. He habitually came from behind, but the jockey had to leave matters very much to the horse. 'If you asked him to go into a fence short, he would stand off, and if you asked him to stand off, he would put in a short one,' Michael recalls, 'but once you were used to him he was a great ride – he was a lovely old horse.'

Traditionally jockeys and trainers took up a dinner jacket to Liverpool with them 'just in case' they were celebrating a winner that night – but not Frenchie Nicholson. 'I've got to go home to feed the chickens,' he would say, and depart, regardless of how well his horse had run. 'He was a marvellous man to ride for,' Michael says. 'I respected him enormously, and you can only really be taught by someone like that.'

So Michael had had two places and two falls from his first four Grand National rides. In 1955 he rode Irish Lizard again, but this time they were only eleventh, behind Quare Times.

In 1956, the year of Devon Loch, Michael was without a ride until the last minute when, on stopping at a café to phone home, he was given a message to phone Neville Crump. Within a few minutes he had been booked to ride Much Obliged, a class horse who had won a Whitbread.

In the race, Michael found himself struggling and, approaching Becher's for the second time, he was thinking that he might soon have to pull up. Then, in a couple of strides, the whole race changed. Two or three fell in front of him, Much Obliged took on a fresh lease, and suddenly they were bang in the picture. But the new vitality proved his undoing – he overjumped at the fourth fence from home and came down. 'We would have gone very close,' Michael recalls ruefully.

Next year, the pair fell at the same fence, first time round...

Michael's ride in 1958 was Valiant Spark, trained by Major Champneys (trainer of the unfortunate Zahir, who, ten years earlier, had taken the wrong course on the run-in), but Valiant Spark fell at the fifth, the fence before Becher's, giving Michael a third successive fall in the race: 'I always used to think I hadn't had my money's worth if I didn't jump Becher's!'

Most jockeys experience enormous tension before the National, but for Michael, who loved it so much, the big thing was just to get there. It was a close thing one year, when he cracked a bone in a leg ten days before the big race. He had a bit of a limp but didn't realise how bad it was until a few days later when, cantering down to the start for a race, he found he could put no weight on it. He didn't have long to get fit for the National, so he did what many other National Hunt jockeys have done before and since: enlisted the services of Mr W. E. Tucker. 'His London address is etched in my memory for ever,' Michael says. 'When lying on the ground, the trick would be to prevent the ambulance people

In 1959 he won the great race on Mr John Biggs' Oxo.

> 'When lying on the
> ground the trick
> would be to prevent
> the ambulance people
> getting you to hospital,
> because you wouldn't
> get out again – you
> had to get to
> Mr Tucker.'

getting you to hospital, because you wouldn't get out again – you had to get to Mr Tucker.'

Early in 1959, Michael embarked upon the long drive to Lingfield from Hereford in pouring rain. It was a journey of over 180 miles, and when he encountered floods at Runnymede he felt sure that the meeting at low-lying Lingfield would be off. But for once it was not. The horse he rode (because Tim Moloney was hurt) won by half a length. 'I wouldn't mind riding *that* round Liverpool,' Michael told the trainer, Willie Stephenson, as he unsaddled. The horse had struck him as a real National sort. His name was Oxo.

Of Willie Stephenson, Michael says simply, 'He was a good man to ride for. He never blamed you if you lost, unless you'd done something diabolical, but if you won he'd just as likely say, 'You came too soon,' if that's what he thought. 'Of them all, he was the one man before the National who was convinced we'd win, rather than just hope.'

Willie Stephenson began with a couple of bad days at Liverpool that year: he lost money on a two-year-old on the opening day (when it was a mixed meeting), and Farmers Boy added to his losses the next. It takes a brave man to attempt to recoup losses in the National, but that's just what Stephenson did. He liked to lead his own horse out of the paddock, something several trainers do nowadays, and, although he was at Oxo's bridle as usual on the day of the big race, he let him go more quickly than normal to nip off and back him some more.

Michael had Oxo held up in about fifteenth place near the outside as they approached Becher's for the first time, but five or six fell there, interfering with other runners on the inside, so that he came out of the fence in about fifth place and far too close to the lead for comfort.

Oxo nodded a bit at the water, but going out into the country for the second time there were only three in front of him – and Tim Brookshaw on Wyndburgh just behind. From the second Becher's it was these two in front together – and, when Tim broke an iron, Michael remembers thinking: Thank goodness, I've got a chance!

But Tim Brookshaw was not to be denied so easily. They jumped the last half-dozen fences upsides each other, with Tim performing miracles to stay on board the gallant little Scottish horse. 'From the last fence to the winning post took ten years off my life,' says Michael, 'because all the time I could hear him coming . . .'

As he passed the post and realised his life's ambition, Michael Scudamore felt almost a sense of anti-climax – what was there left to achieve? But, before long, he was aiming to win another one . . . 'I didn't think I'd be sober for a month,' he remembers.

After the race, Willie Stephenson said, 'You came too soon.' That night, with the revelries at the Adelphi still going strong at 3.00 a.m., Michael approached his trainer. 'Did you mean that?' he asked him. 'Of course I did,' came the reply.

Other good rides came Michael's way, but he was never to win the National again. The year after Oxo, 1960, he rode Wyndburgh, but the pair failed to catch the eye of the television cameras filming the race for the first time, for they parted company at the first Becher's. The next year Michael rode Oxo again, but he was no longer the horse he had been and pulled up after the second Becher's.

Hopes were high in 1960 when Michael had the ride on Wyndburgh...

1961 was the first National in which the take-off side of the fences was sloped, and there are many still who talk of the days when 'the fences really took some jumping', when 'the men were sorted from the boys'. Until that time, the fences had been upright and it was difficult for horses to judge their take-off accurately when at speed or under pressure. It should be remembered, however, that the fences were in no way lowered or softened; they were simply made fairer. And do people really want to see a lot of falls, or does it not create an even greater racing spectacle to have several horses in with a chance in the closing stages instead of a mere procession?

The Aintree fences remain unique, and perhaps it should not be forgotten that, in the early days of the National, most of the fences were flimsy and low. Only the brook fences and the wall (where the water is now sited) offered any real jumping challenge.

In 1962 Michael Scudamore pulled up on Chavara. He finished about seventh on O'Malley Point in 1963. The following year he rode Time, on whom he was going really well until Becher's second time. There, the horse made a terrible mistake, coming down on his nose and belly before rising to his feet, with Michael having performed a superb balancing act, still in the saddle, but their chance had gone. 1965 brought him another fall, on Time, at the seventeenth. When he went out on Greek Scholar in 1966 little did he know that it would be his last National. He was brought down at the second Becher's, going so well that 'I would have won or placed.'

Eight months later, riding at Wolverhampton, Michael suffered a fall on the flat that finished his career. He lost 90 per cent of the sight of one eye, broke his palate and some ribs, and suffered a collapsed lung. The accident brought to an end a series of sixteen consecutive rides in the Grand National – a unique achievement in this century.

Still a young man, Michael was unprepared for a future without race-riding, which until then had occupied most of his time. He had driven an average of 1000 miles a week for over fifteen years and regarded serious in-

... but they were dashed at Becher's first time round.

juries as things that happened to other people. If you started thinking of them in relation to yourself, it was probably a sign of failing nerve and time to quit. Today, racing is bigger business, much more professional than it was then, and many young jockeys have second careers lined up for their retirement or even running parallel with their riding for a few years.

To begin with, Michael did not know what he would do. He supposed he would farm. But racing was in his blood, and a year later he took out a licence to train. He has since turned out a steady stream from his yard, including smart performer Bruslee, who won the Mackeson, and Fortina's Palace, who won the Grand Annual at Cheltenham. He also bred Fred Pilliner, who won eleven races. Nor has he forgotten the National, producing Charles Dickens, who ran third behind Red Rum and L'Escargot in 1974.

JAY TRUMP

1965: American winner

Jay Trump, American victor in 1965, with Tommy Smith up.

THREE YOUNG MEN camped in a shared caravan, while their boss and his family roughed it in two bare rooms as the rest of the house was altered around them. Discomfort meant nothing to them; they were all as keen and eager as prep school boys, determined that their group – or, in this case, stable – should do well.

The guv'nor was Fred Winter, CBE; the lads Richard Pitman, Brian Delaney and Derek King, along with head man Tom Carey, who lived in the bungalow. It was the summer of 1964.

Any day now their first horse would arrive; excitement and anticipation were high, for, by all accounts, this was no ordinary horse. He had swept all before him in America and was coming

His target: the Grand National. His name: Jay Trump.

over to prove that he was the best in the whole world of steeplechasing. His target: the Grand National. His name: Jay Trump.

Although Fred Winter had enjoyed the highest possible reputation as a steeplechase jockey, owners had not immediately flocked to him when he retired to train.

Many of his 930 winners had been helped past the post by the rhythmic persuasion of his hands and heels, by

the clock inside his head, by being taken the shortest route – by sheer jockeyship. He had galloped more than 10,000 miles and over something like 120,000 fences and hurdles, and fallen 300 times.

Fred Winter's first steeplechase came in 1947, when he was on leave from the Parachute Regiment, on a horse called Carton, on which, nine years earlier, his life-long friend and former school chum, Dave Dick, had scored *his* first win as an apprentice on the flat!

It was in the 1961–62 season that he took the racing world by storm: winner of the French Grand National in Auteuil with a broken bit dangling out of Mandarin's mouth – his greatest

Fred Winter, pictured in 1964, the year he retired as a jockey.

racing memory of all; winner of the Turf Writers' Cup in Belmont Park, USA, on Baby Prince; winner of the Galway Plate in Ireland on a mare, Carraroe; winner of the Cheltenham Gold Cup on Mandarin; and, for good measure, of the Grand National on Kilmore (to add to his 1957 success on Sundew). At the same time, he was wasting down to 9 stone 2 pounds and rode successfully on the flat for his father, Fred, and for Sir Noel Murless.

No wonder that, the next year, racing's perfect sportsman with the creased-up smile and calm manner (sadly badly injured in 1987), was awarded the CBE in the Queen's honours list for his services to racing.

And the year after that? He was camping in his new house, Uplands, Lambourn, with barely half a dozen horses in the twenty-seven boxes outside, having been turned down by the Jockey Club for a job as starter, and declining to accept one as a judge. Uplands is now a lovely home, boasting a much nurtured garden and fifty-seven boxes, all of them occupied each winter.

The first few horses included two from Sir Michael Sobell. Mrs Miles Valentine soon became a loyal owner. Another batch came from Ryan Price when he was warned off for six months, including Anglo, who was to give Fred Winter his second Grand National winner in two years as a trainer, following his two as a rider, all in a single decade.

If there had been doubters before that he could train as well as he could ride, they were silenced after those wins. Within another decade a magical era had begun, with the 'famous five' of Pendil, Bula, Lanzarote, Crisp and Killiney, later joined by Midnight Court. 'All those good horses had wonderful manners. They were so easy to do and had no vices, you could sleep with them, only Pendil could nip a bit,' Fred says. Killiney, who was tragically killed at Ascot, was 'so kind, he was just like a great big puppy'.

But all this was a long way off in the summer of 1964 as Fred and his nucleus of staff awaited the arrival of Jay Trump. Far from an anti-climax, his arrival exceeded their wildest dreams. Used to horses who had been 'broken' in a matter of days and asked to gallop within weeks, they found here a beautifully schooled, beautifully balanced, beautifully mannered paragon.

Brian Delaney, Fred Winter's head lad for many years, had served in the King's Troop and soon found that, if he gave traditional aids to the good-looking bay horse with the big white star above his eyes and snip on his nose, he would respond with high-class dressage movements. This was the horse who had been drumming round little dirt tracks in quarter-horse racing, who had been almost killed in a racecourse accident when caught up in tin as a two-year-old, who had changed hands many times – but whose potential had been spotted and noted by one Tommy Crompton Smith, from a long line of American racing and hunting enthusiasts, who bought him for Mrs Mary Stephenson (now Le Blond), herself a former polo player and Joint Master of the Camargo Hunt.

By the time he came to England, Jay Trump had won America's premier steeplechase, the Maryland Hunt Cup, over 4 miles of gruelling upright timber fences, twice.

Tommy Crompton Smith had been hunting from the age of six months, when he was strapped in a basket saddle, and by four was hunting on his own pony. His grandfather was Harry Worcester Smith, who one year had his hounds shipped over to Ireland to hunt, and the tradition continued with Tommy's father, Crompton, a dairy farmer who also rode in the local races. A picture of the Grand National hanging over the family's fireplace fuelled Tommy's enthusiasm for the race, and before long he was riding any and everything in American races.

He joined the renowned Smithwick family and gave up his college course to pursue a career as a gentleman rider, with considerable success. Naturally he jumped at the chance Mary Le Blond gave him to find her a likely steeplechaser. He had seen Jay Trump in a couple of races at Charles Town, West Virginia, and secured him for $2000.

From then on, Tommy worked, trained and practically lived with the horse. Mary Le Blond stipulated that only he should ride him, and after his second Maryland Hunt Cup victory somebody suggested the Grand National as his next target. 'Why not?' came the owner's reply. 'He has done everything there is to do over here.'

Jay Trump arrived in England eight months before the 1965 National and was joined four months later by Tommy, who proved himself every bit as dedicated here as he had been at home. In time he partnered Jay Trump on his first English outing. It was also the stable's first runner. No one knew quite what to expect. The race was at Sandown, and the pair won.

It was clear that this dedicated American was no 'bum' amateur, and that the horse was top class. Indeed, had Jay Trump stayed in England another year, Fred Winter believes he would have won a Gold Cup. He ran second of two behind Frenchman's Cove in the King George VI Chase at Kempton on Boxing Day and in all won three of his five preparatory races before the Grand National. As Fred says, 'It put the icing on the cake' in helping to establish him as a trainer.

Preparation was progressing exceptionally well, when, just three weeks before the big race, anxiety struck. By this time Tommy Smith was an eating, sleeping, walking, talking Grand National automaton, and his horse was as well as could be. But a coughing epidemic hit Lambourn. One by one, good, fit horses were struck down by it, till only two horses in Fred's yard, Solbina and Jay Trump, remained healthy. Then Solbina succumbed. There was only one thing left to do.

Tommy, who with his wife Frances had rented a cottage nearby, moved Jay Trump to an empty stable on his own about half a mile away, and literally moved in with him. The horse anyway had his own fodder flown in from America. Now if Fred Winter himself wanted to see his charge he almost had to make an appointment to do so, and then had to step through disinfectant to reach him. (The vaccinations that the American horses had had proved their worth – it was before they were obligatory here – for soon the only other horse besides Jay Trump in

Tommy Smith keeps a tight hold on Jay Trump's head.

the whole of Lambourn without the flu was an American one in Fulke Walwyn's stable.) The rest of the Uplands team could only look on and admire Tommy Smith's single-minded sense of purpose.

It was the fifth year of the televising of the National and, as part of its build-up, the BBC picked two horses for their cameras to focus on: Jay Trump and Freddie. They could not have chosen better, because the finish saw those two fighting a memorable battle.

In spite of all the films he had watched of the race and all the discussions he had had about it, when Tommy Smith first saw those Aintree fences they were bigger and more daunting in real life than he had ever imagined. But when it came to the race itself he was as cool as a cucumber and obeyed instructions to the letter. It could have been Fred Winter himself riding out there to victory, as he had done only three years before on Kilmore.

Forty-seven horses lined up on perfect ground. The popular Scottish horse Freddie, on 11 stone 10 pounds, was 7–2 favourite, and Jay Trump, carrying 5 pounds less, started at odds of 100–6.

It was a dream ride for Tommy and Jay Trump as they cruised round on the inside. They avoided the melée at the first Becher's, where five horses were brought down; then jumped the

At the last fence Jay Tramp is just ahead of the gallant Scottish horse Freddie (Pat McCarron).

It was a momentous triumph for the American dream – the first American bred, owned and ridden winner – and for the first-season trainer.

Canal Turn at a superb angle – no problem for a horse schooled in dressage and showjumping and a manoeuvre that saved him so many lengths it may have won him the race.

Jay Trump was lying twelfth at the water, from which point, his energy nicely conserved, he steadily improved his position. As they crossed the Melling Road for the last time and came back onto the racecourse proper, he moved smoothly up to dispute affairs with Freddie, the two horses jumping the second last alongside each other. The American went into the last just ahead, jumped it well, and started off up that long, long run-in, apparently drawing away.

Then came the only anxious moment of the race for Fred Winter, when Tommy, a length clear, picked up his whip on Jay Trump. 'He hated being hit,' Fred says. 'I could see the old devil stopping. But Tommy was so efficient and clear-minded, he didn't flap, he just put down the whip. A lot of professionals would have let the situation go to their heads and they'd have lost the race, but not Tommy.'

He passed the post threequarters of a length to the good, with another amateur-ridden, highly handicapped horse, Mr Jones ridden by Chris Collins, 20 lengths or so back in third place.

It was a momentous triumph for the American dream – the first American bred, owned and ridden winner – and for the first-season trainer. Fred Winter didn't jump up and down in the excitement – 'I'm not made that way' – but naturally he was delighted, and his smile said it all.

Fred Winter with Jay Trump's proud owner, Mrs Stephenson.

Jockey Tommy Smith and owner Mary Stephenson in a victory hug.

Jay Trump, Tommy Smith and Fred Winter returned to Lambourn to a heroes' reception, and Jay Trump was so well that he was prepared for the French Grand National at Auteuil in June. He almost won that challenging race too. He landed first over the last fence but Tommy's strength for once failed him, a result of having over-wasted to do the weight, and he finished third.

Jay Trump returned to America for an epic third victory in the Maryland Hunt Cup, and was immediately retired. He was nine years old. He still looks well and, in Mrs Le Blond's words, 'sassy', at thirty-one years old, cared for by her granddaughter, Serena Stephenson.

Tommy Smith's fortunes changed with the retirement of his great partner, for his marriage broke up and he trained for only about a year before quitting the racing scene altogether and going into a job in education.

The loss to the sport of both an exceptional horse and an exceptional horseman, when still in their prime, was keenly felt on both sides of the Atlantic.

FOINAVON

1967: Luckiest winner

THERE HAVE BEEN lucky winners of the Grand National but, of them all, Foinavon must rank supreme – and may also have been indirectly responsible for saving the race.

Sole contender to get over the twenty-third fence at the first attempt in a huge pile-up, the moderate, blinkered Foinavon held onto his unexpected lead all the way to the winning post, seven lonely fences later.

Yet, while Foinavon was indisputably lucky, bravery and, yes, skill, also came into the reckoning. That day in 1967 twenty horses were put out of the race at the smallest fence on the course. All of them had safely negotiated Becher's for the second time. The commentator remarked on the fact that the two loose horses leading had caused no hindrance. They jumped straight and true, as if guided by jockeys. All that changed at the next, as the loose horses stopped and swerved broadside to the take-off side of the fence. The havoc they wreaked was total. Most horses were baulked and refused. Some jockeys reached the landing side without their partners. A few combinations scrambled over only to fall apart on landing.

Into this melée came the backmarkers, Foinavon among them. Much credit is due to the quick thinking of his jockey, John Buckingham, riding in his first Grand National, in steering him over to the wide outside and popping him through a gap; and an equal amount to the horse himself, who had every excuse to stop on the take-off side along with most of his comrades. From a virtual standstill he jumped over. And entirely alone he faced the remaining seven fences: a situation not

---

… the loose horses stopped and swerved broadside to the take-off side of the fence. The havoc they wreaked was total.

---

for the faint of heart, for it is in company that horses race best, their adrenalin stimulated by the competition at their heels.

Foinavon's win may have been due, at least in part, to the somewhat unorthodox, individual training of his young handler, John Kempton. Although his win brought amazed gasps at the time, and returned odds of 444–1 on the Tote, in fact Foinavon had been bought specifically with the Grand National in mind.

John Kempton had a small yard at Compton in Berkshire, and some loyal but unwealthy owners. Originally a Londoner, he studied to be a vet in Epsom but lack of finances forced him to quit and he became a blacksmith. He took out a permit, then, mustering a few owners, one or two shopkeepers who probably could not afford today's fees, he was granted a licence to train and moved to Compton.

First owned by Anne, Duchess of Westminster, Foinavon – named, like Arkle and Ben Stack, after Scottish mountains – had won three chases for Tom Draeper in Ireland but had a tendency to fall, and the duchess decided to sell him. One of his wins had qualified him for the National so, when he came up for sale at Doncaster, Kempton secured him for 2000 guineas on behalf of two of his owners who were keen to have a runner in the race.

John's prime aim was to improve the horse's jumping. He took him hunting with the Old Berkshire, where he jumped all sorts of obstacles and had to learn to look after himself in tricky situations, and he found a new enthusiasm for life. He was lunged a 'fantastic amount' over jumps and popping over little schooling fences became a daily routine on exercise.

A fine, upstanding sort, standing 16.3 h.h., with a bright eye and plenty of heart room, Foinavon was 'one hell of a character' who 'could really talk', and he loved nothing more than the companionship of the goat Susie, with whom he became real friends. Fionavon got very upset if for any reason Susie was taken out of his box for a while, and he looked forward twice daily to her being milked. He looked on virtually drooling, just waiting for his drink, and as soon as she was milked he drank it like lightening, licking his lips with pleasure. Susie even used to accompany Foinavon to race meetings, as usual sharing his quarters; the two were great pals.

Foinavon's form had not been as moderate as all those who wrote him off as a freak National winner claimed. He finished fourth in the King George VI Chase at Kempton on Boxing Day, though he came seventh (last) in the Cheltenham Gold Cup of 1967. He was usually ridden by John Kempton himself, and many times ran in a bitless bridle. Kempton had tried this unusual equipment before on a horse called Seasend with startling results. Anxious not to get into trouble, Kempton had asked the stewards' permission; there was nothing in the

Two loose horses caused carnage and the virtual demolition of the fence but miraculously no horse or rider was seriously hurt.

rulebook to prevent it so it was allowed, with the proviso that, should the horse cause interference, Kempton would find himself in trouble. Far from that, Seasend won by 20 lengths, went on to win about four more, and even finished second in the Becher Chase at Liverpool.

A bit of a psychoanalyst with his horses, John found they responded to him: for instance, in a bitless bridle a poor jumper would no longer fear being jobbed in the mouth at a fence, and performances improved dramatically.

Foinavon ran sixteen times during the season in which he won the National but, once fit, was not trained hard between races, so he stood his racing well. Indeed, he hardly had a saddle on him during the fortnight before the National. He was mostly lunged and got used to jumping on his own – something that was to prove an advantage that even the most clairvoyant could barely have foretold...

John Kempton would have liked to ride Foinavon in the National himself but displayed loyalty to his owners

Only Foinavon avoided this melée, while the crowd rush to help.

on two counts: his minimum riding weight of 10 stone 10 pounds would put him 10 pounds over weight; and he had another horse running at Worcester – 'I had just as much responsibility to the owners of that as to those of a horse in a big race.'

So on Grand National day he went to Worcester, where he rode Three Dons in a novice hurdle race – and won. An hour or so later, he settled in the jockeys' changing room to watch the National on one of several television sets, his father having travelled to Aintree to saddle Foinavon, and John Buckingham having been booked to ride...

'As the pile-up happened, and before the commentator spotted him, I saw Foinavon pop over the fence; he was wearing distinctive yellow blinkers which I had had specially widened for the race to prevent mud blocking his eyes.' John Kempton, normally a cool customer, went 'just sort of loopy': 'I had bought the horse for the Grand National, and here it was coming off. I don't think the implication of it all penetrated my mind terribly quickly, that it was more than just an ordinary race...'

The splash all over the next day's papers soon brought it home. It was at a time when public interest in the race was waning; its future was under a cloud, due to Mrs Topham's negotiations to sell the site for building development. But the sensational pile-up, and the fact that no horse or jockey was hurt in it, sparked the race into new life; the element of luck needed in the National, the belief that 'anything can happen' which gives hope to thousands of the general public who place their ten bobs each year was once more on everyone's lips. 'It was the era of constant "last" Grand Nationals and I believe this happening made people fight for it,' John Kempton says. 'It's possible there would be no National now but an estate of houses had Foinavon's year not happened.'

Foinavon himself ran in the Grand National again but was brought down at the water when in much closer contention. He eventually died of old age and is buried at Compton.

> ## 'As the pile-up happened, and before the commentator spotted him, I saw Foinavon pop over the fence.'

Astonishment shows on John Buckingham's face as Foinavon sails over the last.

With the rest strung out behind, Foinavon holds his lead all the way.

Life took a change of course for John Kempton. For family reasons he had to give up training a few years later and, when David Barons offered him a job as assistant trainer, he jumped at the chance, having got to like Devon in annual summer forays round Newton Abbot, Devon and Exeter and the now-defunct Buckfastleigh. Once in his new job, he made many friends and was persuaded to take up sub-aqua diving as a hobby, his wife, Trish, joining in too. He began to get itchy feet to work for himself again, however, and after about five seasons with David Barons he set up a yacht-chartering business from Salcombe. Now he and Trish take groups of about ten throughout the summer on their 'floating hotel', sometimes nicknamed 'booze cruises', with Trish cooking and John teaching sub-aqua diving and navigating. Throughout the summer it is a seven-day-a-week job, and in the winter Trish is cooking for the freezer, John is painting and maintaining the yacht, and there is little time left for racing...

If racing's loss was sailing's gain in the case of John Kempton, racing has been the winner with John Buckingham. As a fifteen-year-old school leaver, having never sat on a horse, he was faced with the choice of becoming shepherd, gamekeeper or stable boy for Mr Edward Courage. John's mother was a dairymaid on Mr Courage's Edgcote estate in south Northamptonshire, home of great Grand National horses such as Tiberetta and her son Spanish Steps, and it was to the stables that Buckingham went. He has never regretted that decision. For him, racing became, and still is, all-consuming. Although the Grand National victory inevitably changed his life, it did not alter him as a man; he remained modest and cheerful, in love with racing and only too happy to reminisce – for barely a day goes by without some stranger recalling that great event over twenty years ago.

John had ridden Foinavon once, a year before their win, at Cheltenham and in the bitless bridle, but when the offer came to ride the horse in the National it was at such short notice

For a few moments John did not realise he had been the only one to get over at the first attempt.

that all the Aintree accommodation was fully booked. John and his brother Tom had to stay in the sitting room of a nearby boarding house, Tom on a sofa and John sleeping on two armchairs pulled together – hardly ideal big-race preparation!

Although Foinavon's connections fully expected him to get round, victory was so unconsidered that the owner, Mr Cyril Watkins, did not even attend. He was watching at home in Berkshire with his wife, but after the pile-up he could not bear to continue and his wife had to call him in from the garden to tell him he had won! As for Foinavon's previous co-owner, Mac Bennellick, he had found his funds stretched in the autumn and failed to sell his half-share in the horse – so he had given him to Cyril Watkins!

In the race, Foinavon took a fair hold early on; he was in the leading flight over the first fence but the pace increased so much that he quickly dropped back. In fact, the pace was so fast that the race time was 3 seconds faster than that achieved by Anglo the previous year when there had been no mid-race hold-up. Only five horses were behind Foinavon when they jumped Becher's for the second time, but just ahead of him was the fancied Honey End, ridden by that good judge of pace, Josh Gifford.

As they approached the next fence, the twenty-third, mayhem was breaking loose, and when Foinavon drew closer there were horses and jockeys running about all over the place, doing everything except jumping the fence. They were literally piled up on top of each other, bits of broom and gorse everywhere, the fence almost demolished.

John Buckingham could hardly believe his eyes. He had Honey End ahead and to the inside of him; he was roughly central, when he pulled Foinavon over to the outside and, weaving his way as two loose horses trotted back towards him, Foinavon popped over from little more than a trot and set sail the other side.

For a few moments John did not realise he had been the only one to get over at the first attempt, but by the Canal Turn he knew, and by Valentine's he realised that all he had to do was stand up to win.

'It is to Foinavon's eternal credit that he did not refuse, either at the melée, when he had every excuse to, or when he was out on his own and especially as he was tiring,' says John. 'When I saw Honey End and Greek Scholar coming I didn't think they could catch me, but I gave him one slap after the last, just in case. I must admit I was nearly unconscious at the end of it.'

As for Foinavon, he passed the post with his ears pricked – and ate up as well as ever that night, in the company, as usual, of Susie the goat. Altogether, seventeen of the baulked or fallen horses got going again to finish.

It was the fourth time in the history of the race that only one horse had completed a clear round, following Glenside in 1911, Shaun Spadah in 1921 and Tipperary Tim in 1928.

When John and his wife, Ann, returned to Chipping Warden, where he still lives, a stone's throw from Edgcote, they found the house covered in bunting by their neighbours and a notice proclaiming 'Buckingham Palace'. The next day he was invited onto *The Bob Monkhouse Show* at the London Palladium and, wearing a dinner jacket borrowed from amateur

John Buckingham pats Foinavon, winner of the 1967 Grand National.

rider Roger Charlton, he joined in the fun, although confessing the stage fright to be worse than the pre-National nerves. He later opened a few fêtes and knocked down some charity piles of pennies, but he had been back at work at Edgcote the morning after the National. One outcome was that his number of rides markedly increased the following year.

He rode Foinavon several more times, though injury excluded him from the 1969 National, when Foinavon was brought down at the water. Amazingly, he was on when another mini 'Foinavon' happened. It was in a three-horse race at Uttoxeter; he was tracking the other pair three from home when one ran out and took the other horse with him, leaving Foinavon to jump and gallop home alone again. 'The crowd simply went mad,' John recalls. Of the Grand National win, he says, 'It could have happened to any horse in the race, it just happened to be Foinavon. Although he was lucky, I still think he was a good horse who would not have been disgraced; he was one-paced but always stayed on and I'm sure he would have been in the first dozen.'

John Buckingham continued racing for a few years but eventually, at the age of thirty-two, with his rides dwindling and a young family to support, he was offered and accepted a job of jockey's valet – a role he revels in, for it keeps him in the weighing room in the midst of the atmosphere he knows and loves so well. Before retiring, he rode a further three times in the National and remains convinced that he would have won on merit on Limeburner had that horse not fallen at the penultimate when lying a close-up third in 1969 – but then, there are so many 'might have beens' in the National each year, and only one winner . . .

TIM DURANT

1968: Oldest rider

Tim Durant, who at 68 became the oldest rider to complete the National.

WHEN GRANDFATHER TIM DURANT galloped into the Grand National record books in 1968, at sixty-eight years old, he became, at his third attempt, the oldest rider ever to complete the course. For a man who was also a bit-part film actor, financier and the founder of a Hollywood fox-hunt, his was a remarkable achievement in a remarkable life.

Born at the turn of the century in Westbury, USA, Tim Durant grew up in Madison, Connecticut, where he learnt to ride on horses owned by a cowboy-happy uncle. Educated at Hotchkiss as a scholarship student, he completed his secondary schooling at Andover, then in 1923 he graduated from Yale, where he studied Russian literature and was a baseball player.

He married into the smart horsey set of Long Island in the 1920s; his wife, Adelaide, was daughter of E. F. Hutton, who gave Tim a seat on the New York stock exchange as a wedding present, and of Mrs Merriweather Post, whose family had made a fortune from cereals.

Tim became Master of the Smithtown hounds and also hunted with the Middlebury pack in Connecticut. He began riding in timber races and point-to-points and gradually an ambition to ride in the Grand National was born.

But it was only after many years and many ups and downs that Tim Durant was to achieve his aim. After Yale, he went into stocks and bonds but, according to Jim Murray, writing in the *Los Angeles Times* in 1965, he 'couldn't wait to get out of his bowler hat and customer suit and down to the family stable on weekends so he could jump fences and chase frightened little furry animals'. Tim put his business brain to good use, however, soon taking peanut-butter sandwiches with him to work rather than miss earning perhaps $200 at lunchtime. His aim was to earn a million dollars by the time he was

After completing the course, Tim salutes the cheering crowd.

thirty. He got halfway there – and into hospital, suffering from stomach ulcers. Then in the Great Depression of 1929 he lost everything, including his marriage. To stay in Manhattan was to risk joining those jumping from top-storey window ledges... So, penniless and horseless, he headed west.

The tall, lean six-footer soon made his mark in Hollywood, taking minor riding parts in a good many films; and he became, among other things, financial advisor to Charlie Chaplin. In later years, Chaplin wrote the following letter to him, dated 6 July 1971:

Dear Eternal Tim, Not tiny Tim, but Tim the dashing steeple-chase rider. If you lose, you can have a job with me as a leading man!

If you are passing this way, and you are not social, drop in for a drink or a cup of tea. I am very jealous of your stints, your riding – How the hell do you do it?

Your picture is, as usual, quite good looking. I have become a fat old man, so don't expect too much.

However, joking aside, if you're coming this way, jump in – Oona sends her love and our love to Marjorie.

Yours ever,
Charlie

PS: I have a young daughter of eleven who is crazy about horses, but I try to dis-

Tim Durant goes uncomfortably out of the side door, hits the ground but manages to cling on to the reins and gets a hand back into the saddle.

courage her as much as possible as I think it is dangerous.

Tim also became good friends with film director John Huston who, just before his death in the summer of 1987, wrote:

... Tim never rode professionally but he was an outstanding figure among amateur riders.

Tim was a man of distinguished appearance, tall, slim and elegant. He was not a professional actor, although I had him in several of my pictures, notably *The General* and *The Red Badge of Courage*, the reason being that he could ride a horse and I liked his company.

... after his riding in the Grand National, Tim continued to ride as an amateur jockey with his grand-daughter. Very often they would come in one, two in a race.

Tim used to vist John Huston in Ireland when John was Master of the Galway Blazers; and it was from John's house there that he married for the second time, with everyone wearing hunting dress for the occasion. After the ceremony they all rode off to the first covert, including the priest.

Once Tim had moved to the West Coast he remained there. During the Hollywood heyday of the forties and fifties, when gossip columnists such as Hedda Hopper and Louella Parsons were at their height, his name and picture appeared almost daily with the female stars of the time.

Jim Murray wrote, 'He organised drag hunts and enlisted as many of the movie colony as could manage to get on a horse and not fall off to join him.' With film actor Dan Dailey as joint Master, he founded the West Hunt Club, Los Angeles. Among their followers were film stars Jose Ferrer, Joan Fontaine, and one Ronald Reagan ...

In the 1960s, Tim determined to ride in the Grand National, but first he had to prove to his daughter Marjorie, who had considerable influence over him, that he was fit enough to do so. This he managed by taking part in a gruelling 100-mile-a-day race over the Sierra Nevada mountains. Following the old gold trail of Pony Express and Wells Fargo fame, riders had to climb up 9500 feet and down a total of 15,250 feet in temperatures of up to 100 degrees fahrenheit. Horses had to be hard and tough – and so did their riders. Most of them used Western saddles but

not Tim Durant, who rode English style all the way, creeping along narrow mountain precipices with drops of 2000 feet. A cowboy used to mountain riding won the race but Tim, who did not drink or smoke and always retained his lean figure, was not disgraced, finishing in 19 hours 34 minutes. In a field of ninety, he was thirty-sixth of the fifty finishers.

After that achievement, his daughter had to concede that he was not yet ready for a rocking chair. Instead, she supported him financially in his quest for a suitable Grand National horse. The search took him, during the 1965–66 season, to the yard of Roddy Armytage in East Ilsley, Oxfordshire. There Tim found Ariel III, winner of the previous year's Liverpool Foxhunters, the 'amateurs' Grand National', and as such an ideal mount for him. Within half an hour of Tim's arrival at the yard the racing reporter from the local Newbury paper happened to ring on a routine call, and was promptly put on to the American. Not surprisingly, his story was picked up by the dailies, and the Armytages soon found that Tim revelled in publicity.

One consequence was that the Jockey Club discovered Tim's true age to be sixty-six. Roddy Armytage had applied for Tim's amateur licence before his new patron came over and, when asked his age, had truthfully

'After that, they couldn't very well take his licence away.'

replied he did not know – so the age of fifty had been recorded. It was before the era of compulsory medical checks for riders over the age of thirty-five, but when the stewards saw the age of sixty-six splashed across the papers they felt they had better interview the elderly rider.

Luckily for Tim, the date booked for the interview was after the Becher Chase, a now defunct race over the Aintree fences in which he successfully completed the course. 'After that, they couldn't very well take his licence away,' comments Roddy.

Tim had spent some time in California preparing himself for the National. He would gallop his horse along the beach at Santa Monica, followed by a bracing dip in the surf, then he would return home to practise balancing on a bongo board. All this was before he went to work in his office, and even then he would spend his lunch hour toning up his arm and leg muscles. In England, his landlady sometimes heard him doing press-ups in the middle of the night . . .

Tim had proved his fitness to ride in English steeplechases. But then he was dealt a last-minute blow: Ariel suffered tendon trouble and had to be substituted. In the event, an ideal replacement horse was found. 'King Pin was a real Christian,' Roddy Armytage recalls fondly, 'and a blind man could ride him.'

Tim finished second on King Pin at Kempton, and so all was set for the 1966 National. A few days before the big race, television crews and press photographers visited East Ilsley intending to film the Galloping Grandfather's final workout on King Pin. The particular day did not suit for the work Roddy had planned, so the trainer swapped the horse with another of similar colouring called War Lace; the films rolled and cameras

Tim Durant approaches Becher's Brook, still just in touch with the rest.

clicked innocently away, and they all got their pictures of 'King Pin'.

At Aintree, Tim dressed himself in his vertical striped colours and went round shaking the hands of all his fellow jockeys in the changing room and asking, 'Have you made your will?' His friends in America, meanwhile, many of whom had flown over for the race, had formed 'The Society for the Preservation of Tim Durant'. Tim and King Pin safely negotiated two thirds of the course behind Anglo, but then came to a standstill.

Tim was a popular personality wherever he went, and much admired on both sides of the Atlantic, but sometimes his publicity-seeking tested the patience of those around him, as happened during the 1966 National. After jumping twenty fences, he returned to

'... a bit of a film star who rather fancied himself as a womaniser.'

Roddy near the paddock, but – instead of dismounting and handing his horse over to be unsaddled, washed down and cooled off – he insisted on keeping a pre-arranged rendezvous with a photographer and remained mounted on the blowing horse. In the end an exasperated Roddy left him to it and walked off in disgust. The photographer eventually arrived and his picture of Tim 'just coming in to unsaddle' was duly published.

Roddy and Susan Armytage felt there was no harm in the man, just that he was a bit eccentric. Roddy remembers him as 'a bit of a film star who rather fancied himself as a womaniser'. They recall him visiting their yard one Sunday with a female friend on his arm and 'nibbling her ear' all the way round. On another occasion his agent arrived with him to visit the yard dressed in breeches, boots and bowler hat!

After his first Grand National Tim Durant was invited to race in Sweden that summer where, on hard ground, poor King Pin was killed. Then Tim had some bad news: he was told that he had developed bone cancer in an ankle and that his leg would have to be amputated from below the knee. Unwilling to accept the California doctors' prognosis, he flew to New York. There, surgeons operated, removed the lump, and within no time Tim was able to *walk* off the plane which brought him home. He determined that he would have another crack at the Grand National in 1967.

Ariel was fit to ride that year and Roddy Armytage believes that Tim and the horse should have been able to pop over the infamous twenty-third fence along with Foinavon. 'But the silly bugger refused to take a stick; he insisted on hunting round from the start, so he was finding all the trouble and the horse was disheartened.' They refused at the nineteenth fence and had to concede defeat.

Tim returned to the States, where he continued racing, and in October 1967 he won the Prince of Wales Cup in Toronto, beating a twenty-year-old jockey riding the favourite. The victory proved that Tim Durant was not finished yet. Only a few weeks before the 1968 Grand National he found and bought Highlandie, an eleven-year-old gelding trained in Ireland by the late Jack Bamber.

This was the horse who was to make it third time lucky for Tim Durant. It was Red Alligator's year, and it looked curtains again for Tim when he came to grief at Becher's Brook. But the intrepid American, who had taken on a £500 bet to complete the course, hung onto the reins, remounted and finished to tremendous cheers. Nor was he last either, one other horse passing the post behind him.

The television cameras, already focused on Red Alligator's return to the unsaddling enclosure, switched back to the finish as the tall Tim raised his arm in triumph as he and Highlandie crossed the finishing line. He later gave the proceeds of his winning bet to the Injured Jockeys Fund.

Tim Durant continued his riding in America until he was well into his seventies and had become a national celebrity. He found himself much in demand as a speaker to all age groups, showing slides and expounding on his 'impossible dream' at schools, retirement colleges, church groups, even prisons. His own physical fitness, enthusiasm and energy were an inspiration to youngsters and living proof to the older generation that life is for living to the full.

Eventually the bone cancer caught up with Tim, but not until he was eighty-five years old, when he died in Beverly Hills. His character certainly epitomised the spirit of the Grand National.

CRISP

1973: Most gallant loser

WHEN JOCKEY RICHARD PITMAN talks about Crisp the enthusiasm in his voice bubbles as freshly as if the whole thing had happened yesterday instead of fifteen years ago.

The admiration and awe he feels for that magnificent Australian chaser is as strong now as it was then: 'Crisp was incredible. When he first arrived in Fred Winter's yard from Australia, the first thing that hit you was his size; he was so strong, with a great shoulder, and to ride he was exactly as he looked: he would wear you out, he carried his head low and you just had to sit and suffer.'

Within days of his arrival to a British winter as a seven-year-old in November 1970, having won all there was to win in his sunny native clime, Crisp started growing an extra coat. Soon it was 2 inches long and wafted in the breeze like the ripples of a cornfield; but he proved virtually impossible to clip – a normal dose of tranquilliser did not so much as shut one eye, and in the end a drug used by a zoo on elephants and rhinos did the trick.

Brian Delaney, Fred Winter's head lad, also recalls Crisp's arrival at Uplands, Lambourn, admitting that they felt a little sceptical: 'We had heard this horse was coming who was the tops in Australia, but at the time our stable was the top in the world, with such as Pendil, Bula, Killiney, so there wasn't

great anticipation, not like when Jay Trump came in our very first season and we were all agog.' Brian remembers the shaggy coat and the time it took Crisp to acclimatise. He, too, was impressed by the size and strength of the dark brown horse – 'a wonderful

---

'Crisp was incredible. When he first arrived in Fred Winter's yard from Australia, the first thing that hit you was his size.'

---

stamp of English three-mile chaser, the sort that aren't around much'. Tall, angular, with long, slightly loppy ears, kind eyes and a gentle nature, Crisp had character written all over his face.

Crisp's first run in England was a handicap at Wincanton; he was allotted automatic top weight of 12 stone 7 pounds because he had not had the requisite three runs in the country to enable the handicapper to assess him. No one knew quite what to expect. A good round would have been satisfactory. What followed staggered onlookers. Crisp, ridden by Paul Kelleway, took up the running after a mile and then drew clear to win the race

easily. Fred Winter himself had disbelief written all over his face as his horse trotted up.

Fred Winter has ridden and trained a total of four Grand National winners, but he unhesitatingly puts a loser as the best Grand National horse he has been connected with – and considers Crisp probably the best of all National horses in living memory. 'His performance was unforgettable,' he says, and adds with a tinge of real regret, 'the only sad thing is that Red Rum is the one who will be remembered and Crisp is not. People don't realise what his run amounted to. He has to be the best.'

Before the National, Crisp had won the 2-mile Champion Chase at the Cheltenham National Hunt Festival and broken several track records, including at Newbury, by pulverising the opposition into the ground, usually ridden by Paul Kelleway or Richard Pitman. Richard recalls, 'He gave a sensation that money simply cannot buy; his jumping was electrifying and it was all so *easy* to him. He was magical.'

Owner Sir Chester Manifold had sent Crisp over to England – he finished third in the Colonial Cup, South Carolina, on the way – to have a stab at the Cheltenham Gold Cup; he was entered for the race in his second season. But, as he had run so sensationally over 2 miles, there was a fear that he might not last the trip.

Above: Barony Fort takes a mighty leap at the Chair.
Below: Charlotte Brew was the first lady rider in the National in 1977.

Above: Ben
Nevis half way
in the Grand
National of
1979.

Left: All the
dash and vigour
of American
Charlie Fenwick
is shared with
his ex-English
partner Ben
Nevis as they
scorch to
victory in 1980.

*A picture of health, Bob Champion,
now a trainer who devotes most of
his life to supporting cancer
research.*

Right: Aldaniti and Bob Champion soar over Becher's Brook second time round in the 1981 National, enthusiastic crowds lining the rail.

Right: Nick and Valda Embiricos' magnificent Aldaniti.

Below: The Duchess of York (on second horse from right) sets out from Windsor Castle on the London–Aintree walk.

Right: Dick Saunders is seldom seen without a smile on his face – especially when with the Pytchley hounds.

Below: Dick Saunders on Grittar in the 1982 Cheltenham Gold Cup – a warm up for the following month's Grand National ride.

Left: Mrs Tom Shalley and Mrs Charles Mackenzie's Cheers, Geraldine Rees up, pictured in 1982.

Press pressure was part and parcel of early lady riders' lives, but Geraldine Rees faced them with composure and a smile.

*Geraldine Rees surveying the
scene at the start in 1983.*

'The only sad thing is that Red Rum is the one who will be remembered and Crisp is not.'

Sir Chester Manifold with his Australian chaser Crisp.

His rider tried to settle him didn't work. He pulled for a bit, then gave up, like many another frontrunner who feels frustrated when restrained, finishing a disappointing fifth. Unfortunately, the result encouraged the view that the horse did not stay, so it was back to the Champion Chase the following year, when he finished third. His former Australian rider, the ex-British Tommy McGinley, was convinced it was wrong to hold him up.

> ## 'I just thought: he'll never fall. It was so easy to him it was laughable; there wasn't a fence on the course that would even make him blink.'

Anyway, Crisp was entered for the Grand National and, being such a class horse, was allotted top weight of 12 stone. Fred Winter and Richard Pitman discussed tactics at length: if he was held up, there was a danger his spectacular jumping would land him on another horse's back, so it was decided he would do best if allowed to jump off and then slow down the pace from the front. That was the theory. In practice, Crisp had other ideas, resulting in the most breathtaking National run in living memory.

Thirty-eight runners milled round at the start; the joint favourites at 9–1 were the improving Red Rum on 10 stone 5 pounds and Crisp. How right the bookmakers were to be proven.

Richard Pitman lined Crisp up on the inside – always Fred Winter's favoured position – where the drop fences are bigger but the danger of interference less, and they were off.

Crisp devoured the big fences as if they were bales of hay strung across the course. Every time he saw one he gripped harder on the bit and attacked it boldly, always fast, always totally accurate, and he was away from it again in a flash, as well as saving many lengths by going on the inside so that he gained ground all the time without even trying. Big, with a wide open ditch, the third fence is the downfall of many; to Crisp it was no more than an upturned dandy brush. To his exhilarated rider he exuded confidence: 'I just thought: he'll never fall. It was so easy to him it was laughable; there wasn't a fence on the course that would even make him blink.' All Richard could do was try to sit against him, conserving what energy he could, all the time conscious of his stamina limits: had he simply let him go, the horse would have burned himself out before the halfway point. Becher's Brook came and went as if it didn't exist. The Canal Turn was executed in the style of a top three-day eventer taking a corner fence; Crisp went so close to the inside of the 90-degree turn that he brushed the marker post.

The crowds were mesmerised; what a performance! Incredibly the horse drew even further away so that, when they headed out into the country for the second time, he was an amazing 30 lengths clear. As Crisp and his partner went down that long line of fences which culminate in Becher's Brook there were signs everywhere of those who had not been so lucky: big holes in the fences, disconsolate jockeys on their feet, one holding a bridle, not another horse in sight. Richard, out on his own, had time to reflect: poor sod, he hasn't even got a horse under him and mine is jumping as if the fences don't exist. He found the silence the strangest thing of all. Normally there is the crashing of fences as horses plough their way through, the swearing of jockeys, the thud of hooves.

At Becher's second time, another doddle for Crisp, Richard distinctly heard the Irish voice of racecourse commentator Michael O'Hehir, say, '... and Red Rum is breaking away from the pack some twenty lengths behind.' David Nicholson, another jockey who had fallen on the first circuit, called out, 'Kick on, you'll win.'

The brilliant horse jumped the Canal Turn perfectly again and at long last the stands came back into view.

At the first fence Crisp slightly pecked on landing; but he learnt his lesson and did not see another horse until a stride before the line.

But they were still a long, long way from home: six fences and that gruelling run-in of nearly 500 yards.

The mental obstacles were well out of the way now: to get over the third and remain alive; to clear Becher's and have the bogey fence out of the way; to complete a circuit and start being a jockey; to jump the Canal Turn again and know that completion of the course should follow; and, if well in front at that stage, to collect thoughts and make the best way home . . .

It was at the second last fence that Crisp began to falter. The pounding, relentless gallop was at last beginning to tell, and Richard felt the horse's strength 'fall out of him'. It got worse: those loppy ears sagged lower; his legs, instead of stretching out forwards, began swinging sideways; his whole body swayed as if he were drunk.

And now their pursuer was within earshot: Richard could hear the snorts of the 'high-blowing' Red Rum and the rhythmic drumming of his hoof-beats on the firm ground. The threat was still nearly 20 lengths back but

> ## 'It was like being tied to a railway line with an express train coming and being unable to get out of the way.'

drawing ever nearer. Richard describes the feeling graphically: 'It was like being tied to a railway line with an express train coming and being unable to get out of the way.'

They jumped the last all right, but Richard will never forgive himself for what happened next: 'Crisp was out on his feet but I made the basic riding error of picking up my stick in my right hand, with the intention of waking him up. He just fell away from it towards the left and away from the angle of the racecourse. I had to put down the whip, gather him up again, and get him back on course for the elbow, where there was the running rail to guide him. I am stuck with that mistake for the rest of my life and I know that someone like John Francome would not have made it. I lost the National for all those people who so deserved to win it: the owner; Fred Winter, the trainer; the horse's lad, Chippy Chape.'

At that moment, Crisp was still in front. To the thousands in the crowd and the millions watching on television it was the most agonising few moments they had ever seen in the Grand National: if willpower alone could have got Crisp first past the post,

Crisp has given his all and Red Rum gallops to his first victory.

he would have been home and dry. They had witnessed the most devastating, compelling performance under top weight.

All was not yet lost. As Crisp felt his lighter-weighted rival draw up to his quarters, he tightened instinctively and tried to give more when he had in truth already given his all. Red Rum went by, just two strides before the post, in an all-time record time.

Formbook publishers Raceform Ltd paid a vivid tribute to the loser:

Crisp, flicking over these enormous fences like hurdles, pulled his way into a twenty-length lead after jumping the water. Sailing down to Becher's he actually increased his lead and, turning for the long haul home after Valentine's, looked to have an unassailable advantage. He started to tire at the second from home but was still at least ten lengths clear at the last. Then, suddenly, Crisp the flying rocket became painful flesh and blood with air-starved lungs and limbs like stone. Rolling about, out on his feet, he started to hang towards the dolls guarding the Chair and it was all Pitman could do to wrench him back on to the racecourse. Though by now he appeared to be standing still and looked certain to be caught, it was only in the last few agonizing yards of the interminable run-in that the dogged Red Rum finally cut down perhaps the greatest Aintree hero of them all.

To many, the spectacular Australian chaser was the most gallant loser ever. Little did they know how exceptional the horse who had beaten him was to prove... The emotion provoked by Crisp's defeat was overwhelming.

To many, the spectacular Australian chaser was the most gallant loser ever.

From Fred Winter, the best respected man in racing, there was not a word of recrimination. From the owner, there was a cash present 'for disappointment'. For Richard Pitman there was the sorrow at losing for all those people who deserved to have won – and the memory to accompany him all his life as fresh as the dew of the greatest steeplechasing ride any man could experience ...

Sitting at home in his bungalow at Uplands, watching the television, Brian Delaney recalls the agony: 'We were *screaming* for him to last home; my mother-in-law's poodle went crazy and jumped onto a glass ashtray, smashing it to smithereens. We have had some

horses jump round Liverpool, but nothing like that before or since. Crisp made those fences look like hurdles; I hate seeing it all again.'

The night of that epic race, amazingly recovered from his exhaustion, Crisp ate up every oat. And although he did not run in the National again, he gained his revenge on Red Rum in a match at Haydock the next year in yet another bold display, his superior class telling at level weights.

He ended his days with Mr John Trotter and his wife, Joy, hunting with the Zetland in Northumberland, where the wide-open spaces suited him admirably. Within a couple of years Richard Pitman, too, had retired, and quickly established himself as a polished paddock commentator for BBC television, as well as writing for several newspapers and magazines, becoming involved in the bloodstock business, and being much in demand as an after-dinner speaker.

In 1985 Crisp died of a heart attack doing what he loved best, out galloping and jumping with the Zetland. He was twenty-one years old. Richard Pitman was called upon to write his obituary for *Horse and Hound*. 'I'm not normally a sentimental man,' he says, 'but as I wrote I wept buckets, it all came flooding back ...'

RED RUM

1973–74: Part I, Fastest time

Red Rum, an Aintree legend in his own lifetime.

THE LIGHTS DIM, the theme music rises, and the murmurings of the dark-suited business delegates cease as all eyes turn expectantly towards centre-stage. Then into the spotlight walks calmly the symbol of all that is good in British industry – that example of courage, professionalism, of triumph over adversity: Red Rum.

This is the living legend, the horse who won the Grand National a record three times; who landed first over the last fence an unprecedented five years in succession, finishing second in the two he did not win. He slashed the course record by an incredible $18\frac{1}{2}$ seconds; and even after ten years of retirement he is better known and better paid than many human showbiz stars.

Hard-raced under both rules from an early age, Red Rum's future looked decidedly ordinary, but he was blessed with that overriding essential the will to win; he was a survivor no matter what the odds. He is the horse for whom the overused word charisma could have been specially invented.

Superlatives may be showered upon Red Rum but none can do him justice. Few could have foretold his greatness the day he first ran at Liverpool, but

> ## This is the living legend, the horse who won the Grand National a record three times.

the character was already there. 'The horse always had a high opinion of himself, and it got bigger and bigger,' says Ginger McCain, his trainer. 'He just literally shows off; you have only got to put a camera near him and he poses.' He was undoubtedly a bit of an

actor, even in the early days at Ginger's, when his lad, ex-boxer Billy Ellison, built up an enviable rapport with the horse, enjoying Red Rum's bucks as much as Red Rum enjoyed giving them.

From the start Red Rum was a bright spark – not nasty but so cocky and full of himself that his first trainer, Tim Moloney, gelded him as a yearling to settle him down. Although, or perhaps because, he was a bit of a lad, he was well loved wherever he went and never lacked care and attention at home. This must have helped him mentally, for he took some harsh punishment in hard races right from the beginning of his racing career. And although he had five trainers, three of them operated successively from one yard, so that Rummy, as he was to become affectionately known, did not himself 'move house' that many times.

By the miler Quorum, out of a winning mare said to be virtually unrideable, mared (by Magic Red), Red Rum's breeding did not indicate that he would be a stayer, although there was some blood for stamina further back in his pedigree. He looked more of a quality flat horse than a three-mile chaser but, in the same way as a good heavyweight boxer does not look

Ginger McCain, trainer of Red Rum.

heavy, so Red Rum, who in fact stands 16.2 h.h., never looked big because his proportions were perfect.

Born and bred in Ireland, he and his companion, the filly Curlicue, were sold at Ballsbridge Sales, Dublin, as yearlings for 400 guineas each. By a remarkable coincidence they were to dead-heat on their racecourse debuts in England six months later: the venue, of all places, Liverpool; the race a modest two-year-olds' seller run over 5 furlongs. Not waiting for the subsequent auction was fledgling trainer and part-time taxi driver and car dealer Ginger McCain, an integral part of racing's backbone. He was attracted by the two-year-old colt's physical brightness, thinking that he might go on to make a three-year-old hurdler; but 300 guineas was twice as much as McCain could afford in those days. Red Rum was auctioned by John Botterill, for whom the race stands out from countless others because it was a dead heat. With his brother, Michael, he has run Ascot Bloodstock Sales since 1947. 'Just imagine the derision I would have been greeted with if I'd offered the two-year-old sprinter by Quorum as a future Grand National winner,' he chuckles now. 'I'd have been laughed out of the ring!'

So began Red Rum's love affair with Liverpool, and with life. He ran there seven times, won four and was second in the other three. But he was not only a Liverpool horse, although that course was certainly all he lived for in his latter racing years. In his ten-year career, he won three races on the flat, three over hurdles and twenty-one steeplechases, and was placed thirty-five times. He was ridden by twenty-four different jockeys, including Lester Piggott and Josh Gifford, and won over distances from the minimum 5 furlongs

'He just literally shows off; you have only got to put a camera near him and he poses.'

on the flat to the maximum 4½ miles over fences. He was beaten a short head in the Hennessy Gold Cup by Red Candle; he won the Scottish Grand National in the same year as one of his Grand Nationals (another record); and he never fell, once having his jockey knocked off at the first fence and once slipping up on the flat, both at Haydock Park. He had five trainers, Tim Moloney, Bobby Renton, Tommy Stack, Anthony Gillam and Donald 'Ginger' McCain.

It was only by a quirk of fate, through a monumental blunder on Ginger McCain's part, that Red Rum came to his Southport stables at all.

The holder of a full licence to train only since 1969 (and of a permit before that), three years later Ginger McCain had bought Glenkiln for owner Noel Le Mare to run in the Grand National. Naturally, he was anxious not to have anything go wrong but, unused to the extra formalities involved in valuable races, sent off what he believed to be Glenkiln's declaration a full week in advance of the closing date to ensure it got there in time. What he had unwittingly done was withdraw the horse from the race at the forfeit stage. Mr Le Mare discovered the mistake when he tried to telephone a bet and was told by his bookmaker that the horse was no longer in the race. The news came as a bombshell to Ginger: 'I thought: that's it, I've cocked my first big chance and all my owners will take their horses away.' Instead, the magnanimous Le Mare took it like a gentleman and sent Ginger straight out to buy another horse, allowing him up to 7000 guineas to do so, seven times as much as Ginger's previously most expensive horse.

So, at the Doncaster Sales of August 1972, McCain secured Red Rum for 6000 guineas – and twenty-four hours later feared he had made another terrible error. Ridden on the beach that morning by vet's son and successful point-to-point rider Robin Greenway, Red Rum pulled up, apparently lame. Imagine Ginger's dismay; 6000 guineas was a fortune to him – 'and I thought I'd just blown it'. The horse walked into the sea to paddle and cool off – and, miracle of miracles, he emerged sound. 'At the sales when we bought him, Tommy Stack told us he was 'a bit footy' but that took in an awful lot!' McCain recalls.

That seawater was to prove a lifesaver for Red Rum, who in earlier years had been nursed through the serious foot complaint pedalostitis by a girl groom, Sandra Kendall, at Bobby Renton's yard. She was so devoted to Rummy that she refused to get married throughout the time she had him to look after!

Red Rum was housed in the stable nearest to McCain's house and there he has lived ever since. The stables had been converted by Ginger from old brewery-horse stalls and garages; the garden gradually gave way as more stables were built, only a central tree remaining as a feature of the yard. Today there are colourful flowers on the wall and the house has been extended, but it is still modest however one looks at it, set in a shop-lined back street typical of any town anywhere in the country: washeteria, post-office-cum-stores, coal merchant and, just before the level crossing with its old-fashioned gates where trains speed by at regular intervals, there are the modern showrooms of D. McCain, car salesman.

Only a few streets away is the seaside pier and a huge, garish fun-fair on one side of a roundabout; on the other side is a 2-mile stretch of coastal road carving through bleak sand-dunes, uninhabited save for the wildlife and McCain's horses at exercise, until it emerges at a Pontin's holiday camp.

The seawater, sea air, sand and rarity of formal grass gallops stimulated Red Rum's vigour for life and he bloomed so much that he won his first five races on the trot for his new handler, and went from the bottom to the top of the handicap in one season.

Brian Fletcher, the only jockey this century to win three Grand Nationals.

His stable companion Glenkiln, unable to run in the 1972 Grand National because of Ginger's clerical error, had meanwhile requalified for the 1973 event and so McCain's life-

long dream of having a runner in the race came doubly true. Glenkiln carried Le Mare's first colours of maroon with yellow diamond and similar cap, and Red Rum a plain yellow cap, to differentiate them. Each of Red Rum's riders wore that yellow cap ever afterwards for luck, which was apparently questioned only once by a clerk of the scales, who checks the jockeys' colours.

As a boy, the blue-eyed, ginger-haired Donald McCain had first watched the National from beside the canal and had been hooked on it ever since. For the race, canal barges were colourfully bedecked with bunting and had tiers of seats for spectators. Ginger was struck by the carnival atmosphere and afterwards by the camaraderie between fallen jockeys as loose horses were caught and ridden back from way out in the country.

The race took such a hold on him that he went to it even on the afternoon of his wedding, repeating the exercise of two years earlier when he had become engaged to Beryl Harris on National day, then taken her along to watch it. His one ambition as a small trainer was that one day he might have a horse good enough to run in the race and – dreams being free, after all – even to win it.

Ginger had gone to work in stables at fourteen, been a motorcycle messenger, completed his national service, then returned to stables once more. He rode in a few point-to-points but, at 6 foot 3 inches tall, with broad shoulders to match, he was always too big to be a jockey. He built up his second-hand car-dealing business and started a local taxi service. When he began taking fares from Noel Le Mare, their conversations soon revolved around the big race, for it was also Mr Le Mare's ambition to win the Grand National.

Born in 1887, the son of a missionary, Noel Le Mare served as a merchant marine from 1911 to 1918. Before that he had been apprenticed at an engineering firm in nearby Fleetwood and it was there, in 1906, that his Grand National ambition was hatched. Seeing Le Mare standing idle for a few minutes, his foreman told him

Mrs Mirabel Topham admires Red Rum in the winner's enclosure in 1973.

to 'bugger off and find out the winner of the big race'. This was in the days when the quickest way of conveying such news was by telegram, and the young Le Mare was struck by the excitement of it all as a bell boy waved a telegram from some hotel steps, proclaiming Ascetic's Silver the winner.

Most of Le Mare's life was taken up with work, but, once in his eighties, he set about in earnest fulfilling his National dream. A slim, dapper man, he was always immaculately dressed, with starched cotton shirt and silk socks, often wearing a bowler hat and neat glasses. He was a true sportsman. His departing words to any jockey riding for him would be, 'Have a good ride and come back safe,' and his sense of humour was never far away.

Le Mare's one concession to advanc-

ing years was a morning lie-in. He had a housekeeper/companion who would bring him a glass of sherry before lunch and, come 6.00 p.m., he would enjoy a whisky, sitting in a chair by the fire and smoking like a chimney. He kept an

---

'Have a good ride and come back safe.'

---

immaculate Daimler and chauffeur, although he no longer travelled very far. At his family's insistence, he spent his last few years on the Isle of Man, until he died at the age of ninety-two. A grandson, Michael Burns from Burscough, not far from Southport, ran the Red Rum fan club and is now chairman of the company looking after Rummy in retirement.

Thoughts of a fan club were in no way entertained during Red Rum's early days at Southport, though the transformation Ginger wrought in the cocky rich bay was swift. After the horse's fifth win in barely six weeks, on ground ranging from good to hard, Timeform commented that he was 'still cherry ripe and reflects credit on his trainer'. A midwinter break followed, and the ground softened, but when Red Rum was third on his reappearance, the form book noted that he 'refused to give in . . . and looks an ideal National type'.

By Grand National day, Red Rum, ridden by Brian Fletcher and set to carry 10 stone 5 pounds, started joint favourite with the great Australian chaser Crisp, carrying top weight of 12

'Red Rum kept making up just one or two lengths at each fence...'

stone. It was to be the most memorable of Nationals. The commanding lead which Crisp set up is described fully in chapter 20. Suffice to say here that there can have been few watching from the stands or on worldwide television who thought Crisp would be beaten, or who were not saddened as he rolled with fatigue in the final hundred yards.

But there was one man who thought he *could* be beaten. 'From the Canal Turn I thought we had a chance of beating him,' says Ginger. 'Red Rum kept making up just one or two lengths at each fence, although I must admit I also thought: I am going to be second; what bad luck to come up against a horse like Crisp on the day.' But, as the formbook records:

> Red Rum set off on the daunting task of chasing Crisp going to Becher's the last time round. Ridden along, he jumped the remaining fences with precision but came to the last still all of ten lengths behind the leader. With victory in sight as he came to the elbow, he never gave up running and inching back the ground forced his head in front in the last forty yards. An indomitable and plucky win.

Both gallant horses smashed the course record by almost 19 seconds, held for thirty-eight years by Golden Miller, the horse who won steeplechasing's blue riband, the Cheltenham Gold Cup, a record five times.

Asked what his feelings were for Crisp after the dramatic race, McCain says frankly, 'Not a lot. It was a spectacular and tremendous performance, but it's no good saying I was sorry for Crisp because I was pleased for my horse; but Richard Pitman, who is a good friend of mine, was very sporting. And,' he points out with justifiable pride, 'when Red Rum himself carried 12 stone the next year, he didn't go off a true line.'

That was 1974 and it produced a truly outstanding performance from this most professional and courageous of horses. Again ridden by Brian Fletcher, he had 12 stone to carry, giving a pound to L'Escargot, who had won the Cheltenham Gold Cup in both 1970 and 1971. The 7–1 favourite was Scout, and he finished eleventh ridden by Tommy Stack, who was to win on Red Rum three years later. L'Escargot was 17–2 and Red Rum was third in the betting at 11–1.

To quote the formbook again, Red Rum made that Grand National 'look incredibly easy':

> Very much at home on the fast surface, he was going so easily that his rider had to let him hit the front approaching Becher's the last time round. Cruising in the lead coming on to the racecourse, he quickened appreciably and, with his race won long before the elbow, his rider was able to salute the crowd and then ease him back before the post. This was a fantastic performance and Red Rum, whose win last year was rather overshadowed by the gallant efforts of the second, now dominates the Aintree scene as a figure of heroic proportions in his own right. Such dramatic improvement reflects the highest credit on his trainer.

Grand National winners traditionally return home to a hero's welcome, especially those from small stables, but the greeting which the Southport suburb of Birkdale gave Red Rum after his second Grand National was out of this world, quite unlike anything seen before. Crowds thronged the road so many deep that in the end the police gave up trying to let traffic through and closed the road. Even the chimney stacks along the lines of houses were occupied by cheering fans. The only scenes reminiscent of that occasion in Ginger's memory were those of VE day, when he was a lad of thirteen.

RED RUM

1975–77: Part II, Most wins

A LTHOUGH RED RUM was beaten into second place in the next two Nationals, only in one, against L'Escargot in 1975, did he find the going really tough. That was the only year in which he had to contend with soft going; he hated it so much that halfway round Brian Fletcher even thought of pulling him up. Yet Red Rum ploughed on to such effect that again he landed just in front over the last fence. 'But he was a beaten horse that day,' Ginger recalls. And L'Escargot, a dual Cheltenham Gold Cup winner, was receiving 11 pounds.

It was different against Rag Trade in 1976, when Rummy was ridden by Tommy Stack. Carrying top weight, for the third successive year, and overtaken by Rag Trade (receiving 12 pounds) just after the last, he was regaining ground all the way up that long run-in. 'It was lovely to be second,' says Ginger, 'it was still magic, great ...'

B y 1977 Red Rum was twelve years old but felt better than ever. His whole programme was geared to one single race, the Grand National. Yet again he had top weight but it was down to 11 stone 8 pounds. Could he possibly win again? Would his luck in running hold up or would, finally, some faller bring him down? McCain was given a lot of stick from some

uninformed quarters for even contemplating another attempt.

'But he was fit and still relatively young,' says Ginger, 'and Mr Le Mare, at eighty-eight years old, had given up golf. Red Rum was his only remaining pleasure and we were not abusing the horse.'

'Brian rode him superbly, but Tommy had that little bit of Irish magic with him.'

Rummy had had his warm-up races on park courses, where in later years the knowing horse 'switched onto automatic', but when it came to Liverpool he rose to the challenge of the mighty fences and electric atmosphere. 'Brian rode him superbly,' says Ginger, 'but Tommy had that little bit of Irish magic with him.'

'It was lovely to be second, it was still magic, great ...'

For some reason McCain never doubted that his horse would win that day. Possessed of superior intelligence, the horse simply never met his fences wrong; he could shift his shoulders

from four strides out to put himself right, and would change direction in mid-air if he spotted a faller on the other side; indeed, he was his own race-reader. What was more, he was king and knew it, bearing himself with majesty.

D own at the start there was a delay. Red Rum was *bursting*. He was so *sure* of himself. He swaggered round his kingdom and Tommy Stack had never felt anything quite like it in a horse before. It was a mystical moment that brought incredible confidence.

In the event, there was no other horse in the race. From Becher's second time round Rummy drew further and further ahead, making the fences look like matchsticks, and won as he liked by 25 lengths, to tumultuous applause. Here was the little flat-race selling plater turned greatest Grand National horse of all time. Grown men wept openly.

This time the whole of Southport joined in the official celebrations. There were two bands in the parade through the seaside resort's streets, which were lined with cheering admirers. There were people with no interest in horses, those who never so much as had a Grand National flutter, but here they could admire and praise in this horse so many of the qualities that once made Britain great: guts, perseverance, hard work, professional-

In 1975 the blinkered L'Escargot beat Red Rum, seen here jumping the last fence together.

ism, enthusiasm, the ability to come back for more and more – above all, that will to win against all odds, to survive.

Had a minor ailment not caused his withdrawal at the eleventh hour the next year, Red Rum looked all set to win again, at the age of thirteen, and could have done so yet again at fourteen, Ginger is certain.

The season that was to have culminated in the 1978 Grand National progressed much as the last few had done, with just one target in mind. About a week before the race, with all having gone well until then, Rummy came off the sands going a bit 'short' behind. It looked to Ginger as if he might have a bit of stringhalt. Ted Greenway, the vet at whose Cheshire home Rummy used to spend a few weeks each winter, nerve-blocked the foot and located the trouble. The sea treatment was kept up and once again seemed to bring about a miracle. On the day before the National the horse worked so well over 6 furlongs on the Liverpool course that his new lad, Billy Beardwood, had to aim him at a high fence to stop him. But once they were home Ginger noticed with a sinking heart that he was again going short behind; he was definitely sore. Mr Greenway returned and said a hairline fracture in one of the many tiny foot bones was the possible cause. 'If the foot goes in the race,' he reasoned, 'the crowd will hang you.' It was time to say enough is enough and thanks very much old pal.

Rummy nevertheless went to Liverpool next day, immediately starting his new career as a star. He turned himself inside out with excitement as he led the parade, to the extent that there were an unkind few who claimed that the apparent injury had been a bookmakers' ploy! But the country and

the world of racing at large loved the horse as their own and perhaps breathed secret sighs of relief in the knowledge that Becher's and the rest could no longer hold any hidden perils for 'their' horse.

There was never any question of Red Rum retiring to grass. For one thing he was in too much demand as a celebrity, and for another Ginger firmly believed it would not have been the best life for him. 'Racehorses are treated as well as humans, more so in many cases,' he says. 'Sentiment is great, but it's no good putting human thoughts in a horse's head. They have always been mollycoddled, with luxury beds, daily grooming and the best fodder, and they are better off keeping active than out in a field. Racing is what they know; they are old professionals and they do miss it if given nothing else to do. Red Rum eats as much now as when he was racing and his coat is still groomed to burnished mahogany. One day, perhaps, he will throw a great big buck and drop down dead.'

To begin with, as Rummy made numerous appearances, it became apparent that other people were cashing in on the act – Red Rum tea towels and other souvenirs appeared. To prevent this, a company called Red Rum Ltd was formed, with Peter Rougier, one of Ginger's owners as managing director, and members of the Le Mare family. Now only products with the Red Rum trademark may be marketed.

That summer of 1978, a Japanese restaurant owner by the name of 'Rocky' Aoki offered a million dollars (about £500,000 then) for the Red Rum company for promotion purposes, guaranteeing Ginger a say in the horse's movements. When Mr Aoki arrived at the stables, accompanied by

> **'Red Rum is not for sale to anyone at any time or any price; he stays with Ginger for life.'**

a police escort, an antagonistic crowd had gathered. Suddenly a little old lady swung her umbrella in Mr Aoki's direction and cried, 'Remember Pearl Harbor.' It was perhaps not surprising that the deal fell through and Mr Le Mare firmly stipulated, 'Red Rum is not for sale to anyone at any time or any price; he stays with Ginger for life.'

Red Rum's new life could hardly have been more hectic, varied and interesting, and he revelled in it. In one typical week that first summer he went to Ireland by boat, to Exeter the next morning, up to Scotland for the following day, down to Wolverhampton, then home – all the time opening fêtes (he once ate a vicar's buttonhole), parading at shows, opening betting shops and new stores, and so on.

There is hardly a major television programme on which Red Rum has not appeared: *The Generation Game*, *This Is Your Life*, *Sportsman of the Year*, *Tiswas*, *Record Breakers*, *Blue Peter*.

Everywhere he goes reactions are the same: adulation, pride, emotion. At the Cheshire County Show one summer the crowd around his horsebox was so deep that the ramp could not be

Rag Trade (left), who just beat Red Rum in 1976.

lowered to let him out. It took the police a whole hour to move people back far enough to enable their hero to emerge. Each time, as the ramp is lowered, the horse appears at the top ears pricked, bright eyes staring, taking in whatever scene it is this time; he is royalty arriving, pausing to survey his subjects before deigning to step off his pinnacle and join them on the ground.

There was a time in Ireland when Jonjo O'Neill was riding Red Rum during a parade at Cork Show. Beyond them, a man lay collapsed on the ground. 'Come this way,' the police said to Jonjo, indicating the direction of the inert figure. 'Sure, an' don't be worrying about him, he's dead, let the horse step over him ...' Afterwards, the

horse box was in a rush to catch the boat back, but was mobbed as it came out of the ring; there were seemingly thousands of ginger-haired, blue-eyed, freckled-faced Irish kids swarming around.

William Hill, the bookmakers, regularly booked Red Rum whenever they had a new office to open. Peter Rougier inquired, out of interest, why they kept on having the horse, as opposed to a human celebrity. 'We could have anyone we liked and top stars draw a fair crowd,' they said. 'But the crowd doesn't own a star, and they feel they own a part of Red Rum, they can touch him and crowd around him.' On one occasion crowds parted for a wheelchair-bound woman to come through and touch him – she left with tears pouring down her face.

In Wales, customers of a pub wanted to arrange for a dying young boy to see Red Rum. Rummy was fully booked and could not let down people with existing engagements, so instead the pub customers brought the boy to Southport, to see Red Rum in his own stable. The boy was gravely ill, but as his mother lifted him up at Red Rum's stable door his face burst into a smile. 'It was the first smile the mother could ever remember her son giving since he became ill,' says Peter Rougier.

A favourite type of engagement has been the conference appearance. Delegates are seldom told Red Rum is coming. The lights are dimmed, the Red Rum song crackles over the loudspeakers and, as it ends, with Peter Bromley's exciting, emotional radio commentary of Red Rum's epic third victory, so the curtains part and Red Rum strides confidently onto the stage, led by his handlers. Sometimes Ginger goes too, to give a talk – 'but we don't get as much for him,' laughs Peter Rougier.

At sales conferences such as these

Red Rum is used to illustrate the 'Rolls Royce' syndrome: he epitomises all that is best in professionalism. 'Even at international conferences people from Japan or Australia or wherever all seem to have heard of him,' says Ginger with an air of mild surprise.

And how does Red Rum, whose exuberance and bucks and kicks are the trademark of his love affair with life, cope with slippery stages, narrow doors, bright lights, hotel foyers, lifts, shop floors and clapping and cheering? 'It is the survival thing,' says Ginger. 'He will turn himself inside out on grass or sand but he won't act the fool when

Red Rum sails over the water, left, with Roman Bar (centre) and Brown Admiral.

he's unsure of his surroundings and thinks it may be slippery. He's very intelligent.'

When Red Rum celebrated his twenty-first birthday in 1986, it was done in superb style. A huge marquee was erected at the Burscough

think it has given me some standing in racing. Obviously I've had some wonderful times with him and through him, and our whole year revolves around the build-up to Liverpool. But I must admit I wouldn't want to be so intense, so personally involved, with a horse again. As for the training, it was

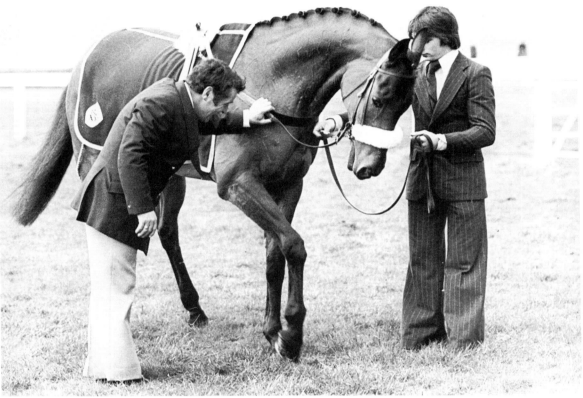

home of Mr and Mrs Burns, whose grandfather, Noel Le Mare, had died in 1981 at the age of ninety-two. Everyone who had ever been connected with Red Rum in any way was invited. 'It was the biggest success,' recalls Ginger with great affection, 'and of course Red Rum stole his own show.'

It was thirteen years since Red Rum's first record-breaking National victory. His surroundings and that of his trainer had changed little; nor had Ginger McCain changed inwardly, though Red Rum's achievements had certainly altered his life. 'It has all been tremendous,' says the affable man with the amused grin and modest manner – there is nothing cocky or big-headed about Ginger. 'It certainly opened doors I would never have been through and allowed me to meet people I would

otherwise not have done, and I like to very satisfying; it gave me the confidence that, given the material, I can do the job.'

Public demand is as great as ever for Red Rum, but by 1987 some of his more demanding appearances had to be cut out, and for the first time he was unable to parade before the National. He suffered a setback with a slight blockage in an artery in a hind leg. For the first time he was not ridden in exercise and had to be excluded from parades, always so popular with the masses, instead being limited to 'walk on, walk off' appearances.

There could be no more fitting tribute to mark the 150th anniversary of the unique race than to have the statue of its greatest legend unveiled at Aintree.

Red Rum 'takes a bow' before his worshipping fans.

CHARLOTTE BREW

1977: First woman to ride

Charlotte Brew walks to the paddock for the 1977 National.

THE NEW MOTHER hoisted her baby onto her hip as she made her evening check round the yard, which was full of young horses. Seeing all was well, she returned indoors to put baby Katherine to bed and prepare supper for her GP husband, who is also doctor to Taunton Racecourse.

This is Mrs Jeremy Budd in 1987, ten years on from her historic ride in the Grand National, when, as Miss Charlotte Brew, she became the first woman to take part – ten years since she and Barony Fort had had to contend with a press barrage far more fearsome than the National fences.

Ten years – and still this handsome housewife finds it irritating to remember the way she was ridiculed. She is annoyed that some people still tend not to take her seriously; that there are those who know her for what she did rather than for what she is.

But Charlotte was in the line-up in 1977 strictly on merit and within the rules. When the Sex Discrimination Act came into effect in January 1976, it meant that, overnight, women were suddenly allowed to take on men as equals in the world of race-riding. Many experienced point-to-point riders were swift to do so, with immedi-ate effect; and when Charlotte Brew and Barony Fort finished fourth in the Liverpool Foxhunters that year, they automatically qualified for the next year's Grand National.

For Charlotte, it was literally a dream come true. She could not remember a time when she had not wanted to ride in the great race and, knowing that women were not allowed in it, her family for years indulged her pipedreams with gentle 'there, theres'.

Now the councillor's daughter from Coggeshall, Essex, could do so. Although Barony Fort had been last of four finishers in the Foxhunters, he had been beaten only 16 lengths overall by two of the country's top hunter chasers of the time, Credit Call and Creme Brule; he had actually jumped his way into the lead three out, but had then gone wide on the last bend. As Char-lotte said, he had proved himself cap-able and was not disgraced.

Once Charlotte's parents, Richard and Judith, had agreed to the previ-ously inconceivable – that their daugh-ter should ride in the Grand National – they backed her wholeheartedly, and proved a great source of strength. Charlotte, for her part, spent months training herself as well as her horse,

> ... he 'looked as if he'd come straight from pulling a float; he was hideous, with that enormous goose-rump.'

learning all she could about the big race, and studying the course.

Although not from a particularly 'horsey' background – her mother hunted a bit – Charlotte never outgrew the 'pony-mad stage'. All her spare time at Benenden School in Kent had been spent in the nearby stables of Cherrie Hatton Hall. She had run the usual gauntlet of Pony Club activities until, at eighteen, she was old enough to ride in a point-to-point. She then set about looking for a suitable mount to start on.

The horse she came up with was the impeccably bred Barony Fort, from Mr Richard Redgrave. By Fortina, he was out of Sunset Slave, a full sister to Arctic Sunset, by Arctic Slave. Richard Redgrave, outgoing Norwich garage owner, farmer and permit holder, had bought Barony Fort sight unseen for £1000, after seeing him advertised in *Horse and Hound* as a Grand National prospect. The big horse had not long been over from his native Ireland and, when Mr Redgrave first set eyes on him, he 'looked as if he'd come straight from pulling a float; he was hideous, with that enormous goose-rump'. His new owner decided to 'sling him in a field and forget him for a bit'.

On Barony Fort's second run in England, Dick Saunders rode him, found he lacked finishing speed, and reported, 'He wants a hell of a long trip.' He ran in the 4-mile National Hunt chase at Cheltenham, and by the finish he was flying; he then went on to win a 3-mile chase at Folkestone thanks to his superb jumping.

Richard Redgrave remembers being approached by the Brew family, who were seeking a safe conveyance for their daughter to start

point-to-pointing; he took Barony to Newmarket Links for them to see and for Charlotte to school. 'Charlotte was a good pilot but had only evented before and had never ridden anything at 35 m.p.h.,' he says. 'As she approached the first fence there was a look of sheer horror on her face, but she had the good sense to sit still and as they flew over her expression changed to one of sheer delight.' He adds, 'The horse really went for that girl, on rock hard or bog deep, week in, week out.'

> 'Charlotte was a good pilot but had only evented before and had never ridden anything at 35 m.p.h.'

Charlotte won several races on him, mostly modest members' events, but, although he was strong, with a tendency to hang right-handed, he jumped well and stayed for ever.

In answering some of the critics of her entry in the Grand National, she admitted that he was slow, but pointed out his attributes, adding, 'Anything can happen in the National, which is why he's in that and not the Gold Cup.' When some jockeys threatened to 'lynch' her if she crossed them in the big race, the quiet-spoken Fred Winter commented, 'If professional jockeys can't keep out of her way, then *they* don't deserve to be in the race.'

The lengths to which Charlotte went to prepare for the National surely went beyond the bounds of duty, and would have silenced many of her critics if they had realised just how much effort she had put in.

Charlotte was no weakling. Indeed, at 5 feet 10 inches, she was tall for a jockey of either sex. She underwent rigorous training in a local gymnasium, under the eye of physical trainer Keith Allison, who even watched her gallop so that he could see exactly which muscles were called into play and devise exercises for them. She also swam, ran and, of course, road work. With all this physical training came another problem: weight. Charlotte's horse was on the 10-stone minimum, and just imagine what cannon fodder there would be if she went out overweight! But her muscles were getting so strong and hard that she was actually gaining weight. In the end she managed on a paperweight saddle with about 2 ounces to spare.

Already she had taken a huge hiding from the press – until she took upon the expedient of not reading their reports. Many critics had claimed that the fairer sex were too weak to ride in the National; others that she was too inexperienced (to which she replied: how many male jockeys have much experience of Aintree?); others that she and Barony Fort were too moderate a pair to be taking part, that they were 'courting disaster'. Even fellow female jockeys were against it.

Happily, not all the publicity was bad. There were those who admired her pluck and courage. The inhabitants of her home village of Coggeshall adored her; and she received two pre-race telegrams she will always cherish, one from the (late) Ryan Price, the other from Bruce Hobbs, who won the race when only seventeen, both admiring her and wishing her luck. She had never met either of them.

But in the big build-up in the months before the race, she found that her

Although she had no hope of winning, she was determined to get round...

riding was suffering, for she was becoming neurotic about not making a fool of herself in public. She won an amateur race at Fakenham but, finding the critical glare at other times such a strain, she mainly confined herself to point-to-points: 'I became frightened of doing something silly. Any mistake got glaring publicity and nerves about it made my riding suffer appallingly. Instead of going out and taking the risks necessary to win races, I just sat there like a dead duck. It was awful.'

Barony Fort and his human entourage set off in their old trailer from Essex to Aintree on the Wednesday before the race – and were greeted by stable manager, Ossie Dale, who had helped Charlotte so much the previous year to prepare for the Foxhunters, with a bottle of champagne.

Charlotte spent most of her time with Barony, and listening to Ossie's Grand National tales. She and her mother stayed at the Park Hotel right by the course, where they were able to get some much needed peace and quiet. It was the same when she was exercising Barony – she took him right down to the far end of the course where they did not encounter any hassle.

The night before the race, jockey and long-time pal Ian Watkinson persuaded her to go dancing ... and some of the press even berated her for that. In Charlotte's words, 'It really was the right thing to do, rather than tossing and turning in bed.'

She rode out once more on Saturday morning, then returned to the hotel for breakfast, one cup of black coffee in her case. Afterwards, she had another walk around the course, this time with Richard Pitman and Ian Watkinson, and the reality and enormity of the whole thing began to dawn on her – there was no turning back now. The Chair looked enormous, and Ian clowned

about in it, pretending to be mountaineering. 'Don't. You're tempting Providence,' cried Charlotte. It was at the Chair that Ian fell in the race...

The short walk from the weighing room to the paddock was a nightmare, with police warding off the mob around Charlotte. Once she had the familiar feel of Barony Fort beneath her, she felt better and, after the parade, they cantered nicely down to the start. She was struck by the tremendous noise of the crowd. Soon the forty-two horses moved into line: they would be off any second now...

Suddenly a protest group marched out in front of them, waving banners. Jockeys turned their horses in anti-climax, as police removed the demonstrators. They were called into line again, then – 'Hold it!' rang out the cry. A policeman's helmet was lying on the grass in their path. For Charlotte, the last remnants of tension disappeared with that sight, and within moments they were off.

Because of all the haranguing she had received, Charlotte settled at the back on the wide outside. Her horse was soon loving it all, and jumped superbly. Although she had no hope of winning, she was determined to get round...

They avoided a seven-horse pile up at the first fence, and thereafter managed to steer clear of the loose horses, but she was soon slipping further and further behind. She needed to have jumped off smartly at the start for such a one-paced horse as Barony to get into the race properly.

Throughout the race, a separate television camera was focused on Charlotte, to record the historic ride for posterity. As she approached Becher's for the second time – 'It was like jumping off the end of the world' – there were three horses ahead of her,

Nerves fly away once a rider is united with the horse. Charlotte Brew and Barony Fort look relaxed in the parade.

'It was like jumping off the end of the world.'

Barony Fort's retirement race: he won his hunt members' point-to-point.

but two refused and the other fell. To his eternal credit, Barony kept going and the crowds cheered the pair as they conquered each fence.

Barony Fort negotiated the Canal Turn expertly for the second time, but as they approached the fourth fence from home, which was the final big open ditch, he was losing more and more impetus. To Charlotte's despair,

she could not get him over it. To her, it was failure. In fact they had reached the twenty-sixth fence, further than any other non-finisher. 'The last three fences all had big holes in them, but not that ditch. I felt a terrible sense of anti-climax as we returned to the stables; I'd set my heart on getting round, and we so nearly did – but Mother and Ossie came rushing out to greet me and

they were over the moon that we'd got so far.'

Meanwhile, even greater history had been made, as Red Rum galloped to his unique third win.

Charlotte's effort, although disappointing to herself personally, was to be the best by a woman for a full five years. In 1979, Jenny Hembrow, a

Press pressure for Charlotte Brew weeks before the National.

talented former champion point-to-point rider, took a terrible first-fence fall on Sandwilan – imagine the outcry there would have been had that been the first lady rider's effort. The next year, Jenny pulled up at the nineteenth with the same horse. In 1982, mother of twins Linda Sheedy reached the same fence, where Deiopea refused. Then, in 1982, when Charlotte was again in the line-up (she was unseated off Martinstown at the third), Geraldine Rees became the first girl to complete the race, coming eighth on Cheers.

In the October following Charlotte's brave effort with Barony Fort, the pair set off for Czechoslovakia, where they tackled even bigger obstacles in the Pardubice, including the incredible Taxis fence. Charlotte comments, 'I thought it really would be a race for him to take advantage of his jumping and staying ability, without a premium of speed.' Of the Taxis, she says, 'When I got there and someone said, "That's it", I thought they were joking. It looked unjumpable. I am 5 foot 10, and I couldn't see over it. It was as broad as it was high, with a yawning ditch on the other side.'

The Taxis has been the downfall of many, many horses, but Barony jumped it fine. All the big fences were behind her. Ahead lay only the final river crossing and a circuit of hurdles – and still Charlotte had a double handful, while everything else looked cooked – but they were brought down in the river . . .

Barony Fort now lives in honorable retirement, leading a life of luxury as he deserves at twenty-four, stabled in winter and occasionally ridden by Charlotte's father. Charlotte's life is more hectic than ever and 'lots of fun'. Apart from caring for Katherine, she breaks in racehorses and for good measure runs a catering company.

Of her Grand National effort, Charlotte says simply, 'I'm glad I did it.'

BEN NEVIS

1980: American winner

FOR HORSE LOVERS the world over Maryland is synonymous not with crabs, or Baltimore, or the Blue Ridge Mountains, but with the Maryland Hunt Cup.

The state is a land of white-painted, panel-fenced 'horse farms', of the best of American foxhunting, and home to the stiffest timber race in the world.

Charles C. Fenwick (pronounced Fen-wick) Junior, whose land borders the Hunt Cup course, is from a family as steeped in hunting and racing as the history of America itself. He has won the Maryland Hunt Cup five times and the American Grand National an unprecedented eight, yet, as his father-in-law, Redmond C. Stewart, once said, 'The whole of foxhunting America would rather win your Grand National than any other race.'

For Charlie Fenwick, that ambition began to take vague shape over a dinner party in August 1974 some 3000 miles away from Maryland, when Mr Stewart bought Ben Nevis, untried, after a day's shooting on the Yorkshire moors. 'What did not appear to be one of the wiser moves on his part at that time turned out to be very successful,' says Charlie with masterly understatement.

It transpired that, although the chestnut six-year-old had won a point-to-point, he had fallen in his other two races and the formbook could hardly have been more damning: 'speedy, a bad jumper and only able to stay a bare three miles'. Hardly the recipe for a winner of either the Maryland Hunt Cup or the Grand National.

'The whole of foxhunting America would rather win your Grand National than any other race.'

But that dinner-party transaction paved the way for Charlie's two most abiding memories of his remarkable racing career: 'Ben Nevis was brought down by a loose horse at the Chair in the 1979 Grand National. My family and I had been living in England for four and a half months in preparation for this event and the frustration after the first National was unlike anything I have experienced before or since ... I might add that the thrill resulting from his win in 1980 is also unsurpassed.'

Ben Nevis was bought originally through British Bloodstock Agency's Herbert Clarkson as an unbroken five-year-old by Yorkshire point-to-point rider and civil servant in the Manpower Services Commission Mrs Jane Porter. From the start he was very quick-witted, lit-up and sharp. 'You had to be very quiet with him; if you wanted to blow your nose you more or less had to ask him first,' Jane Porter remembers. Being so much on edge, he was difficult to keep flesh on, which made his light frame look lighter than ever.

He was broken in by Billy and Angela Hope, then trained for point-to-points by Shirley and Harry Hindle at Guisburn, and Mrs Porter hunted and point-to-pointed him herself. It was clear early on that he had ability, although the formbook belies that; his nervous energy needed only to be tapped and channelled in the right direction.

Jane Porter was comparatively inexperienced, but soon discovered the horse was so responsive that if you gave him more than a gentle nudge approaching a fence he would take off there and then. That is exactly what happened in his first race. It was snowing, the ground was greasy, and Ben took off outside the wing and landed in a heap the same distance the other side of it. It looked as if horse and rider had got their act together next time, but Ben spread a plate, fell and was winded. Not deterred by that experience, the brave little horse maintained great trust in his rider, who used to talk to him as they went round, and in their third race, in which several horses fell, they won by 10 lengths.

At the time, Mrs Porter wanted to sell one of her two horses and remembers Mr Stewart coming to see them in their field. 'I whistled and Ben came cantering up, and we sold him there and then,' she says. Having followed his later career with interest, was she at Liverpool the day he won the National? 'We were at a sheep society meeting and didn't even see it on television until the evening, she remembers, but it was very thrilling!'

So the fiery horse with enough spunk to compensate for his small size crossed the Atlantic – with startling results.

When Ben arrived in America, Charlie Fenwick thought his father-in-law must have been carried away at that dinner party. The horse was not just small but looked weedy and was very hot and excitable. Yet one thing Mr Stewart did know about was horses suitable for timber racing. His father, Redmond C. Stewart Senior, Master and amateur huntsman of the Green Spring Valley Hunt in Maryland at the age of eighteen, was second in the inaugural running of the Maryland Hunt Cup in 1894 and won it or was placed nine times. Mr Stewart Junior was placed in it three times as a rider then won the race twice as an owner prior to acquiring Ben Nevis.

Flat racing had begun in America a century before the Revolution, when colonists imported stock, then had to race in matches down the roads

Ben Nevis avoids trouble at the Chair in 1980.

because the countryside had not yet been cleared. Steeplechasing started in the mid-1840s; the first race in Maryland was held at Pimlico in 1875 for a purse of $875.

Hunting, which had been a part of the colonists' scene from the beginning in Pennsylvania, Virginia and Maryland, brought English customs and traditions across the Atlantic along with the hounds. It became almost extinct in the Civil War of the 1860s, with packs dispersed and hunters drafted for cavalry, and 'many stout hearts' who had ridden boldly across country went off to war.

But the sport picked up again after the war, and the Elkridge Hunt in Maryland is reputed to have become the 'Melton Mowbray' of America. Sitting on the steps of the Elkridge Hunt Club one day, a group of members were discussing the relative merits of various hunters. A certain amount of heat entered the argument, and so it was decided to organise a race to test their jumping ability and endurance to see who really was the best. Thus was born the Maryland Hunt Cup, with a trophy valued at $100 to be the absolute property of the winner. The race was to be 'about four miles, flagged at intervals, with no artificial jumps'.

The following year the Maryland Hunt Cup Association was formed. The course had different venues in early years, but in 1922 moved to its present site neighbouring the Fenwick farm.

In 1926 Charlie's grandfather, Howard Bruce, a Baltimore industrialist, won the race with Billy Barton, a small horse with decent flat form, and the next year sailed the horse to England for the Grand National, in which he was one of only two survivors. He was with Tipperary Tim at the last fence, where he fell, leaving victory to the 100–1 outsider and remounted to finish second.

The Maryland Hunt Cup course is all solid timber. Some of the fences are 5-foot-high split-oak rails, and there is precious little margin for error when jumping those at racing pace. It took a brave man to ride a horse like Ben Nevis over such obstacles.

Small and excitable Ben Nevis may have been, but he quickly showed he had the guts and the spirit and the ability to adapt, achieving an impressive sequence of victories.

In Charlie Fenwick he had the ideal partner. A youthful-looking, vibrant personality with fair hair and bright, quick eyes, Charlie was raised on a diet of hunting and timber racing and loved it. He also took the attitude that if something was to be done it should be done well and to a budget. 'I thrive on it,' he says, 'especially chasing. The next chance is the next race as far as I'm concerned. I get a real kick out of it. You have so much racing in England, you don't realise how good it is, and the depth of competition is enormous – although I think our best horses can compete with those in Great Britain. Fort Devon was the best horse ever to go from America to race in England; he was grade one.'

He draws an example of the competitive spirit from a memorable day's hunting he had with the Quorn during his stay in England while preparing for the National: 'Hounds ran for two and a half hours. There had been 250 people at the meet and within five minutes of the kill at least 50 of them were there. That shows some competition; the strength in depth is so impressive.' Charlie remarks on the British character too. 'They are so enthusiastic in National Hunt racing, yet only two per cent of them will have a winner!'

Incredibly, Ben Nevis ran up a sequence of twelve wins in America, including the Maryland Hunt Cups of 1977 and 1978 (the latter in record time). Charlie decided to establish if he really did have a world-class horse, one that could win the National, and set about finding an English trainer.

He chose Tim Forster at Wantage, Oxfordshire, renowned for training big, old-fashioned chasing types, who thought Ben Nevis was the smallest, lightest horse he had ever seen, barely a half-brother to a racehorse. Charlie recalls his arrival: 'When I said the horse was cold-backed and difficult to get on, Captain Forster obviously thought: we'll soon have this American like the rest. We lunged him, but even then when I mounted he walked

Ben Nevis skips over Becher's Brook second time round.

An elated Charlie Fenwick romps to victory on Ben Nevis in 1980.

around on his hind legs and he never did change!'

The wiry chestnut was as tough as they come, and would rear, buck and pull hard. 'He always felt as if he was running off, but he usually ended up doing the right thing,' Charlie recalls.

The horse had arrived with those twelve successive wins behind him. There followed twelve failures over here. He detested mud, but in that English winter kept coming up against it.

The dedicated Charlie, wife Ann, and children, Beth, Charlie and Emily, plus nanny Rita, moved virtually lock, stock and barrel to England for four and a half months to prepare for the race with single-minded sense of purpose, riding out daily, playing squash – all to no avail.

Ben Nevis was not unfancied when he went to post that last day of March in 1979. He had his favoured good

going, carried 11 stone 2 pounds, and started at 14–1. But all those months of preparation, planning, talking, walking and sleeping the Grand National came to nought at the Chair. A horse was in the ditch on the take-off side, and Ben found the task of jumping horse, ditch and biggest fence on the course impossible. In his frustration, Charlie remounted, jumped the water, then, realising his task was hopeless, turned back utterly deflated and watched with envy as the Scottish horse Rubstic held off Zongalero and Rough and Tumble.

So Charlie was down but not out. He would try again. But while the horse could stay in England, there was no way he could repeat the time-off of the previous year. He had to become a transatlantic commuter jockey, taking up cheap stand-by tickets. It was not easy for Tim Forster. With his rider at

such a distance, he had to make decisions about running days in advance instead of waiting to see which of two or three races might be more suitable. Also, it often meant running Ben Nevis on the soft ground he detested.

By the time the 1980 Grand National came round, the horse had still not won a chase in England. He was twelve years old, probably past his prime, his weight had reduced to 10 stone 12 pounds – and the going was heavy. He started a barely considered 40–1 outsider. To make matters worse, as he went out for his thirteenth race in England, Ben Nevis was sweating profusely.

Of the thirty runners, only four finished – not through any multiple pile-up, for the twelve fallers came down at eight different fences and only one, Churchtown Boy, was brought down. Of the others, five refused, two unseated their riders and five pulled up,

'He gave me a fantastic ride.'

Charlie Fenwick junior, winner of the 1980 National with Ben Nevis.

so it was probably the heavy ground which had taken its toll.

It was a year, surely, for a mudlark to triumph – yet here was that avowed mud-detester kicking it out of the ground, still hating it but somehow determined to get the better of it. Ben Nevis hesitated momentarily at the Chair, probably remembering his previous experience at that fence, but he jumped brilliantly thereafter. Another superb jump at Becher's second time took him into the lead as Delmoss crashed, and there he stayed, drawing ever further away from his pursuers.

Charlie was sure that John Francome would be poised to pounce on Rough and Tumble but, as he crossed the Melling Road and gave Ben Nevis one slap down the shoulder, the little horse took hold of the bit again, felt

stronger than ever, and galloped on to a memorable 20-length victory. 'He gave me a fantastic ride.' Charlie grins broadly at the memory.

A couple of years after that victory, Charlie extended his racehorse enterprise, building a new 'barn' which now houses twenty steeple-chasers in the lap of luxury and making himself into one of the biggest jump trainers in that part of America, where the sport is now growing rapidly.

Walking up the stairs to the office within the all-under-one-roof training complex, the first thing one sees is the print of Dick Saunders and Grittar winning the 1982 Grand National, signed by Dick. 'I met an awful lot of nice people in England that we really miss,' Charlie says. He listened live to

Grittar's National, thanks to a tele-phone link-up with firm friend Graham Thorner, at that time Captain Forster's stable jockey and now a trainer himself. 'I had just been think-ing that if I was lucky enough to have the right sort of horse again soon enough, I could just get in another Grand National. Then along comes Dick, at forty-eight, and wins!'

At the age of forty, and with Ben Nevis retired to his farm following Mr Stewart's death in 1986, Charlie Fen-wick himself shows no sign of retiring from the saddle, having, in 1987, won the Maryland Hunt Cup on Sugar Bee and the American Grand National on Local Kid. 'I'm still enjoying it enormously,' he says enthusiastically, as he prepares for another crack at Aintree in 1988 with Sugar Bee.

ALDANITI/ BOB CHAMPION

1981: Greatest fairytale win

WHEN BOB CHAMPION went out for the 1981 Grand National, defeat was unthinkable. Victory was as certain to him before that race as death had seemed in his fight against cancer less than two years earlier.

All the ingredients of a fairytale were there: the broken-down horse, recovered not once but *three* times from leg trouble; the back-from-death jockey; the incredible loyalty and patience of the supporting cast; and a girlfriend waiting in the wings.

Of the seventh generation of a hunting family, Bob Champion loved riding to hounds by the time he was nine or ten years old. But something stirred him even more. Seeing Pathe news film of the Grand National, he thought: I'd like to ride in that one day.

His first race was an unofficial one, but he won it just the same. His father, Bob senior, was huntsman to the Cleveland and at the end of the hunt's annual point-to-point Bob and two or three other whippers-in set themselves a 2-mile course over the track. 'I've got to be fair and admit that I was on the best horse and was also considerably lighter than my

'I'd like to ride in that one day.'

opponents,' grins Bob, 'but I just got up in a stirring finish and thought: 'this is fun.'

The real thing was not at first so jolly. Bob took such a purler when disputing the lead at the last fence at Larkhill, after which the horse rolled on him, that he began to think he was

'You never heard about the people who recover.'

not cut out for racing after all. But, as was to be the case so poignantly in later life, he soon came back – and, what's more, he won on his first ride as a professional.

Bob built up a solid career as a freelance, taking a retainer from Josh Gifford at Findon on the South Downs. He was regularly finishing in the first half-dozen in the jockeys' table, riding forty to fifty winners, and enjoying life to the full, when he re-

ceived the jolt that was to alter his whole future and bring his life to the very brink: the seemingly fit, healthy young man had developed cancer. 'You just think you are going to die when you are first told,' he recalls. 'You never heard about the people who recover.'

Because of this, after his recovery, Bob agreed to help publicise the cancer survival rate, helping to make a film, promoting it all over the world, and setting up a trust fund in which his winning ride, Aldaniti, himself played an integral part. One thing the film did not portray with total accuracy was the ghastliness of the treatment – though, goodness knows, the portrayal was harrowing enough – because they did not want to put people off. But, Bob says, that was in the early days of chemotherapy, and its side-effects have been vastly reduced now. 'Yes, I felt like death during the treatment, but even at the lowest ebb I felt I would get better; I just didn't want to die, basically,' says the master of the understatement.

When that traumatic, harrowing, painful period, which he had borne so bravely, was over, he had to regain fitness; the thought of riding

Aldaniti overjumped and 'paddled along with his nose on the ground, but we got away with it'.

Aldaniti, himself sidelined through injury, in the Grand National, was the invisible spur. 'And that was even harder,' says Bob, whose muscles had wasted, his whole body washed out and limp. Aldaniti was slowly but surely getting better from breakdown, retoning lost muscles, hardening the damaged leg, so Bob just had to make it. His turning point was a spell in America with trainer friend Burly Cocks, and the magic tonic of riding a winner on his comeback ride, and on the flat too!

It had been a full three years earlier when Bob had predicted that Nick and Valda Embiricos's Aldaniti would win the National. 'I really meant it, ask anyone,' he says. 'I had won the Eider Chase on Highland Wedding. I won Rag Trade's first novice chase. I "did" Rubstic at Toby Balding's as a two-year-old, when he was the slowest thing on four legs! I even fell off Corbiere in a novice chase. They all shared common likenesses: they had low head carriage, were very well balanced, and gave the same type of feel. They all won the National, and when Aldaniti came along and felt just the same I was always certain he would win too.'

Bob had not, of course, been on any of those earlier winners and his own National record was mixed. Riding Country Wedding his first time, he decided to follow a proven Aintree horse, picked the previous year's winner Gay Trip, tucked in behind him – and when Gay Trip fell at the first, he was brought down. He got further the next year on the same horse, falling at Valentine's – 'but at least I'd jumped Becher's!' With Hurricane Rock, Money Market and Manicou Bay he finished in the first half-dozen or so, but then it was back to a first-fence fall with Spitting Image. Purdo fell at the first Becher's when in the lead. Then it was

all up to Aldaniti – amazingly, he also fell at the first fence in his second National.

But it was the horse's first National that mattered. Could it be done? Could this pair of former crocks, who had had just one pre-National race together and gloriously won it, really make a fairytale come true? There are so many imponderables and bad-luck stories in a race like the National that, to the huge crowds and watching millions, it seemed to be asking too much of fate, but if their collective wish could bring about the result they would make sure it did.

It was much simpler for Bob Champion. There was no bated breath or jangling nerves for him. 'The race was just a formality, I simply couldn't see myself being beat,' he states, dismissing the loose-horse factor and admitting that his first-fence bogey was the only thing he was genuinely afraid of. 'But that's where Fred Winter won it for me. He said you've got to "break the horse's jaw" after crossing the Melling Road approaching the first fence, to get it back on its hocks. It's a long, long way to the first and such a cavalry charge that most horses are on their forehand.'

Even with this good advice, the pair nearly capsized at the first. Aldaniti overjumped and 'paddled along with his nose on the ground, but we got away with it'. Bob will never forget the moment. At the second he dropped his hind legs, and the thick stakes obviously hurt him; the next was the big ditch – and from then on he jumped to the manner born.

For the early part of the race Aldaniti tracked popular amateur John Thorne on the favourite Spartan Missile, both of them going down the outside, which trainer Josh Gifford favoured for his horse. The ground was

Aldaniti, right, lands over the water alongside Sebastian V (R. Lamb).

good, Aldaniti made light of 10 stone 13 pounds, and as early as the twelfth fence had jumped his way to the front.

It was plenty early enough to be leading but the horse was obviously loving it and so were the crowds. He gave them an extra treat by jumping the huge Chair in front of the stands superbly. 'He gave me a dream ride,' says Bob. But there was one more anxious moment to come. 'We were on the wrong stride going into the last and I didn't know what to do; but he sorted it out himself, drifting left and he fiddled it.'

Now there remained that long run-

Victory salute: Bob Champion and Aldaniti gallop to win the National.

in. Bob knew the horse nearest to him, Royal Mail, was a spent force – 'that's who I thought I was beating' – but, unbeknown to him, it was John Thorne and Spartan Missile who were eating up the ground in hot pursuit, having been badly hampered at the Canal Turn. 'I knew if I got to the running rail after the elbow first I would win,' says Bob – and it was by 4 memorable lengths that he did so, arm raised in triumphant salute, that always-engaging smile spread across his face for the world's cameras to capture.

The crowd applauded to the skies. It was the perfect result; and there were many who felt that John Thorne's turn could surely come in next year's National. But, shortly before then, the true amateur was killed in a fall at his local point-to-point...

Now all eyes were on Bob Champion and Aldaniti, trainer Josh Gifford, owners Nick and Valda Embericos, lad Peter Double, stud girl Beryl Millam, doctors and nurses from the Royal Marsden Hospital for cancer sufferers, the vets, the families: it was a happy ending for the press to lap up and the whole world loved it. And it heralded a new role in life for Bob Champion.

A picture of perfection, Corbiere and Ben de Haan canter composedly down to the start.

Above: A magnificent spectacle in front of the packed stands as three horses clear the water in superb style. Winner Corbiere is number 6.

Right: Corbiere is given a rapturous welcome home from trainer Jenny Pitman, jockey Ben de Haan and a host of fans.

Right: The 1983 winner Corbiere gives a useful lesson in jumping Valentine's to Hallo Dandy who was to win the following year.

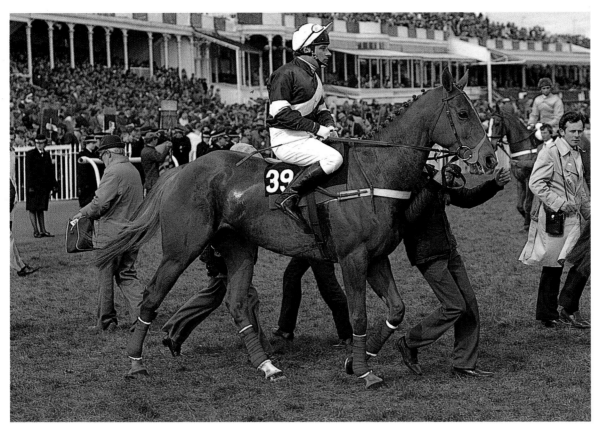

*Above: Parading before the start of the 1984 National is Canford Ginger (Colin Brown up).
Below: Mr Richard Shaw's Hallo Dandy, ridden by Neale Doughty.*

*The Chair is the widest fence on
the course but Canford Ginger
negotiates it safely.*

Right: Caviare and champagne are all part of Hallo Dandy's celebrations in London.

Below: An understandably happy Richard Shaw proudly holds aloft the magnificent Seagram Grand National trophy in 1984.

Left: Part of the magnificent Childwick Bury Stud, home in retirement to 1987 Grand National winner Maori Venture.

Below: Mr Jim Joel's Maori Venture (Steve Knight up) at the East Hendred stables of his trainer Andy Turnell.

Right: Maori Venture on his way to victory in 1987.

Below: The grand old man of racing, Mr Jim Joel, flanked by trainer Andy Turnell, left, and jockey Steve Knight, surrounded by media and well-wishers.

> ... he was the inspiration for cancer sufferers, who saw that they could get better and lead a normal life again.

Jonjo O'Neill, Tommy Stack, Bob Champion and John Francome.

From then on he would find himself telling and retelling his life story. He was to fill the role of ambassador for the cause of cancer research; he was the inspiration for cancer sufferers, who saw that they could get better and lead a normal life again. But, for Bob his life was no longer to be his own – privacy was a thing of the past. His marriage, which set such a happy seal on the story, was to last only three years; the work for cancer increases rather than lessens; he has become public property.

Bob Champion has a shy manner, and he found more loneliness than glamour as he travelled the world, shaking countless hands, giving numerous interviews.

He has set up as a trainer in an attractive hamlet near Bury St Edmunds, but his life at home is little more his own than when he is away. An average of three nights a week are taken up attending some function or other, balls, race-nights and so on, and many days he will be parading Aldaniti somewhere such as a county show, or attending a cricket match – not his favourite game, but it is all for the cause. Such engagements hinder his training and, inevitably, his income; he needs better horses to make his mark; in many ways the freshness has gone.

Bob Champion, OBE, victor over both Aintree and cancer, outside Buckingham Palace after his investiture.

'You get used to it,' he says resignedly, but a lacklustre element has crept into the once-ebullient frame, more portly now than it used to be. 'The reaction was far more than I expected, especially in the length of time it has gone on,' he admits. 'Every charity wants you and you are always expected to go. It was all forced on me a bit, but I'm glad really.' Speaking in 1987, he calculated that he had had just twenty-six days off since 1977.

'I know I've been round the world promoting the film and so on, but that was twenty-five-hours-a-day stuff, no glamour but bloody hard work.' The film was called, appropriately, *Champions*, and had a moving theme tune of the same name; it kept closely to the true story and brought hope and inspiration to admiring viewers round the globe.

Bob's promotional itinerary ran something like this: depart London; five-hour delay Bahrein; 10.00 a.m., first interview in Sydney, Australia, interview's all day; film premiere in the evening; 6.00 a.m., plane to Melbourne; 7.00 a.m., breakfast television; more interviews through the day; another late-night premiere, another early morning flight for the next stop: a continuous whirl, taking in Adelaide and Perth, on to Christchurch and Auckland in New Zealand – Hong Kong, Tokyo, South Africa. It was enough to bring the toughest spirit down, and took some getting over.

Bob may have experienced first-class travel and top hotels but sleep became a thing of the past. 'I slept more on planes than in bed and once, in order to do any sightseeing at all, I was taken round a city, Perth, at 3 a.m., just so that I could see something for myself.'

Very much on his own, Bob never knew from one day to the next whom he would be meeting, but always it was the same round of handshakes and the same set of questions. In Tokyo, instead of having one press conference and photo call, he was required to speak to each reporter and pose for every cameraman separately: 'It was in a riding centre and I was meant to pop a horse over a pole; I must have jumped it three hundred times and it took five hours... Yes, it does get boring; I can see why actors go funny. It is such a false life.' But then his face lights up again as he says, 'Home is still a haven.'

Shortly after the National victory, Professor Peckham, finding that so many uninvited donations were being sent to the Royal Marsden Hospital, suggested a trust fund should be formed. Thus came into being in 1983 the Bob Champion Cancer Trust, with Bob as patron and Clive Nicholls, QC, chairman of nine trustees and two executives. It has raised over $£1\frac{1}{2}$ million since then, including a staggering £814,000 (and rising) from an ambitious, far-seeing 250-mile charity walk with Aldaniti from London to Aintree. The walk ended minutes before the 1987 Grand National, with Bob himself in the saddle for the last mile; horse and rider cantered past the packed, cheering stands. Bob and Aldaniti are still an inspiration wherever they go.

The walk caught the public's imagination, and was boosted enormously by the participation of two popular princesses: the Duchess of York, the former Miss Sarah Ferguson, and HRH Princess Anne, now the Princess Royal, a world-class rider in her own right.

The 250 people who rode one mile each came from all walks of life, ranging from famous film stars and celebrities to Pony Club members. For every

***Aldaniti, ridden by the Princess Royal, at Cheltenham on his
London–Liverpool walk.***

yard of the 250 miles, stud girl Beryl Millam was at Aldaniti's side. 'Aldaniti and I were both very fit by the end of it,' says the woman who has looked after him devotedly since he was a five-year-old and nursed him through his various injuries. 'Everybody used to like to ride or groom him, he is so kind. He just wants to please. He rises to the occasion and is the most wonderful horse ever to look through a bridle.'

The idea of the walk was for each rider to raise £1000 in sponsorship, with the aim of netting a quarter of a million pounds. That it raised three times as much is testimony to the Bob Champion story. It was fitting that Bob should ride the last mile. And it was particularly moving that Jonjo O'Neill, whose sparkling Irish eyes and nicest of all personalities have added such depth to the English scene, should ride the first mile while fighting his own successful battle against the illness.

DICK SAUNDERS

1982: Oldest winning rider

TO HAVE ONE RIDE in the Grand National; to win the race at twice the age of many jockeys; and then to retire ... Dick Saunders, cheerful Northamptonshire farmer and lifelong hunting man, did all this and more. At forty-eight years old, he was by far the oldest winning jockey (Tommy Pickernell was forty-one when he won on Pathfinder in 1875); he was the only serving member of the Jockey Club ever to have won; and he was the only current Master of Foxhounds to have done so. Two other amateurs have won on their only ride: Mr E. C. Hobson on Austerlitz in 1877, and Lord Manners in 1882 on Seaman.

But there was nothing either *old* or flukish about Dick Saunders's win on Grittar in 1982. One of nature's gentlemen, with an abiding interest in racing and all things rural, he was a consummate horseman with a practised eye across country, who had already, from seven attempts, filled the first five places in the Liverpool Foxhunters over part of the Grand National course. This meant that he had had more experience of the course, if not the National, than many professionals. His win in the Foxhunters had been on Grittar himself, in 1981, and so the scene was set...

The scene shows a man who goes out of his way to give time to people and energy to projects; efficiency lies behind his lively blue eyes and ever-ready smile, and a direction of purpose so strong that, once he decides something is worth doing, he will make sure he does it well. That has been the clue behind his success in farming and racing, his involvement in the Jockey Club and with the Injured Jockeys Fund, and as a Master of the Pytchley Hunt for ten seasons.

The horse scene began for Dick, as for many a farmer's son, with Pony Club, hunting and a natural progression to point-to-pointing. He used to win the Pytchley Hunt members' race quite regularly until, as a young man, he was given 10 acres of his beloved Northamptonshire by his father, use of farm equipment, and left to get on with it.

Get on with it he did, fulfilling his ambition to farm 1000 acres within ten years (he now has around 3000), but it meant hanging up his boots during that period, without any thoughts of ever returning to riding, bar in the odd members' race.

Any idea he may have entertained of winning the Grand National was more dream than ambition, for, like many an amateur, he would not be able to make the minimum weight – and horses with a good chance and bigger weights were mostly claimed by top professional jockeys.

But in Grittar he had the ideal partner, similarly from an 'amateur' background, that of Leicestershire farmer Frank Gilman in the Cottesmore hunting country. Gilman not only owned him and trained the horse under permit, but had bred him too, his dam, Tarama, having won two novice hurdles for him. Grittar was by a sprinter, Grisaille, who got little else besides a few hurdlers.

A neat, compact bay with an attractive white star, and a good buck in him, Grittar stood only just over 16 h.h., but was beautifully made and balanced, capable of adjusting his stride as the occasion demanded, an attribute which time and again has proved its worth at Aintree. He started his racing life early, running unplaced twice as a two-year-old, ridden by Pat Eddery, and began to show some form after a switch to hurdling.

Frank Gilman's stable jockey at the time was Terry Casey, now a successful trainer himself in south Northamptonshire, and his head lad was Derek Lane, who now holds the same position at Terry's stables. It was Terry who rode Grittar to his first two victories in large, competitive, novice-hurdle fields, and placed six times in sixteen outings.

In 1979, Grittar began point-to-pointing. As Dick Saunders had ridden Mr Gilman's point-to-pointers and hunter-chasers for about fifteen years, he was the natural choice as jockey,

Congratulations heap on Dick Saunders, at 48 the oldest winning jockey.

But after his last run at lowly South-well on firm ground, and unbeknown to the racing press, both Grittar's front legs blew up. Frank remembers showing him to Dick a few weeks later at grass. Dick's face dropped. Grittar's tendons were bowed. It would be long odds against getting him fit to race next year, let alone tackle the Grand National.

'If he runs, you ride him.'

It was not surprising, therefore, that the two men did not immediately think of the Grand National after that successful 1981 hunter-chasing season; but when the horse got off to a good start under rules next season, having made a complete and speedy recovery, the whole racing world was talking of him as a Grand National prospect.

As his chances were more and more widely discussed, so was the question of his jockey. Surely the best professional should be put up rather than an ageing amateur, the pundits urged. Dick raised the question with Frank just once, suggesting he book the best professional available, probably John Francome. Frank replied, 'If he runs, you ride him.' End of conversation.

Frank Gilman says, 'There was never any question of a professional riding, and you don't want to put a professional on an amateur-ridden horse – it wouldn't know what was happening. Dick is anyway one of the finest horsemen I have ever seen, with marvellous hands.'

Frank Gilman was a man of his word, even though John Francome did ride Grittar once before the race, to do a lower weight, which further fuelled speculation about the horse's Grand National jockey.

getting off to a highly promising start in a quiet run at Newton Bromswold, one of the best-tended point-to-point courses in England. For Grittar's next run, Dick was sidelined through injury, so the ride went to his young daughter, Caroline, who was then twenty, and during two successful seasons they won several point-to-points and hunter-chases and placed many times. By the end of that period, however, Grittar was beginning to get a bit 'knowing' often

finishing second when perhaps with stronger handling he might have won.

The female touch had worked wonders mentally on Grittar after some hard hurdle races, but it was agreed that the time had come for Dick to regain the ride – which, in 1981, he did with devastating results. After an initial fifth, the pair were unbeaten in four races, including the two prestigious Foxhunter events at Cheltenham and Liverpool.

'Dick is anyway one of the finest horsemen I have ever seen, with marvellous hands.'

At the Chair, from left, Tiepolini, Loving Words, winner Grittar and Tragus.

Dick Saunders rode Grittar into a highly satisfactory sixth place in the Cheltenham Gold Cup as his warm-up race, then, on the opening day of Aintree, drove up to walk the course. He went alone, in peace and quiet, to chart out his intended route, to plan and hope and, very privately, dream. His wife, Pam, did not walk round on that occasion, having been frightened enough by the fences during previous Foxhunter forays.

Dick's Foxhunter rides had stood him in good stead. He had learned the hard way that it was worth dozens of yards to go on the inside; and that, in so doing, he was less likely to come up against the dodgy jumpers or timid riders. He had hunted all his life, had raced now for many years, and in the early days of team chasing had been without peer in planning and riding the stiffest cross-country courses.

Three horses headed the market

betting in the weeks leading up to the race: Grittar; the previous year's winner, Aldaniti; and a good class horse trained by Stan Mellor, Royal Mail, third the year before. But the punters' choice on the day was Grittar, and at the off he started clear favourite.

Once Dick had weighed out for the race and handed over his saddle, the daunting task he faced suddenly dawned on him. Not exactly the first jockey in the history of the race to do

Dick Saunders gives Grittar his head as they land safely over the last.

so, he found himself thinking: what the hell am I doing here? The tension remained until the jockeys were called out, and Frank Gilman put his jockey at ease. 'Instructions?' says Dick. 'There were no instructions, he just told a few jokes and was nice and relaxed, and left the riding to me.'

Naturally, they had discussed tactics beforehand and agreed to keep Grittar 'in the van' to make the best use of his stamina; not that he had ever tackled this distance before, but they both felt, correctly, that he would stay for ever.

As they lined up, and the thirty-nine jockeys jostled for position, Dick managed to obtain the berth just two off the rails, with Bill Smith on Delmoss, a proven pair, hugging that number-one position.

Within moments they were off, and both Delmoss and Grittar got a good break. Grittar was at full stretch over the first two fences, then, as the race settled down, and with Aldaniti a faller at the first, Dick found he could track Bill Smith. Grittar jumped accurately and economically and had soon settled into an easy stride; he was still behind Delmoss as they came back onto the racecourse towards the end of the first circuit, and approached the mighty Chair fence in about fifth place.

By the second fence second time round, Dick could see that Delmoss was tiring, so he drew out a bit to pass him; Grittar met the second Becher's on such a good stride that he jumped into the lead and landed running. Dick recalls, 'I decided at that point that the race was hardly being run fast enough, so I took it up to make it a staying race.'

From then on the pair were never headed, though they had to survive

'It felt as long as the whole of the rest of the race, I was sure we were going to be swamped by horses, but luckily Grittar had got them at full stretch.'

one anxious moment. It was not a jumping error; Dick takes up the story as they were approaching the Canal Turn for the second time: 'It didn't go quite to plan, as you want to jump the fence at an angle with your foot brushing through the inside flag, to get the shortest way round the right-angled bend; but Grittar met it on a long stride, and I didn't want to disappoint him by checking him, so over we flew, jumping too well and landing right out so far that we had to come round wide; but luckily, as we were in the lead, all the others followed us, and so we didn't lose any ground!'

Although Dick remained in the lead, he could always hear horses just behind him, waiting, he was sure, to pounce, while he willed them not to. He met the last just right, popped over it and set off up the interminable run-in. 'It felt as long as the whole of the rest of the race,' says Dick with some feeling. 'I was sure we were going to be swamped by horses, but luckily Grittar had got them at full stretch.'

As he pulled up in triumph, the first person to come down the course and congratulate him was Bob Champion – and that was the first time Dick knew that Aldaniti had fallen, along with nine others, in a first-fence pile-up. Royal Mail had fallen at Becher's.

Immediately after the race, Dick Saunders, the ever-youthful forty-eight-year-old, announced his retirement. He and Pam drove home to Northamptonshire that night, scarcely able to take it all in, but soon had to face that greatest of all levellers in racing: their daughter, Caroline, after watching the National on a huge screen, had had a horse she was riding

killed at the local point-to-point. In addition, they had to spend most of the evening taking entries for their own point-to-point the following weekend, a difficult task with the phone going non-stop with calls from well-wishers.

That same evening Dick received a telegram of congratulation from Her Majesty Queen Elizabeth the Queen Mother. Countless letters followed, from old friends, acquaintances, and people they didn't know at all; they included cartoons of old men jumping fences and, most special of all, a four-page personal letter from Prince Charles.

Dick secretly hoped that, with his retirement, Grittar would be retired too, but he ran in the race twice more, completing the course both times, for John Francome and Paul Barton. Grittar never won another race, and eventually broke down and retired on the farm.

Why did Dick Saunders, after seven broken collarbones, a number of broken ribs, a punctured lung, broken shoulder and back injuries during his career, retire at that time? 'I could never cap that, there was nowhere else to go.'

Since then, Dick's life has been taken up increasingly with work for the Jockey Club – he was a steward and chairman of the licensing committee for two years to the end of 1987 – and as a trustee of the Injured Jockeys Fund; he is still involved with hunting, racing and point-to-pointing, to say nothing of having his farm to run. Does he have time for any other interests? 'Occasionally I manage to cook the breakfast.' He smiles, those blue eyes twinkling . . .

GERALDINE REES

1982: First woman to complete

LIKE CHARLOTTE BREW, who was the first lady to ride in the Grand National, Geraldine Rees, the first to complete it, had to contend with enormous prejudice and some extraordinarily antagonistic statements.

What both women found most galling was those decriers who claimed the lady riders were only in it for the publicity. For both were accomplished horsewomen in their own right, well used to the hurly-burly of equestrian competition, simply exercising their deserved prerogative to take part when the right opportunity presented itself. One can only take a hat off to them for their bravery and sheer guts in tackling fences that would be beyond the mettle of many mere male mortals.

Lancashire lassie Geraldine was like a breath of fresh air in the sport. Refusing to lose any part of her femininity, Geraldine piled up her long blonde hair under her crash cap rather than cut it all off. There was nothing hard-bitten about this girl with the husky voice – not that she would give any quarter in a hard-fought finish.

There were those who contended, in 1982, when she rode Cheers in Grittar's Grand National, that she was 'just a housewife who thought it would be fun to hop on a horse and pop round Aintree'. Nothing could have been further from the truth. In fact she was

stable jockey to her trainer-father, Captain James Wilson, and had been the leading female National Hunt rider. She had in fact started her career in three-day eventing and represented her country in junior eventing teams.

'I wouldn't swap the racing world now. I love it, and the people.'

To begin with, she preferred the discipline of riding round tough event courses like Badminton and Burghley to the tumult of racing, but is now totally committed to racing – quite a transformation from that Easter Monday in 1977 when she travelled to Carlisle with her father.

At that time she had an amateur rider's permit, with the vague intention of riding one day, and her kit was stowed in the car 'just in case'. As it transpired, on the busy Bank Holiday racing day, no professional was available for one particular horse and, after a hurried consultation with the stewards, it was agreed that the twenty-one-year-old Mrs Rees, whose racing experience was just two point-to-points, could ride against the professionals in the novice hurdle. This was before the introduction of A and B permits, according to which amateurs can only ride against professionals once

they have proved themselves. So Geraldine was legged up onto the unconsidered outsider, Twidale – and proceeded to lead from start to finish for a fairytale ending.

The next few years brought relative obscurity for her – coping with the frustration most jockeys have faced of poor horses and even poorer luck – but, now bitten by the bug, and determined to prove herself, she steadily built up her experience. 'I wouldn't swap the racing world now. I love it, and the people,' Geraldine says.

It was her switch to chasing from hurdling, and the even greater feeling of elation that chasing brings, which changed her fortunes in spite of an inauspicious start. 'My father, who has been the greatest help in my racing career, was not keen for me to ride in novice chases, and I promptly fell at the first fence at my first attempt and broke my thumb!' Three days later, she rode at Cartmel and finished third, but her arm then had to be put in plaster and she missed Twidale's winning debut over fences. Compensation was soon on its way and, although her old pal, Twidale, could be a distinctly hairy ride, she went on to win on him at Perth. Gordon's Lad and James Ward provided more good wins, and Geraldine was on a crest. Her ambition was simply to ride as well as the professionals. She was quick to stress that

Geraldine Rees became the first lady rider to complete the National.

her success was due to team effort: 'It could not have happened without the help of my family, staff and owners.'

When Captain Wilson was granted a full licence to train (he formerly held a permit), Geraldine played even more of a key role, combining head lad's position with that of work rider, jockey and, of course, housewife. A close family unit made her work in the yard possible. Her mother, Mrs June Wilson, and grandmother gave untold help in the house, which is right by their yard in Preston. Meals were taken as a family in her parent's home. (Her husband, Henry, himself a racehorse owner, is Northern Sales Manager for Dickins Ltd.)

In Gordon's Lad, Geraldine felt she had a live contender to fulfil her ambition of riding in the Grand National, and so he was entered. Geraldine says of the horse, 'He was very headstrong, but I would have liked to have ridden him in the Grand National. It might have been something of a kamikaze job, but I felt the big race and fences would bring the best out of him.'

Once she had got the bit between her teeth, it was a bitter disappointment when Gordon's Lad went lame shortly before the big race – he was, like Red Rum, trained on Southport sands, where the seawater could generally be reckoned to work wonders on 'iffy' legs – and so she resolved, if possible in the short time remaining, to buy herself a horse already entered for

the National. On such occasions fairly moderate horses can fetch inflated prices simply because they are entered for the Grand National. Geraldine was in for another blow. At Doncaster Sales she was underbidder for Cheers, a nice-looking chestnut who had finished last in the race the year before. She was outbid by Mrs Tom Shalley and Mrs Charles Mackenzie, who were equally determined to have a runner.

So a newly disappointed Geraldine returned home in time for the evening stables. News of her thwarted effort, however, leaked out to the new owners, who had as yet to decide on a jockey for the race. And who better than Geraldine?

A week before the National itself, Geraldine travelled to the Newmarket

'It was like going
down a funnel and
was deafening – but it
was also euphoric and
the crowd carried us
on, willing us home.'

But in 1983 her mount, Midday Welcome, fell at the first fence.

Links, where, in a much publicised session, she teamed up with Cheers for some schooling and a bit of work. He was like a cat on hot bricks, jumping sensationally, and Geraldine thought: this is the horse for me. To her intense delight, she was then officially offered the ride at Aintree. 'The big thing for me then was that I had made it,' remembers Geraldine. 'After all, it is every National Hunt jockey's dream to ride in the National, and it was a tremendous relief after all the build-ups and let-downs.'

But as the race was just about to begin Geraldine was suddenly full of fear – not of the fences, but because for a few awful moments it looked as if Cheers might not start at all. He had been worked up in the paddock, and 'frozen' until the girths were loosened a hole, but down at the start it happened again, through excitement or perhaps some discomfort from the girths.

Whatever it was, poor Geraldine suddenly found herself on a horse going backwards, right in front of those packed stands. I'm going to be left at the start like the horse in the Hamlet cigars advert, she thought in rising panic, shouting out, 'No sir!' to the starter, Captain Michael Sayers, who fortunately had seen her plight.

She trotted Cheers in a circle at the back and just as she was returning to the line-up, Captain Sayers's hand poised on the starting tape, she shouted, 'Right, sir,' and with the rest roughly in line she got off to a flyer, right next to 'Big Ron', Irishman Ron Barry.

Cheers was one of those neat, agile horses who gave a tremendous feel, as if he had springs in his heels, and, apart from pecking slightly as he landed over

> '**I would have loved
> the chance to have
> him myself; he holds a
> very special place for
> me. He was a
> wonderful horse.**'

the crucial first fence, he was foot-perfect.

He felt good and he gave her confidence – as did Ron Barry, calling out to her in Irish all the way down the first three fences. 'I couldn't understand a word, but the effect of it was "stick with me",' says Geraldine. Unfortunately for Ron, they stuck together too much at the third, where his horse, Brod Munro-Wilson's Coolishall, jumped crookedly and collided with Cheers in mid-air, ejecting Ron from the saddle. Geraldine herself took a fearful knock, and had to 'hail a cab' and stick like glue (she had actually smeared resin on her breeches before the event and, who knows, it may have helped in this predicament!).

It proved to have been the worst moment. Jumping Becher's felt like flying and she was 'in the van' and experiencing the exhilaration of riding a good jumper in the world's greatest steeplechase.

The pair stayed in contention until the water jump in front of the stands, with a circuit to go; by the time they were approaching Becher's for the second time they were at the rear of the field, with loose horses running around everywhere: 'I kept thinking they were going to cause a pile-up, so I pulled towards the outside rail and jumped safely through. Sure enough, there was a melée there, and it left just Pat O'Connor on Three of Diamonds and me together behind the leading six.'

It was from the second Becher's onwards that Geraldine encountered an Aintree phenomenon – the cheering crowds. 'It was like going down a funnel and was deafening – but it was also euphoric and the crowd carried us on, willing us home.'

As they were crossing the Melling

Road for the last time with just two fences and the infamous long run-in left, Three of Diamonds found an extra spurt, and Cheers was left on his own.

Still he did not falter, and jumped the last fence with feet to spare, but it was then that fatigue set in. 'I was exhausted too. In hindsight, I know I could have trotted past the post, but I was caught up in it all, the adrenalin was flowing, and the crowd was literally roaring us home.' There was, too, no end of housewives' money riding on her to complete the course and, as she passed the post in eighth and last place, they were able to collect at odds of 5–1.

Afterwards, as the euphoria died down, Geraldine was afraid she should not have pushed him on, and asked Dick Saunders if he thought it would have been better to have pulled up. He told her that a sportsman or woman is always competitive and, with adrenalin flowing, it was not hard-hearted but natural to keep going. Inevitably, there were those who criticised her for completing on such a tired horse – yet he still jumped the last fence fresh. She had proved herself, on a 'spare' ride, and created turf history.

Amazingly, Geraldine rode in the very next race, a hurdle, but still 'shell-shocked' – her fine achievement having barely sunk in, and having hastily grabbed her crash cap after being bundled up to the television cameras for an interview – she was, in her own words, 'simply not with it', and fell at the first!

That evening, she found the celebrating something of an anti-climax: 'I was just longing to go to bed.'

Throughout the ordeal (which it was, as far as the press pressure was

concerned), Geraldine received the support of her husband, Henry, and parents, James and June; and they were all behind her again when 1983 saw Geraldine preparing Gordon's Lad once more along the Southport sands, ready for another tilt.

Sadly, the horse had another set-back, but some loyal owners specially bought Midday Welcome for her to ride. He should have been ideal, but, just to rub in the ups and downs of racing, he fell at the first fence.

As for Cheers, he only ran in one more race, again with Geraldine riding, but he went lame and a few days later he was put down. 'I was devastated when I heard,' Geraldine says. 'I had a phone call from the press and it was they who told me. I would have loved the chance to have him myself; he holds a very special place for me. He was a wonderful horse.'

Although she would jump at another chance of riding in the National, Geraldine's race-riding activities have wound down considerably since her father switched almost entirely to the flat.

'But I find I'm very involved with the young staff and I love helping bring them on,' she says. Indeed, their highly proficient girl apprentice, Julie Bowker, became the first girl to ride in the prestigious Gimcrack Stakes at York in 1986 – 'and she couldn't ride at all when she came to us'. Geraldine goes on, 'I love teaching the kids, they're great, and the two-year-olds, so I won't miss racing too much when I retire.'

In March 1987, poor Geraldine lay prostrate at home, nursing a broken pelvis, sustained in a fall at Ayr. To laugh was excruciating, to sneeze was surely to die ... 'But I'll be back, I'm not giving up yet,' she said.

JENNY PITMAN

1983: First winning woman trainer

JENNY PITMAN nearly gave up horses to work in a shoe shop. She thanks Fred Winter for jolting her into making a go of things as a professional trainer.

That was in 1975. As a girl in Leicestershire, Jenny, one of seven brothers and sisters, had grown up with ponies, ridden in a point-to-point at fifteen, and worked in racing stables. After marrying Richard Pitman she produced two sons and started taking in a few liveries, building up into a successful point-to-point yard and then becoming a private trainer.

This worked out fine while she was married, but it was not enough to make a living after her marriage broke up. She had been a relatively big fish in the short-seasoned point-to-point pond; she would be small fry in racing. And earning an income was no longer an extra but a necessity. Some well-meaning friends advised her to quit. She was wavering. Working in a shop might not be lucrative, but it would be steady and safe. One day Jenny was given a lift to the races by Fred Winter, to whom she confided that she was considering packing up the horses. 'He turned round and gave me the biggest bollicking of my life,' she says. 'It saved me.' She responded with guts, enthusiasm and common sense that are her distinctive characteristics. But with the decision came plenty of worries and rock-bottom moments: 'I was skint,

but I always fed the horses the best and I always gave my owners a fair deal; luckily they paid me promptly.'

She moved to Weathercock House, Lambourn. It was derelict. Outside there were nineteen dilapidated boxes. There were no roads or paths to them

> ## 'I was skint, but I always fed the horses the best and I always gave my owners a fair deal; luckily they paid me promptly.'

and no drains; the whole place was up to the knees in slurry. The house was no better; a survey was dispensed with – it would have been too depressing.

Today the house is a picture, tastefully furnished and decorated, and ruled over by a cheery assortment of dogs. Outside is a model yard, or rather several yards, new additions in smart red brick having been built as more money was earned along the way, totalling sixty-five boxes in all.

Just eight horses occupied the rundown stables when Jenny moved in, and six of those were swathed in bandages. For most of them it might have been the last stop before the knacker's

yard, but soon Jenny started winning races with them. Her first winner was Bonidon, in a moderate selling race at Southwell.

Soon after she met a Shropshire owner considering putting two horses with her. Over lunch he changed it to six and Jenny nearly fell out of her chair. In time, that owner's string built up to fourteen. It was the sort of break she needed; when all fourteen were eventually taken away over a point of principle, it was a desperate blow.

In the 1980–81 season, Bueche Giorod won six races, including the Massey Ferguson Gold Cup at Cheltenham. The racing world was beginning to sit up and take notice of Mrs Jenny Pitman.

There were lean spells, there were crises. Somehow, something always came along to pull her out of the mire. Horses such as Fettermist, one of the unsung heroes of National Hunt racing doing a job of work, could be relied upon to provide the odd win or two when most needed. 'If a carpet was pulled out from under my feet and I was slapped down and feeling desolate, there would be a horse like him come along, as much loved in the yard as the Corbieres of this world.'

Corbiere joined Jenny's yard as a three-year-old and has been there ever since. He had been given as a twenty-first birthday present to Brian Bur-

'When he was learning, his gallop was like a baby elephant's, even the labrador could go faster.'

Corbiere gathers himself after landing awkwardly over Becher's Brook.

rough, a member of a Henley brewing family, and, from day one, Corbiere, or Corky as the stable knows him, was a 'character'. A chestnut gelding standing just over 16.1 h.h., with that familiar broad white blaze down his face, he looks almost as broad as he is high, certainly more of a hunter than a racehorse. That was how it seemed on the gallops, too. 'When he was learning, his gallop was like a baby elephant's, even the labrador could go

faster,' recalls Jenny. 'But whatever the weather, come snow or driving rain on the downs, he never turned his head away but always faced it head on.'

And that was the way Corbiere was to face his racecourse battles: head-on. He never did become a fast galloper, but he was a gem with a heart of gold, a will to win, guts that told him never to give up. It was not easy for a horse like him. While Burrough Hill Lad could cruise in third gear for most of a race

Corbiere wins from Greasepaint in a close finish in 1983.

before moving into top gear (and even had fifth gear to call up if needed), Corbiere would be there galloping his heart out right from the start of the race until the end, just in order to keep up.

Conditions contrived to be the worst imaginable for his first race, a 2-mile National Hunt 'bumpers' flat race at Nottingham. 'It was like a ploughed field', recalls Jenny. 'The jockeys' colours were so plastered in mud it was impossible to tell who was who, and then coming out of the pack, stomping his way home, was Corbiere.'

When Corbiere was turned out to summer grass as a five-year-old, farmer Alan Davies, who was keeping an eye on the horses, predicted he would be a Grand National winner. There was an avenue between two fields bounded on both sides with fencing at least 4 foot 6 inches high; Corbiere kept jumping out of his field, crossing the avenue in one stride and jumping into the opposite field, where a filly was the subject of his attraction.

Jenny believes Corbiere would have been a star in whatever sphere he went into; from the start he would do any-thing to please – although he could show a bit of cupboard love, too. 'If you had a packet of sweets for him, he would rob you until they were all gone, then he wouldn't want to know you.'

He was a crackerjack when he was pulled out for exercise in the morning, bunching himself up and arching his back. After he had worked on the gallops, he would regularly buck the whole way home, and the lads on his back often reckoned they had seen all the way to the Severn Bridge. If there was an audience, he would rear and plunge and generally show off.

He built up a solid race career, mostly in long-distance events, always doing it the hard way, gallop-ing resolutely, never giving up. By the start of the 1982–83 season, when he was rising eight years old, he had won six races and had been consistently placed. That season he added the Welsh Grand National to the list, and became a firm favourite for the Grand National. When the weights were pub-lished and he was allotted 11 stone 4 pounds, support for him was greater still.

The ebullient Jenny told the world and his wife that he would win – 'a dangerous thing, which I don't do any more'. She goes on, 'Everyone knows that the Grand National is a lottery and a horse can be brought down at the first fence, but I did think he had a real chance.'

She arranged for her parents, who had given her much moral support, to attend, but as the day grew closer so the nerves became worse – not least because the young owner and his parents would not contemplate defeat! To them victory was a foregone conclusion and Mr Burrough senior not only arranged a party at the Bold Hotel, Southport, where they were staying, but also brought up two coachloads of his brewery's workers complete with crates of champagne! 'If we lose, I think the safest place I can escape to is the car park,' Jenny confided to her friend, assistant trainer David Stait, as the pressure mounted.

She need not have worried. Stable jockey Ben de Haan rode a peach of a race on the stable favourite, always well placed, jumping superbly, and at halfway he was lying third. Excitement and tension was heightening in the box where Jenny and her family were watching. Approaching Becher's for the second time, Corbiere took a fractional advantage. I'll give up smoking or anything, Lord, for a safe jump now, Jenny prayed fervently, the race suddenly making her very religious. Inside the box was pandemonium. Every time somebody said, 'He's going to win,' Jenny pleaded with them to shut up, fearing such predictions would bring bad luck . . . The Canal Turn was past, the last big ditch, they were back on the racecourse with two to jump.

Mandy, Jenny's sister and her secretary for six years, burst into tears. It set Jenny off, as her Corky jumped the last and touched down in front . . . Her family were hysterical now, all hell let loose, shouting until they were hoarse – and here was Greasepaint coming. He was catching up. 'It's going to be another Crisp and Red Rum,' groaned Jenny, 'it can't happen again.'

It didn't. That most courageous of horses hung on, finding that little bit more from his drained reserves when

There's my Corky! Jenny Pitman welcomes home Corbiere in 1983.

he felt his rival at his quarters. He won by threequarters of a length.

Victory didn't sink in for a minute. Then David Stait burst in, calling, 'You've done it!' It hit Jenny then, although she felt as if in a dream world while the two mounted policemen escorted her hero in and she scrambled through the crowds to reach the winner's enclosure. She was then swept up in a whirlwind of interviews, television, radio, press reporters, being led from one assignment to another in the protection of two burly policemen. She was overwhelmed. All she wanted was a cup of tea, a fag, and moment's peace. 'Hang on. I've got to go in there!' she said to them suddenly as

Jenny Pitman interviewed in 1983; rider Ben de Haan looks on.

they passed the queue for a ladies' loo. 'You can't, the television crew is waiting.' – 'I must.' And with that the women patiently waiting parted to let her through, slapping her on the back as she went. She leaned against a basin for a moment, gathering her thoughts. It was a haven. She lit a cigarette, laughed and joked with the rest of the women, and emerged refreshed.

Jenny herself, not a great drinker, drove home that night, leaving about midnight, and soon her passengers were curled up sound asleep. She imagined what it must be like to be on drugs, for she was on a high all right as her adrenalin flowed and she sang the whole way.

When she reached home at about 3.20 a.m., she found, to her amazement, the house filled with flowers. 'Where anybody had been able to get them from on a Saturday night I don't know,' she says. She was far too alert to go to bed, and sat mesmerised, watching the video of the race through several times. After a shower she was in bed by 4.30, totally at peace and contented, but quite unable to sleep!

At 6.30 she looked out of the window and found a crowd already gathering to welcome Corbiere home. When he arrived, many motorists having hooted and waved out of their windows en route in tribute, people crowded so close that she was afraid Corbiere would kick out, but he seemed to know not to.

'Burrough Hill Lad was like a Ferrari, Corbiere a Ford Escort beside him, but he's been a magic old horse...'

By the time Jenny went back into the house, it was high time for food; but, save for one crust and a piece of old Brie, the house had been eaten and drunk dry!

Jenny was staggered by everyone's kindness and especially moved by the amount of mail she received. It came from all over the world, from people she had never met; it took four people two hours each for two days to open it all: 'It was wonderful to know thousands of people are supporting you; I had felt alone and fighting my own battle in the past. They did me a world of good, and it couldn't have been done without a good team around me.'

For Jenny, the best thing of all was that her parents and sons, Mark and Paul, had been at Aintree for the race; and the next day her three brothers and three sisters arrived to join in the celebrations at Lambourn.

Corbiere ran in each of the next four Nationals, and, save for an uncharacteristic fall at the fourth fence in 1986, he showed all his courage, finishing third under big weights in both 1984 and 1985, and completing safely in 1987. He was then deservedly retired, Brian Burrough giving him to Jenny, and he now acts as a schoolmaster to the young lads and loves going hunting in the winter.

Only one year after becoming the first woman to train a Grand National winner, Jenny Pitman pulled off a similar record in the Cheltenham Gold Cup. 'Yes, the horses have been good to me,' she says. 'Burrough Hill Lad was like a Ferrari, Corbiere a Ford Escort beside him, but he's been a magic old horse ...'

RECORD NUMBER OF FINISHERS

1984

RACING IS FUN for Tony Sykes, mine host of the Savernake Forest Hotel near Marlborough. He holds the Grand National record for being the only person ever to own a horse who finished twenty-third in the race. The horse was Canford Ginger, the year Hallo Dandy's, 1984.

Tony, a lover of congenial company, good food and fine wine, which he dispenses convivially at his delightful Victorian country hotel on the edge of the ancient Savernake Forest, is one of those myriad 'small owners' who make up the backbone of National Hunt racing.

For some time he had hankered after having a horse in training, when he read an article about the then up-and-coming trainer David Elsworth. When they met, Tony immediately liked David and realised that he would enjoy having a horse with him. 'Half the fun of owning is visiting the stables and feeling involved and being made to feel important, even if you only have a moderate horse,' says the jovial Tony. He had a useful hurdler in Remezzo, then David bought back Canford Ginger on his behalf.

David Elsworth had originally bought the bright chestnut as an unbroken four-year-old at Doncaster Sales for a firm of solicitors in Canford, Dorset, hence his name. After a while the horse was switched to Jim Old's yard, nearer his owners; but, when he

> 'Half the fun of owning is visiting the stables and feeling involved and being made to feel important, even if you only have a moderate horse.'

came up for sale again, David, who always had regard for him, bought him back for about £1500 – 'One of my better purchases,' he muses.

To begin with, it appeared that the horse simply did not stay, even over the minimum 2-mile trip. Eventually he was tried over a longer distance as a last chance; if he failed again, it would be off to the sales ring.

In November 1982 he ran over the 3 miles 2 furlongs of Fontwell, where the course arrangement, three times round

an attractive figure-of-eight, means that the gallop is unlikely to be exceptionally strong. Canford Ginger hacked up, and duly saved his bacon.

He won two more chases and was beaten a short head in the 4-mile amateur race, the National Hunt Chase, at the Cheltenham National Hunt Festival, at last showing the potential David Elsworth had believed he had.

Canford Ginger was always a superb jumper, and it was decided to let him take his chance in the 1983 National for experience, in preparation for a serious crack at the race a year later.

Tony Sykes and his family love the atmosphere at Liverpool, not so much the race itself – 'it's impossible to really see anything' – but all the build-up. In 1983 they stayed at the Black Swan, Bucklow Hill, where among other guests was Ben de Haan, who won the next day on Corbiere, as well as their own jockey, Colin Brown. They walked the course the night before, Tony's wife, Isabelle, then vowing not to watch the race itself.

Early on National morning the family were back on the course, where all

Twenty-third to finish – but Canford Ginger clears the last well under Colin Brown in 1984.

Hallo Dandy and Neale Doughty are clear of trouble at the Chair on their way to victory in 1984.

the horses were being exercised, the trainers were exchanging good-natured banter, and bacon sandwiches and brandy-laced coffee were being passed round.

Canford Ginger himself was unlucky, being knocked out of the race by a loose horse at Becher's Brook first time round. What was supposed to have been an educational experience proved just the reverse. Canford Ginger lost his form so completely that, when he did return to Liverpool for the 1984 National, David Elsworth was feeling, in his words, 'very negative about his chances'. His one asset was his jumping, and so his connections

backed him at about 10–1 to complete the course.

Colin Brown, his rider, takes up the story of the 100–1 outsider: 'I knew the connections stood to win about £1000 if he completed the course; I'd known the horse since he was a three-year-old and he was a superb jumper. He was not far off them when he started to tire after Becher's second time and got a bit slow; but I didn't pull him up because I kept thinking of the money on him. If he'd been out for the count, I wouldn't have been cruel and continued, but he was still popping away and anyway there wasn't much birch left in the last two fences. By then I was trying to look

after him and just get him round.'

That year, Tony and Isabelle, busy at their hotel, did not attend. Various guests at the hotel shared in the thrill which goes with having a runner in the National, watching the race on television with Canford Ginger's owners, after enjoying a special Scouse lunch prepared by the chef.

Tony Sykes, delighted at winning his bet, did not immediately realise that his horse had set a new National record, but when David Elsworth mentioned the fact that evening it made as good an excuse as any to carry on with the celebrations!

As for strategy, the first part of David's instructions had been complied with to the letter: to run the horse at the back to help him get the trip: 'The only thing is, the back was where he stayed!'

Later that year the horse was sold at Ascot Sales for 5000 guineas, a considerable profit, to go point-to-pointing, which he did without success in Essex for a couple of years.

The twenty-three horses who completed, in the order in which they finished, were: Hallo Dandy, Greasepaint, Corbiere, Lucky Vane, Earthstopper, Two Swallows, Fethard Friend, Broomy Bank, Jivago de Neuvry, Grittar, Hill of Slane, Tacroy, Doubleuagain, Beech King, Eliogarty, Spartan Missile, Yer Man, Fauloon, Another Captain, Mid Day Gun, Poyntz Pass, Jacko and Canford Ginger.

Hallo Dandy was the first horse Richard Shaw ever owned – and he had been bought with the specific intention of winning the Grand National.

Richard Shaw's sporting passion had always been golf until a good friend, (the late) Tim Sasse, talked him into buying a Grand National prospect as they imbibed at a dinner party one day in 1982. Chief executive of Lowndes Lambert, the insurance broking subsidiary of Hill Samuel, Shaw was far more used to frequenting the likes of Sunningdale than Catterick or Cumbria. It was at Catterick that he first made the acquaintance of his pur-

'I tried to pat him but he threw his head up and hit me in the face – that's how little I knew about horses.'

chase, Hallo Dandy, when Mr Shaw flew up to the Yorkshire track: 'I tried to pat him but he threw his head up and hit me in the face – that's how little I knew about horses.' Investments may have made up most of the broker's business life, but this was one he was pleased to leave in the hands of his Cumbrian trainer, Gordon Richards.

For a man who had undergone massive open-heart surgery, Richard Shaw stood the strains and stresses of Aintree remarkably well. Later in the year after Hallo Dandy's win, he had the victor brought to the City of London, where the horse paraded with a police escort right from Tower Bridge to his owner's office in Cheap Street, so he could be seen by staff and clients, many of whom had had a bet on him. The parade had also been organised to raise money for the British Heart Foundation.

Hallo Dandy is a gelding by Menelek, out of Last of the Dandies. He was bought as an unbroken three-year-old at Ballsbridge Sales for £10,000 by Mr Jack Thompson, who initially put him into training with Ginger McCain, for whom he won three races and was consistently placed. But he developed a spot of leg trouble and was fired; when he came back into training he was sent to Gordon Richards at Greystoke, Cumbria.

After a couple of seasons, in which Hallo Dandy won another three races and again was consistently placed, Gordon Richards told his owner, 'I think your horse could win the National.' – 'Terrific,' was Mr Thompson's immediate reply. But a few days later he said, 'My wife will divorce me if we run a horse in the National.' However, he told Gordon he could sell Hallo Dandy to someone who *would* like a runner in the race, on condition that the horse stayed in the stable. It was a magnanimous gesture that was to have a totally satisfactory outcome.

Gordon Richards's phone was red hot when news first got about that Hallo Dandy was for sale, but, while most thought they might be able to buy him cheaply, he was only for sale at a price. Once Jack Thompson, former chairman of David Brown tractors, fixed it, he would not budge: £25,000 or nothing.

Richard Shaw asked for a few days to think about it and put down the phone. Within an hour, he had rung back and agreed the deal. It proved to be genuine beginner's luck.

Hallo Dandy finished a creditable fourth in the 1983 National in the heavy ground he hated, behind mudlark Corbiere. After that encouraging effort, Mr Shaw gave Gordon a free hand in his training, which was all geared to the 1984 National. The horse had an ideal preparation with the perfect outcome.

There was an anxious moment in the race – but only for his connections, not for the horse. With so many runners still standing after the second Becher's, owner Richard Shaw lost sight of Hallo Dandy for a moment. 'I don't think we're there,' he said anxiously. Gordon was briefly unable to see him either and feared the worst. Then Mr Shaw's black colours emerged from behind other horses. What was more, Hallo Dandy was in a perfect striking position to wear down the weight-carrying Corbiere and the Irish trier Greasepaint.

So it was victory for Richard Shaw, the second-season, one-horse owner. Struck by the terrific atmosphere of Aintree, he hosted a hospitality tent for his colleagues, clients and,

Hallo Dandy and Neale Doughty clear the last fence.

not least, his family, including his eighty-one-year-old mother, two sisters, wife Yvonne and son Rupert, who were all there for the great occasion.

It was a memorable day, too, for jockey Neale Doughty and his proud parents, retired Welsh steel worker Arthur and his wife Joyce. They had scrimped and saved so that their son could have the pony he longed for as a kid, and here he was, twenty-six years old, riding the winner of the Grand National.

Neale Doughty, who had taken over as Richards's stable jockey on the retirement of Ron Barry, having been his 'understudy' for a couple of years, had

produced Hallo Dandy at precisely the right moment. At what point in the race had Gordon Richards first thought he might win? 'Well,' he says cautiously, 'you never know until you're past the post; but from a mile out he held a lovely position and I knew he should win if he proved good enough.' Once past that post, Richards relaxed and joined in the euphoria: 'It was great to have pulled it off for my owners and all very exciting.'

Those celebrations were not to be repeated the following year, alas, for Hallo Dandy joined the roll of past winners to become first-fence fallers! He completed the course safely in 1986

and now greatly enjoys his retirement, hunting in Surrey for Lord Onslow.

Gordon Richards, who never rode in the race himself, had already trained Lucius to win the 1978 National, and the brilliant Dark Ivy, who was second favourite but killed in 1987 – 'the best horse of the lot'.

Richards does not disguise the regard in which he holds his horses: 'I loved Hallo Dandy. He was a real gentleman and anyone could handle or ride him; he was never a tearaway. He used to go out for the odd hour by day and he loved to roll. He certainly did us proud.'

JIM JOEL

1987: Oldest winning owner

The Shoe Room at Childwick Bury Stud. The door is devoted to shoes of Classic winners.

WITH A SLIGHT AIR of bemusement, calm and quietly smiling, Mr H. J. 'Jim' Joel, the grand old man of racing, gave his first-ever television interview the week after the 1987 Grand National. He had become, at ninety-two years old, almost certainly the oldest winning owner, through Maori Venture, ridden by Steve Knight and trained by Andy Turnell.

To the owner-breeder of every Classic except the Oaks and several hundred flat winners from one of England's finest studs, it had come as a complete surprise, for Maori Venture, class horse that he was, had not really been expected to cope with the Aintree fences. That he did so was great credit to trainer and jockey and to the horse's own intelligence.

Mr Joel's National Hunt enterprise, which had started as a hobby to while away the winter months, had produced 300 winners and had now culminated in jumping's biggest prize. It could not have happened to a more deserving gentleman, one of a dignified breed of whom all too few survive.

For Mr Henry Joel Joel – 'H.J.' or 'Jim' to his staff and friends – racing has been an immensely satisfying life's passion, a diversion from his taxing involvement in the family diamond business. Even now, at ninety-three years old, he commutes daily to the City of London, leaving his home near St Albans at 9 a.m. – a shining example to many men half his age. He has lost none of his sagacity and he likes, as he puts it, to keep his ear to the ground in City affairs. At weekends he enjoys nothing better than to wander round the stock on his stud, be they old retired faithfuls or the latest crop of yearlings.

To visit Childwick Bury Stud is itself a memorable experience, for Mr Joel sets a high standard and, even as the pace slackens in deference to his advancing years, there is still not a blade of grass unmown, not a flower-bed untended, not a patch of gravel soiled. Mature shrubs and rhododendrons bloom.

Holding pride of place off the immaculate main yard, and the first spot visitors are shown, is the 'shoe room'. Here, filling three walls, are the racing plates of all the winners produced by himself and his father, Jack, since 1907, with thirteen Classic plates filling a door.

Two former selling platers formed part of the foundation of Mr Jack Joel's stud when he emigrated from South Africa. One was Sundridge, which he bought for 1450 guineas and went on to become a high-class sprinter and sire, getting the 1911 Derby winner Sunstar. The other, Doris, Sunstar's dam, was little bigger than a pony and produced nine other winners. Jack Joel also bred the 1921 Derby and 2000 Guineas winner Humorist, who died shortly after his victories, from a broken blood vessel.

'H.J.' inherited the stud in 1940 and bred the 1967 Derby and 2000 Guineas winner Royal Palace, as well as Major Portion, Welsh Pageant, Connaught, Fairy Footsteps, to name but a few.

As Peter Willett wrote in the *Sporting*

Jack Joel, who bred two Derby winners at Childwick Bury.

Chronicle in 1970 when discussing Mr Joel's stud:

One of the fascinations of thoroughbred breeding is continuity and tracing the chain of heredity from generation to generation. This fascination is bound to be enhanced for the owner who is able to watch, always with anxiety, sometimes with the joy of highest hopes fulfilled, his finest bloodstock reproducing themselves.

In the mid-1950s Mr Joel put one or two jumpers with Bobby Renton (who was later to become involved with Red Rum) and at his first attempt in the National, in 1957, his Glorious Twelfth finished fourth behind Sundew. Several years later he put a few jumpers with Bob Turnell, recommended to him by a friend. As fine a judge of a man as a horse, Jim Joel forged a firm friendship with Turnell. Like Bob, Jim Joel had loved his hunting, from a box in Leicestershire in the inter-war years of his prime, having served as a sub-altern in the Hussars during the First World War.

The jumping string went from strength to strength, with such as May-fair Bill, the ill-fated Buona Notte, Bowgeeno, The Laird (beaten a short head in the Cheltenham Gold Cup), Arctic Beau, Kilvulgan, Beacon Light – horses that made Andy Turnell's name as a jockey, too, and some of

them home-bred coming on from their flat-racing careers to add a further dimension to Mr Joel's interest.

His famous black colours with scarlet cap were inherited from his father, who in turn was given them by one William Sutton, winner of the 1886 Triple Crown with Lord Lyon, with the words, 'I hope they are as successful for you as they have been for me.'

Besides some 800 flat winners, over 500 of them home-bred, for Mr Joel, the colours have been carried on twelve Cheltenham National Hunt Festival winners. That course is top of Mr Joel's 'league' with thirty-three winners in all, followed by thirty-two at Sandown and twenty-nine at Ascot, up to the end of the 1986–87 season.

Bob Turnell trained 233 winners for him before his untimely and unexpected death at the age of sixty-seven in 1982. Andy had ridden ninety-eight of them, his century so close, but on his father's death he immediately switched exclusively to training.

Almost every owner nurtures a dream of winning the National, but it was to be exactly thirty years before Mr Joel reached that goal after his promising first attempt – and then he was not there to see it. Of several runners in the race over the years, his 1986 contender Door Latch had looked the best prospect of all, and Mr Joel braved the huge crowds at Aintree to watch him run – only to see the horse fall at the first.

In 1987, Mr Joel was on board a jet flying home from a pre-arranged holiday in South Africa, when his horse Maori Venture won. When told the news, he could scarcely believe it. 'I was flabbergasted and thought: have I heard right? It was amazing, I couldn't sleep a wink all night.'

The disbelief was still with him days later but his obvious affection for his horse, his trainer, who had been in need of a change of fortune, and his unsung jockey Steve Knight, was apparent for all to see when he welcomed them home from Liverpool on the Sunday morning at Andy's stables near Wantage. The rapport between non-agenarian owner and equine hero, whose retirement he immediately announced, was an endearing sight.

The race itself had been a superb spectacle, with over half the runners completing. Out in front for most of the way, Lean Ar Aghaidh had given the youngest jockey in the race,

'It was unbelievable; the whole thing was so unexpected,' says Andy. 'It's the sort of thing that happens to other people but not to you.'

had been trained by Andy Turnell for his previous owner, Major Rubin. When Major Rubin died, the horse went to Ascot Sales, having won several nice races, and Andy bought him from Botterills on Mr Joel's behalf for 17,000 guineas.

Mr Joel, with the horse's welfare at heart, felt that, at twelve years old and with inevitable extra weight to carry, it would be asking Maori too much to win the Grand National again. The rich chestnut now roams the large paddocks at Childwick, his legs as clean as the day he was born, his health excellent, in honourable retirement along with other good old servants such as Beacon Light and Secret Ballot.

One of few, if not the only, Grand National winners to be born in Wales, Maori Venture was bred by publican and rugby player Dai 'Maori' Morgan; the foal was named after Mr Morgan's spell of jackarooing and playing rugby in New Zealand. His sire was St Columbus, who stood in Warwickshire until his owner John Thorne was killed in a point-to-point fall. The grey then moved to the south Northamptonshire stud of farmer and point-to-point enthusiast 'Bunny' Tarry, where he still stands.

Maori Venture won and placed in some good races under National Hunt rules, including a third in the Hennessy Gold Cup, but a tendency to make mistakes at speed produced doubts about his suitability for Aintree. When he won the Mandarin Chase at Newbury in January 1987, however, his trainer and jockey persuaded Mr Joel that a crack at the National was worthwhile. Tracy's Special was also due to represent the stable and, if either could run well, it might prove just the tonic they needed.

For some sort of injection was vital if the East Hendred yard was to survive. Before Bob Turnell died, Andy had expected to ride for a few more years before becoming his father's assistant. Instead, he was thrown in at the deep end and, to make matters worse, he was given notice to quit the beautiful old yard they rented at Ogbourne Maisey just outside Marlborough. The horses dwindled. At one time the ratio of staff to horses was one to one, 'but

Maori Venture, ridden by Steve Knight, on his way to victory.

Guy Landau, a superb first ride and it was only on the infamous run-in that he succumbed.

Though achieving the third fastest time on record, Steve Knight had not hurried his chestnut, and in a classic piece of patient race-riding he steadily drew towards the front rank on the second circuit. Poor Dark Ivy, tipped to be only the third grey ever to win the National and starting second favourite, was unsighted going into Becher's first time, fell and broke his neck.

Up front, Lean Ar Aghaidh skipped merrily along, with the previous year's winner and favourite, West Tip, going

well; so was Classified, a good class horse, but he was out of it with a slipped saddle after the Canal Turn. The Tsarevich was hot on their heels, and Maori Venture moved ever closer, along with his stable companion, Tracy's Special. Attitude Adjuster, the youngest horse, had been driven up, only to weaken quickly.

Going to the last it was clearly a three-horse race, as first Maori Venture and then The Tsarevich overhauled Lean Ar Aghaidh and drew away in that order to be separated by 5 lengths and 4 lengths, with West Tip fourth.

The eleven-year-old Maori Venture

the staff were old friends, not just servants and I didn't want to sack them,' Andy recalls.

Eventually, thanks to Mr Joel and several other owners, he was able to set up at East Hendred. But the first season was a disaster, as horse after horse succumbed to a virus infection. Maori Venture's Grand National victory, in Andy's second season at the village near Wantage, could not have been better timed. Andy and his attractive wife, Louise, had been thinking seriously of quitting.

The secret to Maori Venture's victory was that he was never hustled and therefore not forced into blundering. Always a superb jumper at his own pace, his extra class was able to tell in the National, enabling him to move up a gear when others were grinding.

In the unflappable Steve Knight, he had the ideal partner. Steve had been second jockey to Andy when Bob Turnell was alive and it was natural for him to move into the number-one slot when that became vacant. The promotion was just reward for loyalty, for, after a flat apprenticeship with Richard Hannon until he became too heavy, he had never worked in any other stable.

After the race Steve went home to Hungerford with his girlfriend, Josie, but instead of indulging in alcohol, which he would normally have enjoyed, he was so overcome by it all that he sat up half the night drinking black coffee and watching replays of the race. The couple married soon afterwards, as did Maori Venture's stable girl, Jill Anderson, to head lad Stan Wallsgrove.

Andy and Louise Turnell returned home the night of the race after celebratory drinks with the sponsors, Seagrams, at Aintree and crossed the road to their local pub, the Plough, for a quiet steak, only to find the place bedecked with bunting and a great reception awaiting them.

Next morning, Andy was confronted by the local policeman. 'Where are you going to put the cars, sir?' – 'What cars?' a still-stunned Andy replied.

By 11.00 a.m. Andy knew. The village street was blocked as he tried to

PC Richard Mason congratulates Maori Venture after his 1987 success.

return to his stables after a late breakfast at home half a mile away. The pavements were thronged with pedestrians. Altogether nearly a thousand people milled around the entrance of Orchard Stables awaiting the return of the hero of the hour. 'It was unbeliev-

able; the whole thing was so unexpected,' says Andy. 'It's the sort of thing that happens to other people but not to you.'

Its ability to induce that sense of euphoria is what makes the Grand National a unique attraction.

BIBLIOGRAPHY

AINTREE IRON
Fred and Mercy Rimell. W. H. Allen, 1977.

BRITISH RACECOURSES
B. W. R. Curling. Witherby, 1951.

CHELTENHAM RACECOURSE
Alan Lee. Pelham Books, 1985.

DIRECTORY OF THE TURF
Pacemaker Publications, various editions.

THE GRAND NATIONAL
David Hoadley Munroe. William Heinemann, 1931.

THE GRAND NATIONAL: A HISTORY OF THE WORLD'S GREATEST STEEPLECHASE
Vian Smith. Stanley Paul, 1969.

THE GRAND NATIONAL: AN ILLUSTRATED HISTORY OF THE GREATEST STEEPLECHASE IN THE WORLD
Clive Graham and Bill Curling. Barrie and Jenkins, 1972.

THE GRAND NATIONAL: ANYBODY'S RACE
Peter King. Quartet, 1983.

HEROES AND HEROINES
Finch Mason. The Biographical Press, 1911.

THE HISTORY OF STEEPLECHASING
Michael Seth-Smith, Peter Willett, Roger Mortimer, John Lawrence. Michael Joseph, 1966.

HORSE RACING
Peter Churchill. Blandford Press, 1981.

LONG LIVE THE NATIONAL
John Hughes and Peter Watson. Michael Joseph, 1983.

THE MARYLAND HUNT CUP PAST AND PRESENT
John Ellis Rossell Jr. The Sporting Press, 1975.

NO SECRET SO CLOSE: THE BIOGRAPHY OF BRUCE HOBBS
Tim Fitzgeorge-Parker. Pelham Books, 1984.

ONE HUNDRED GRAND NATIONALS
T. H. Bird. Country Life, 1937.

THE QUEEN MOTHER'S HORSES
Ivor Herbert. Pelham Books, 1967.

RACEFORM UP-TO-DATE
Sporting Chronicle Publications, various editions.

RED RUM
Ivor Herbert. William Luscombe, 1974.

ROYAL CHAMPION: THE STORY OF STEEPLECHASING'S FIRST LADY
B. W. R. Curling. Michael Joseph, 1980.

SECOND START
Bobby Beasley. W. H. Allen, 1976.

THE SPORT OF QUEENS
Dick Francis. Michael Joseph, 1982.

WINTER KINGS
Ivor Herbert and Patricia Smylye. Pelham Books, 1968.

INDEX

INDEX

INDEX